Creating an Eco-Friendly Early Years Setting

T0333852

This book offers a comprehensive guide to becoming a more eco-friendly setting, from small steps that can be taken to reduce waste and improve efficiency to setting up partnerships. It illustrates how sustainable choices can become a natural part of every child's education and how children, parents and staff can all inspire sustainable behaviour across local communities and at national and international levels.

Covering all aspects of practice including colleague and parental engagement, the environment, routines, resources, and teaching and learning, the book helps readers and practitioners to embed a sustainable approach in day-to-day practice. It draws on recent research, studies and stories of success and failure that can be adapted to fit everyone's own journey towards a more sustainable world. The chapters address topics such as:

- plastics and their alternatives
- sustainable food
- sustainable resourcing
- transport and trips
- waste management.

Drawing on the experiences of real nurseries and including a wide range of activities and lists of resources, this is an essential read for practitioners, leaders, policymakers and all settings that want to help make sustainable choices a natural part of young children's lives.

Cheryl Hadland is the Founder and Managing Director of Tops Day Nurseries, Aspire Training Team and Hadland Care Group, and the early years sustainability charity, GECCO, UK.

Creating an Eco-Friendly Early Years Setting

A Practical Guide

Cheryl Hadland

Routledge
Taylor & Francis Group

LONDON AND NEW YORK

First edition published 2020
by Routledge
2 Park Square, Milton Park, Abingdon, Oxon, OX14 4RN

and by Routledge
52 Vanderbilt Avenue, New York, NY 10017

Routledge is an imprint of the Taylor & Francis Group, an informa business

British Library Cataloguing-in-Publication Data
A catalogue record for this book is available from the British Library

Library of Congress Cataloging-in-Publication Data
Names: Hadland, Cheryl, author.
Title: Creating an eco-friendly early years setting : a practical guide / Cheryl Hadland.
Description: First edition. | Abingdon, Oxon ; New York, NY : Routledge, 2020. | Includes bibliographical references and index. | Identifiers: LCCN 2020003097 (print) | LCCN 2020003098 (ebook) | ISBN 9781138333697 (hardback) | ISBN 9781138333703 (paperback) | ISBN 9780429445842 (ebook)
Subjects: LCSH: Nursery schools–Administration. | Nursery schools–Environmental aspects. | Environmental responsibility. | Sustainable living. | Children and the environment. | Environmental education.
Classification: LCC LB2822.7 .H33 2020 (print) | LCC LB2822.7 (ebook) | DDC 372.12–dc23
LC record available at https://lccn.loc.gov/2020003097
LC ebook record available at https://lccn.loc.gov/2020003098

ISBN: 978-1-138-33369-7 (hbk)
ISBN: 978-1-138-33370-3 (pbk)
ISBN: 978-0-429-44584-2 (ebk)

Typeset in Melior
by Wearset Ltd, Boldon, Tyne and Wear

Printed and bound by CPI Group (UK) Ltd, Croydon, CR0 4YY

Contents

Introduction   1

1 Parents   9

2 Working with colleagues   17

3 Pedagogy   33

4 Plastics, and their alternatives   43

5 Nappies and wet wipes   57

6 Play activities   71

7 Children's gardening   87

8 The natural world and pets   103

9 Electronic equipment   116

10 Building design   124

11 Cleaning, sanitising and disinfecting, personal care   136

12 Sustainable food   155

13 Sustainable resourcing   167

14 Transport and trips   183

15 Waste management   195

16 Legal framework and relevant accreditations (not early years specific)   204

17 Advocacy   209

18 Standards, curricula and accreditation specific to early years   219

Summary   239

Appendix I: Suppliers' sustainability and eco-grading   243

Appendix II: Tops Day Nurseries Corporate Social Environmental
Responsibility (CSER) Policy   245

Appendix III: Tops Day Nurseries and Aspire Training Team
Sustainable Travel Plan and Policy   254

Appendix IV: Environmental dates to celebrate   259

Appendix V: Useful websites   262

Appendix VI: Sustainability checklists   267

Appendix VII: Children's books   273

Appendix VIII: Educators' resources   274

Index   277

Introduction

I run a group of day nurseries in the UK called Tops Day Nurseries. I started the first one in 1990, inspired by the need for quality childcare for my own children: a familiar start for many! We now have around 3500 children in 30 settings across the South Coast.

Nearly 30 years later, my grandchildren attend Tops Day Nurseries. Like all parents, grandparents, and colleagues in the sector, I strive to provide an environment that will inspire them and enable them to lead fulfilled, happy lives and develop to their best potential. In recent years, I have come to reflect deeper on the environments we provide, the way we educate small children, and indeed the way we support and enable our professionals who care for them.

I had amazing freedom in my own childhood. Despite being brought up in a land foreign to my parents, Hong Kong, I was free to roam for miles around. I remember being given a watch for my 5th birthday, being taught how to read it, and given instructions to be home by 5. I explored under the blocks of flats, where huge spiders spread nets between the foundation pillars and streams trickled with foul smelling liquid. I explored in the mountainside forests, where I ran down winding paths through what I now know to be snake- and insect-infested undergrowth. I clambered into old war-time pill boxes, dug caves, climbed trees, and got dirty and scratched. Ultimately, I developed a resilience and self-sufficiency which has stood me proud for my whole life – thank you, Mum and Dad.

Unfortunately, my children had a lot less freedom. There were many more cars on the roads and as a parent I listened to advice to teach my children to be wary of strangers and to guard them more. Now a grandmother, I see that my grandchildren have even less freedom. They are brought up within a culture that does not let children out of parents' sight. We try to protect our children from strangers, from sickness, from bacteria, from animals, from falling, ... but we do not protect them from the steady poisoning of the world they inhabit and I think we must try.

I am a keen scuba diver and amateur underwater photographer and videographer. While I used to believe I was fairly forward thinking environmentally (I fitted my first solar panels back in 2005), I had my eyes fully opened in 2016 when on a diving trip organised by David Jones, who worked as diving supervisor and scientific advisor to the production team for the film *A Plastic Ocean*. Thanks to him, his academic dissertations, his film and others he recommended, and his passion for the oceans, I started to notice the dire levels of plastic pollution around me. I finally began to recognise the impact that my actions had, both as an individual and an employer. I was shocked. I'm trying not to beat myself up over it and I don't think anyone should, but I did immediately start changing my ways. Like a recently converted non-smoker, I became passionate about changing 'the world'. I wanted to change everything immediately, and it left a bitter taste to realise it isn't that easy. Family, friends and colleagues couldn't help but notice my change of focus and my personal changes.

I studied a distance learning course through Cambridge University and received a postgraduate certificate in Sustainability Leadership, attended conferences and read widely. I repeatedly discussed the issues with colleagues and academics. With a growing body of information, a book and a website seemed a natural complement to share the knowledge with others who might be interested. I firmly believe that with knowledge may come caring, and with caring may come action, which is what I am hoping for. My peers in the sector voted me the most influential person in early years in the UK in 2018, and I'm sure that was largely due to my passion on this subject.

The journey towards sustainability

One of my key realisations was that you need your friends, family, colleagues and community to understand **why** you want to make changes, and indeed to wave their own banner in support. It is impossible to make significant impact on your own. I also discovered that some instant decisions were neither wise nor correct. There is lots of 'greenwash' about – products and services being sold as 'eco-friendly', without justifying the label. You can discover you've been conned by clever sales techniques!

Sustainability is a complex subject and every decision will come with counter-arguments. The best anyone can do is to be pragmatic, and make the most informed decision they can at the time. Be prepared to reflect and to continuously try to improve what you do. Inevitably, you will make some mistakes along the way, and that's normal – that's how we learn after all.

While our prime focus in early childhood education is still, of course, to enable each child to develop to their best potential, by providing a safe, but fascinating, learning environment, I also believe the time has come to lift our heads and set our sights outwards. We have a duty to educate ourselves and our children to be responsible for our environment, and to include this in the everyday lives of children and adults. We do not need permission from anyone else to make the world a better place for our children. Some changes are small, and cost nothing other than a change of mind and a bit of effort. Other changes of course require investment, collaboration and permission – more of all this in due course.

Not everyone who knows about environmental pressures will care enough to do anything. Some will have far more pressing concerns, such as their survival, poverty, violence, feeding and housing themselves and their families. Some people will simply not care. But those of us who have the ability and will to choose what we buy and use can make a difference. If we spend a little of our time and effort being more sustainable, together with our children, we can all enjoy a healthier lifestyle.

We can also use our individual and group consumer power, political votes and influence to make a difference. Indeed, as Mahatma Ghandi said:

You must be the change you wish to see in the world.

I'm trying to lead a more sustainable life myself, and to cascade this into my world with children, parents and colleagues in the early childhood sector. I am far from perfect and I often learn from making mistakes, but I hope that writing about what I have learned will help you to bring about the changes we need to make our world a more sustainable place for our children and grandchildren.

I feel we need to do something to stop our children inheriting a world where current lifestyles mean we have polluted our rivers and oceans with plastic and poisons; where some people starve and others get fat and waste food; where the air is poisoned by exhaust fumes; where there are no animals over 50kg, other than methane-producing dairy cows and animals kept for food, entertainment or sport; where biodiversity has been decimated, even losing the bees that many plants depend on; where global climate change has killed off the coral, caused massive storm damage, and covered some of our lands with rising sea water.

This book is a call to action. We can make changes to help our environment, and our children, now. It's the responsible thing to do. We do not have to wait for politicians, or police, or local authorities to just start. My hope is that we will continue to learn from each other, and to innovate and develop innovators. Changing our own behaviour, one thing at a time – just start!

The global warming 'story'

Humans are brilliant at making up 'stories', and equally brilliant at believing 'stories'. Even with science, we can arguably manipulate the facts. Global climate change is a story that I believe is true. I am not a scientist, but from my perspective, there is more scientific evidence that supports climate change happening now (and the human contributing factors) than doesn't.

Environmental sustainability

Sustainability is not just about climate change, but also about the health of our children, our food, and our oceans. It relates to every part of our lives. I have considered it from plastic pollution to building eco-nurseries, sourcing sustainable food, toys, materials and equipment, renewable energy, to low-impact furniture and clothing.

The concept of sustainable development was first put forward in the 1987 report *Our Common Future* – prepared for the World Commission on Environment and Development. The report recognised the links between inequality, poverty and environmental degradation. It seeks a way forward towards a fairer world with less damage to the environment. The report defined sustainable development as 'development that meets the needs of the present without compromising the ability of future generations to meet their own needs'.

The first United Nations Climate Change conference was held in 1995 in Berlin, called Conference of the Parties (COP) 1. The purpose of the conference and subsequent conferences was to assess climate change and to discuss global actions. In 1997, COP3 adopted the Kyoto Protocol, where most industrialised countries agreed to legally binding obligations to reduce their greenhouse gas emissions. Unfortunately, not all countries ratified the agreements on their return. While the US agreed to reduce emissions down to 7 per cent below 1990 levels, Congress did not ratify it after the president had signed it and it was then explicitly rejected in 2001.

In September 2015 a United Nations General Assembly Resolution created 17 global goals, called the Sustainable Development Goals (SDGs). Each of the goals has its own targets – 169 in total.

The UNCC conferences and lately the International Conference on Climate Change (ICCC) continue to be a hub for academics, scholars and activists who present papers on climate change. It is a place for peer review, and for politicians to debate and try to agree actions. It's not just about politicians agreeing to take action when they return to their countries, though; states within countries, green parties, not-for-profit groups, charities, companies and individuals around the

Figure 0.1 Sustainable Development Goals

world benefit from reading the papers and discussions. California, for example, continues its sustainability work along its coastline, despite the current president's opposition.

The Bonn Climate Change conference (held 30 April–10 May 2018) and a number of reports (such as the Adaption in Human Settlements) focuses on increasing urbanisation worldwide. More than 50 per cent of the world's population lives in urban areas, which is expected to increase to near 70 per cent by 2050. This exacerbates our vulnerability to human-made hazards, especially in developing countries, coastal and delta regions, and small island developing states (SIDS), such as those in the South Pacific.

The more we pump carbon and methane into the atmosphere (from burning fossil fuels like oil, coal and petrol, and methane from cows) and the more we deforest the world, the warmer the world will get. The more ice that melts in the polar regions, the higher the sea level will go, and the more extreme the weather will get. Ocean currents will be disrupted, and we will be under enormous threat to life as we know it, particularly around our coasts. Costs just to protect our coastlines will be enormous, and we need to start spending now.

In order to reduce our production of greenhouse gases, we need to stop our dependence on fossil fuels for making electricity. We need to stop using petrol and diesel to power our cars, we need to reduce the number of cows making methane, we need to grow more trees and we need to protect the coral. We also need to develop our coastal defences to prevent our homes and workplaces being flooded by the sea. Some areas are already under water. If we wait for these conferences, and for politicians to pass the relevant laws, we will wait too long. Our world, and our children's future, will be ruined.

All this in a world where the population is currently 7 billion people and expected to grow to 9 billion in our lifetime. Billions are living in poverty and lack the resources to choose sustainability. This puts pressure on the developed world to make amends for the damage we have already caused, as well as to make better provision for the future. A lot of the argument at conferences is about how much money the developed countries are prepared to contribute to developing countries to help them make the necessary changes. Currently, we are underinvesting by billions of pounds. Of course, taxpayers who do not know or understand, and those in poverty or living beyond their means, are unlikely to vote for politicians promising to increase taxes. This instant-gratification, consumer mentality has to change and we need to invest in our world if we want to continue living on it in the matter to which we have become accustomed.

Politicians are beginning to see the advantages in tackling sustainability issues, particularly as some actions might even offer economic advantages. More and more, one-use plastic is being banned around the globe. They wouldn't have done that if they had thought it would jeopardise their next election. The tide is turning in favour of the planet!

Humans also have a capacity for thinking 'out of sight, out of mind', even once we have learned the concept of permanence. Once we stuff things into our bins at home, we think it is gone. Sadly it hasn't.

Some of the wealthiest nations in the world, such as the Scandinavians, are leading the way to a happier, healthier, and less wasteful lifestyle through more conscious, sustainable purchasing. Being thrifty is now a compliment. Spending time at a repair café rather than retail therapy is a respectable choice, one that's more likely to yield financial stability instead of fleeting excitement.

We know that there are some decisions we are currently making that are negatively impacting the environment. Information about alternative choices would help us make more informed decisions going forward. Every choice we make as individuals and as professionals in the early childhood sector can make a positive difference. Each chapter of this book considers a real issue for childcare professionals, to help provide the information needed to make good, sustainable decisions. Our duty of care is not just for our children now, but also for our children's children.

In conclusion, I'd like to refer to an original presentation I saw delivered by David Jones, of Just One Ocean, at the National Oceanographic Centre at Southampton University in May 2018. He was speaking on plastic pollution and he referred us to his theory that there is a priority order we need to be aware of in order to effect change:

1. 'Science – let's get our facts right (spot the greenwash)

2. Education – we need to educate ourselves and others, of all ages, on the facts

3. Innovation – we might not need to make some changes if innovation can fix the issues

4. Alternatives – we should use alternatives that are more sustainable

5. Participation – we still need to participate to make the difference, on an individual level, family level, work place level, as a community and as a country/worldwide.

6. Legislation'

He argues that in order to get legislation through our various governmental and political institutions, we need to go through the five previous stages.

Certainly discussing what we know and why we need to take action is a first priority in this book, **the science**, and the purpose of the book is to **educate** ourselves so we can educate our children and also work with the families/communities within which we work.

Where I can, I offer **innovations and alternatives** that I have learned about. I've also become an early adopter where I can, for example with electric cars, solar panels and replacements for plastic glitter. Fortunately this is an area that is currently moving fast and, as our children mature, my hope is that they will also be able to move the baton further along, quickly.

We all need to **participate** in this movement in order to make a difference, right now. There are dozens of big and little changes we can make, every one of us, at home and at work and in between. I have included some resources we have developed at work in the nurseries and also as part of our charity GECCO to help you along, but the choice is yours. You cannot do it all at once, so I recommend you decide what is most important to you and your children and start there.

Legislation is constructed by politicians, but politicians need votes, which come from popularity, in order to stay in power. The politicians need to know that we want them to enable sustainability to protect our planet, and that unless they include sustainability in their manifesto, and in their actions, we won't vote for them.

Thank you so much for reading this – I sincerely hope I can be a help to you.

1 Parents

Introduction

> Of course, when using the word 'parents', I mean adults with parental responsibility for the children in our care; they could be foster or adoptive parents, grandparents or extended family, so please read all of these into any descriptor saying just parents, just for brevity.

Parents are our customers, our key stakeholders. They choose us to look after their children and they pay the bills either personally, via their employer or as taxpayers. Like any business, communication is two-way. We need to listen to what their needs are and we must communicate how we can meet their needs and, in the early years sector, of course the needs of their children.

Sometimes there is an educational aspect to our communications with parents. They come from all backgrounds and levels of experience; from young mums who need childcare while they do their school exams, to experienced, mature mothers of four who may have strong opinions on what they require from us for their children, and everything in between, each one an individual. Some parents might have English as a second language or have sight or hearing limitations; some will be highly educated, some will be competitive, tiger mums; others will be laid back and very relaxed, but all will have subscribed to the ethos that we are offering. But we have to adjust our messages and the way we communicate them, potentially to every individual, to ensure we are understood and working together for the child.

This chapter looks at how we might communicate our vision on sustainability to parents. This poses the same challenges as for general communications. Some parents may be totally unaware and new to the concept; some may be CEOs who have written their own CSR document; another might have a master's degree in environmental science, or marine biology, or be the sustainability coordinator of a local charity or business. How can we adapt to engage all of these?

Role-modelling within the nursery

Environmental stewardship for their children is a concept that parents can appreciate; it shows we care about the environment that their children will inherit. When you show parents into the nursery, whether new or existing parents, it is an opportunity to speak about why environmental stewardship is important to you, on behalf of the children, and what you are doing – point out the composter, the children's garden, and the plants inside, all those little things as you go around: it can only be appreciated.

Questionnaires

Questionnaires to existing parents, manually on paper, or preferably online such as Survey Monkey, are a normal element of administration for your service. At the end of 2017, we added the question on whether the nurseries being eco-friendly was important to parents into our annual Survey Monkey questionnaire – 86.48 per cent said yes! And in 2018 it was slightly higher. We will be asking the same or similar questions every year from now on and we will be very interested in the answers. Now if 86 per cent of your parents said they wanted to buy t-shirts for their children, would you try to supply some? We started selling t-shirts successfully at only a 54 per cent 'yes' response, so a result this high indicates a strong and existing interest, and we also know some were not interested

If you can include some open questions, you will get indications of what objections and what support you might expect from the parents as well, and you can engage accordingly. For example, you might find one parent fits solar panels and might do you a deal; another loves gardening and might be prepared to come in sometimes to show colleagues and children how to plant some vegetables; another might make soap and be happy to do a demonstration or to provide some. Parents can really help with the sustainability journey.

Key workers

Key workers, by definition, will be learning all about the child's and parents' needs on a day-to-day basis. They are the front line; they are the ones who can speak to parents bringing in plastic bags to stop them and suggest alternatives, to encourage them to try out cloth nappies, and to explain why we don't have balloons. They can also introduce parents to each other for mutual support and advice, for example the experienced mum using cloth nappies might well be happy to share advice and tips with a new mum thinking of trying them.

Listening to parents

Parent power stopped us serving beef a few years ago, in the days of mad cow disease in the UK. New Zealand still doesn't allow beef imports from the UK due to this disease. There is a balance required here; we must listen to parents, and we also need to be pragmatic in order to protect our business and our own livings.

Sometimes, sustainable actions that we would like to put in place are just not viable because parents do not support the idea, or do not fully understand the benefits. You either have to try again to sell the benefits, perhaps in a different way, or bide your time and try again in a different way. If you force change on parents, they might leave the nursery – and you almost certainly don't want that to happen. So don't be afraid to sound parents out, verbally via the manager, or even the owner speaking to them one-to-one or by arranging a parent meeting. You want to hear the objections so that you can offer answers or alternatives.

Noticeboards

Just in case the key workers miss the conversation, or parents are waiting for something in a corridor with a noticeboard up, don't miss the opportunity to have an attractive and interesting noticeboard, and/or posters around explaining what we are doing with sustainability, using the 'whys' that you've already shared with staff. Companies such as Lush sell soaps with a price point about four times the price of supermarkets and in chemists. The perception is that an eco-product is worth more than a non-eco-product, so make this point to your parents. Your environment and teaching is worth more if it's eco; even if you don't charge more, it's beyond the average expectation – at least currently it is. In fact, looking forward, those who do not start to act sustainably could find themselves losing children to those who do. As we know from our survey, parents include sustainability as part of their criteria for choosing their children's provider.

Newsletters

Whether these are emailed, Facebook, printouts once a week, or glossy magazines once a year, these are of course prime opportunities to explain your vision, mission and objectives and to engage parents in your progress. However, if it is at all possible to send these out electronically, this is far more sustainable – by creating an e-version of our welcome pack for parents, with information such as terms and conditions, enrolment forms, policies and more, we saved £750 on printing per 500 visits.

Website and social media posts

If you use these, they will all need updating once you start your sustainability journey. The message needs repeating, and explaining, many times, in many different ways, in order to attract parents on board if they aren't interested. You may want to post not only in Facebook, but in Instagram, Twitter, LinkedIn, etc. as you discover which forms of communications your parents like to see.

Sustainability will be a source of interesting news, some lovely pictures of children with their plants, or in the sand, or sharing stories about turtles and whales, and these are likely to engage prospective parents as well as your existing parents.

Online presence is a great way to communicate with parents. Parents need to know what's in it for them and their children, so blogs that tell them this will help get them on board.

Events

Some parents really appreciate and enjoy being part of nursery outings and meeting other parents – and sustainability activities can be an opportunity for this, such as having pop-up shops selling sustainability items (eg real nappies) set up in the nursery, or inviting parents to join with you and the children on a beach clean. Figure 1.1 is a photograph of a parent and her daughter on such a trip to our local beach in Bournemouth. The story of this beach clean, which we held in collaboration with our local university, was also press-released. Various articles and photographs were published as a result, showing other parents how responsible we are, which led to more footprint on our website and more enquiries on our phones.

Figure 1.1 Parent and child during a Tops Day Nurseries beach clean on Bournemouth beach

Extending into the home

You can now offer a different kind of homework to engage parents with their children between attendances at nursery. We can ask them to bring in boxes, tubes and cartons for us to recycle in our craft activities – and this is part of sustainability. You probably do it already!

You could design helpful resources in line with your actions in the nursery to continue the learning at home, such as 'switch it off' or 'recycling' posters that the

Figure 1.2 Sticker to place near light switch, issued to all children/parents at Tops Day Nurseries

children have drawn and then take home to their parents to continue the message there. The children could then remind their parents, and older siblings perhaps?

We also found that showing off our bamboo toothbrushes at nursery inspired some parents and children to ask to buy one for home as well. We then started sharing all the other money-saving and planet-saving opportunities with them as well, such as re-useable wet bags instead of nappy sacks, eco eggs for laundry, re-useable cloth nappies, coconut husk scrubbers, and started putting our partnerships with sustainable suppliers on our website – as we aren't retailers, after all. This is all above and beyond normal service and is likely to impress your parents.

A blog that we posted for parents, produced by the United Nations, which covers quite a lot on sustainability, is the following:

The lazy person's guide to saving the world![1]

Want to make a difference but don't know where to start?
Here are some simple things you can do … with minimal effort.

From your sofa

- Save electricity. Turn off the lights when you don't need them and plug appliances into a power strip. By turning them off when not in use, including your computer, you'll save power and money.
- Follow local news and share. If you see an interesting social media post about climate change, share it so others in your network see it too.
- Don't print. Use a digital notepad and spare the paper.
- Stop paper bills and statements. Paying your bills online or via mobile means no paper, so no forest destruction.
- Shop smart. Plan meals and avoid impulsive buys. Buy from companies that you know have sustainable practices

From your home

- Use energy efficiently. If you're using the washing machine, make sure the load is full, and if you use a dishwasher, don't rinse your plates before running the machine.
- Plug air leaks in windows and doors to increase energy efficiency.
- Take showers. Baths require gallons more water than a 5–10-minute shower.
- Eat more fruit and veg. More resources are used to produce meat than plants!
- Freeze fresh produce and leftovers. If you've not had the chance to eat them before the best before date, freezing them for another day will save both food and money.

- Compost food scraps. Composting can reduce climate impact while providing nutrients for the soil.

- Reduce. Re-use. Recycle. Reduce waste. Re-use – no single-use items. Recycle paper, plastic, glass and aluminium to keep landfills from growing.

- Avoid pre-heating the oven. Unless you need a precise baking temperature, start heating your food as soon as you turn on the oven.

- Replace old appliances with energy-efficient models and LED light bulbs.

- If you have the option, install solar panels in your house. This will also reduce your electricity bill!

- Use a rug. Carpets and rugs keep your house warm and lower your thermostat.

- Choose re-usable nappies. With a variety of options available, these are a big money-saver and often a healthier alternative to disposables.

When out and about

- Shop locally. Supporting local businesses keeps people employed and prevents unnecessary travel.

- Bike, walk or take public transport. Save the car for trips when you've got a big group.

- Buy strange fruit. Fruit and vegetables are often thrown out because their size, shape, or colour are not 'right'. Buying this perfectly good food at the farmer's market, etc., utilises food that might otherwise go to waste.

- Shop for locally sourced produce and sustainable seafood. When shopping or visiting restaurants, ask for the source. Let your favourite businesses know that local farming and ocean-friendly seafood are on your shopping list.

- Use a re-usable water bottle and coffee cup. Cut down on waste and maybe save money at the coffee shop!

- Take fewer napkins. You don't need a handful of napkins to eat your take-away. Take only what you need.

- Upcycle. Shopping new isn't necessarily best. See what you can remake from second-hand shops.

- Maintain your car. A well-tuned car will emit fewer emissions.

- Donate. Local charities will give your used clothes, books and furniture a new life.

Conclusion

We seek to educate children and sometimes their parents, in order to achieve the best outcomes for future generations. But we respect every parent's opinion and, of course, their right to remove their children from our care and therefore stop paying our bills, so we must tread carefully. But these were some tried and tested ideas to help you engage your customers with your sustainability journey.

Note

1. Tops Day Nurseries, 2016. *The Lazy Person's Guide to Saving the World!* [online]. Hadland Care Group. Available from: www.hadlandcaregroup.co.uk/lazy-persons-guide-to-saving-the-world/.

2 Working with colleagues

Introduction

Apart from solo childminders, we work in a team in the early years sector, so even if you are converted to the sustainable journey yourself, you are likely to need to do some work to bring your team along with you. You will have change management to consider, as this is likely to be a cultural change for some. This chapter offers some key areas for you to consider.

First, you need to start with WHY? What is it about sustainability that you feel is relevant to them, what is in it for them? Do they want to protect the planet for our children? What would help inspire them? Do they know enough to care?

And next you need to envisage where you are going and offer them that vision to follow. Start with the end in mind.

This chapter looks at these questions: it is about onboarding your team, your organisation, to sustainability.

Vision

As leaders, our vision needs to be clear and something that we can communicate clearly.

But what is the definition of 'sustainability' as it relates to the environment? I did a bit of research and realised that there are many definitions and interpretations of this word. I found the original Bruntland Report's definition of sustainable development – **'development that meets the needs of the present without compromising the ability of future generations to meet their own needs'**[1] – and this might be useful for you too. How can we establish an environment where we can develop future generations without compromising what they will need in the future?

Each organisation needs to develop their own vision, one that is personal, that they care about, that is relevant to them, to protect future generations.

Mission

The mission is what you are doing now. So what actions are you taking? Can you include something sustainable or environmental in those? Our first step was to look at our existing mission statement and consider if it needed revising. Fortunately, it already had the word sustainable in it, but it had originally meant financial not ecological sustainability, in that we had to focus on being profitable, or at least not making a loss. After all, any business that doesn't financially sustain itself will quickly go bankrupt. Even charities, not-for-profits and social enterprises cannot make a loss unless they expect to achieve donations to make up the difference, in which case they haven't made a loss at all. Perhaps putting the word in green or adding pictures or diagrams would help communicate that the word 'sustainability' can be about the environment, not just about finances.

Values

If you are a UK-based company, you also need to consider how this new purpose affects the fundamental British values that must underpin your work, and I take the liberty of providing in this book the 'Fundamental British Values for Colleagues' poster that we developed to help ourselves focus on these. Shockingly, the original values do not include any reference to the environment ... so I added it in myself! Sustainability can be incorporated as part of the cultural capital in your setting, something that Ofsted are looking to see on their inspections.

In the UK the EYFS also currently fails to consider sustainability. Thankfully, this is not a global omission; for example, the Australian National Curriculum and Guidelines and the New Zealand Te Whariki both make reference to sustainability. The UK primary curriculum also includes sustainability and many primary teachers are now tuning in to this aspect of our work. More about this in Chapter 18.

Who needs to be on board?

It would be useful to consider who the key people are that you need on board, and then how to 'sell' them this new way of looking at things through a sustainability window. The ultimate aim would be for them to become engaged, as well as accountable. The organisation will need their commitment and involvement to help develop appropriate strategies, put them into action and then measure their effectiveness – all without compromising the fundamental purpose of providing great childcare and education. A change of purpose, something embedded in the culture, is a significant change for any business.

The board of directors were the first group I needed to inspire, but they also needed to be considered as individuals, as each would have a different perspective on the change.

The operations team (area managers) and the specialist managers (health and safety, information technology) would be the next group.

And then the managers on the coal face – who would be the ones cascading to colleagues within each setting – had to be considered, along with practitioners working with the children as well as administrators, cooks, domestic staff and maintenance teams.

In a larger organisation there are the head office departments to consider, including accounts, administration, human resources, training, marketing and sales. Each department would have a slightly different perspective.

In a big organisation it's just not possible to meet with every colleague individually, but with a significant cultural change you have a significant time impact on leaders to put the work into communicating at least with the groups and supporting cascading mechanisms, bearing in mind that talking about it once is not sufficient. The message will need to be repeated many times and in different ways to ensure people have a chance to digest, ask questions, reflect, ask more questions, and hopefully take it on board!

Recruitment

Your website needs to reflect your ethos to help potential employees assess whether this is an organisation that they would like to work within. After all, the millennial generation often need to feel that they are making a difference, so making your sustainability ethos as well as your other vision, mission and values clear is essential if you are to move your organisation forward in this direction over time.

We added a couple of questions about sustainability into our recruitment interview questions, and you could include environmental awareness as a recruitment criteria. After all, if a potential member of staff really doesn't care about the environment, would you want them on your team if sustainability is part of your ethos? It is more difficult to change people's attitudes than to teach them skills, and although I do believe you can teach the various ways that you can make your environment more sustainable, the caring attitude in the first place can make all the difference.

Induction

The induction system for new employees now includes a presentation on the company vision, mission and values, which of course includes an explanation of why sustainability is important to us and how we demonstrate this in our daily work. If sustainability is to be embedded in everything you do, it does, of course, need to be embedded during induction.

Leadership

Leadership style is a huge influence on how new ideas are effectively passed onto teams. I prefer to use the leader–leader style of leadership, rather than an autocratic style. As a young managing director I delegated effectively and knew when it was best to abdicate entirely. I am rather good at designing new systems but not so good at consistently following through. Knowing your own strengths and weaknesses as a leader is pretty crucial for success. I have a really strong team of directors who know what I am good at and what I'm not so good at: we balance out well.

The leader–leader style was described and developed by David Marquet, an astonishing US Navy submariner famous for his 'turn the ship around' talks.[2] I'm also strongly influenced by David Rock, a doctor of leadership neuroscience, who considers how to lead so that people can respond with their brains rather than their fight, flight or freeze instincts. Both schools of research celebrate and value colleagues, in all their diversity, but also lay responsibility at the feet of the leader for communicating the vision and ensuring appropriate training and support is in place to enable colleagues to do what they do best for the business. With this grounding, these are some of the things I tried:

How might you implement sustainability into your culture

A **five-year plan** meeting is a good opportunity to present a change like this. If you presented your ideas to your board off site in a nice hotel, perhaps with support from a mentor, you could inspire your top team, aiming for an enthusiastic support and leading from the front. Be ambitious! Explain why it is important and what is in it for each of them, but also be prepared to open up the floor to disbelief, objections, and refusals before achieving a united front with the next group of colleagues.

Give **examples** of other companies who have successfully integrated sustainability into their ethos. Lush, for example, was formed around the same time as ourselves in the 1990s, and has since become a global success. They use as little packaging as possible, their ingredients are sourced sustainably and they charge and achieve premium rates compared with less ecological household names. Another example is Organix baby food; organic food sourced sustainably, doing well financially, and also local to our business centre. Differentiating ourselves from the childcare competition and giving us another unique selling point would be good for business, at least until others caught us up. I hoped to provide enough evidence to satisfy the finance director.

For the **marketing and sales director**, the new purpose would provide a whole **new area for press releases, social media messages**, and would likely attract the millennial generation – those born between 1980 and 1996 – who are the majority of our customers (parents of children) and the majority of our staff. According to the World Economic Forum Annual Meeting in 2018,[3] the millennial generation views climate change and conflict as amongst the most critical issues we face. On that basis, selling our early childhood education as helping to address climate change must surely be a customer-winning formula?

And a similar message for the **human resources director**: *Harvard Business Review*[4] research found that 21 per cent of millennial workers left their job in the last year (more than three times older employees) to shop around for **careers that best aligned with their needs and life goals**. They consider the most important aspects of a job to be how an organisation will help them learn, grow, develop and further their careers, as well as the quality of their manager. So it could be argued that by being more sustainable we would attract more customers, improve their learning opportunities and the quality of their manager – perhaps?

Another interesting piece of research I found focuses on the meaning of **'meaningful work' to different generations**.[5] Myself, I have no doubt that providing a sustainable education for young children is meaningful. According to this study:

- *Traditionalists* (born 1922–1945) were typically quoted as: 'I can't even imagine going to a job that … I didn't think had value.'

- *Baby Boomers* (1946–1964) most often talked about their work with phrases like: 'If I didn't get personal fulfilment and feel like I was doing something good, it would be miserable to put that much time and effort into something.'

- *Generation X* (1965–1983) answered questions about their commitment to their job with: 'if your job is without meaning, what would get you out of bed?'

- *Millennials* (1984–2002) talked about their employment with comments like: 'I would rather make nothing and love going to work every day than make a ton of money and hate going to work every day.'

The main finding was that 'meaningful' work meant something different to each generation. Traditionalists felt it needed to be challenging, the Baby Boomers tended to be slightly more goal-oriented, Generation X were more about work–life balance, whereas millennials thought 'the most meaningful job is a job of service … if you can do something that you know in one way or another directly benefits somebody else, it can be very rewarding.'

For our **commercial director (a traditionalist)**, the new challenge of sourcing products and equipment sustainably was enticing. He has since gone on to source electric cars, bamboo toothbrushes and all sorts of things that I will detail in due course.

He and the **FD were also challenged to provide the data** we would need to measure in order to define our success in becoming more sustainable. For instance, you cannot declare a reduction in electricity usage/carbon footprint unless you know what each site used before and after the implementation of a new procedure or practice.

To take on board this whole concept in one chunk is much like 'eating an elephant'. You can only make a cultural change of this size 'one bite at a time': the number of changes and the speed that they're implemented has to be an individual or group choice. You might choose to pilot some of the changes in one centre, or sometimes even in just one room, to try and work out the practicalities and impact before making massive changes across the whole organisation. However, do not ever think that a little step is of no significance and is not worth doing! Every small action by every individual person is important, something to hold onto in this journey.

One director recommended we **prioritise actions** by considering actions which cost nothing, actions which just cost a little, and actions which were an investment. Another colleague recommended we prioritise actions by those most accepted by the local community as being good practice, and another by those which would attract most press interest; I am sure you can guess which department each of these colleagues was from. I don't think it matters from which perspective, or why, you seek to make change, as long as you do it. Don't just dream about change or it won't happen. Remember that *every single person in an organisation can lead sustainable change.*

Change philosophy

When proposing a change in the way you purchase your resources or a way to manage your setting more sustainably, you first need to reflect on the reason you wish to make this change. This reasoning behind the desire is what must be communicated, even sold, to your colleagues. You need to consider what their objections and questions might be before you present to them so that you have your answers ready. For example, do you have a manager or colleague who is reluctant to support ideas they didn't have a hand in creating? How could you present the idea for them to take it on board as one of their own?

When we announce a big change, such as a change towards being a more sustainable childcare setting/service/centre, we need to explain why and then expect people to object. Some people will get upset or angry because the change is away from what they've always done. Some may go on strike and just not do as you ask, and some may even quit. This isn't because the change isn't a good one, but just because it is a change. We know this. We know people feel threatened by change, no matter how beneficial it might be, and we also know there are ways to help change go smoothly – but don't ever expect it to go totally smoothly! I think it is well worth spending some time reflecting on reactions to any previous changes in your setting and considering how to avoid the same outcome again. You know your colleagues: some will be on board with you really quickly, others need time to consider the research carefully themselves, others need to discuss it at length to iron out any implications, some might like to role-play or set scenarios, some would object to that. I would suggest a combination of as many or as few of these plus your own ideas to suit your own team.

A staff survey could include a question on sustainability, and will indicate where your colleagues are already, and improvements over time. Our staff survey in 2018 returned an overwhelming 92.5 per cent saying that they try to be as sustainable as they can in their daily routine by recycling, re-using materials and/or refusing single-use plastic. The survey also generated a significant number of suggestions as to how we could improve on what we are doing already. You can either construct your own survey, or you could work with a company that does this independently such as CEEDA, specialising in child-related surveys, which can then also enable you to benchmark results against other companies.

On our side is the fact that research on millennials has identified that this generation are in favour of eco-sustainability. Indeed, when we surveyed our parents in 2017, 86 per cent of the parents using our service wanted their children to have an eco-sustainable/green education. We believe this eco-sustainable focus helps sell our service to families in the community and is currently giving us a market edge. It's important to share this information with colleagues too, as it helps give them the confidence to support the changes to parents.

Reasons for making the change towards being more sustainable need to be presented or even sold to colleagues; they need to understand why this vision is important. It's easier to approach an issue of this size from a familiar angle; try to consider which reasoning hits closer to home for your first pitch:

- Save the planet from global warming – is your setting near sea level and therefore threatened by it rising? Is your water getting warmer and therefore coral is dying?

- Save the seas from plastic pollution – save seals, turtles, whales – is there one you are more passionate about that you can structure your campaign around? Are you water enthusiasts like I am and therefore even more passionate about saving our seas and the creatures in them? Do you eat fish that are increasingly polluted or harder to find because there aren't so many in the sea? Are your beaches being ruined by plastic rubbish?

- Save the air from pollution – do you have asthmatics at your centre?

- Save people from themselves – the phalates in plastic are known to confuse our hormones and cause fertility problems – is anyone in your centre affected by fertility problems? Have they had to suffer IVF to conceive?

- Are you being hit with increasing bills for lighting, heating, waste disposal, resources – is the financial sustainability of your organisation under threat?

- Does it concern you that the population is increasing from 7 billion to 9 billion in the next few years and we already have 2 billion people struggling with food shortages and lack of fresh water?

- Do you love animals and hate the increasing numbers of animals, birds and insects that are threatened or extinct?

Films and documentaries

There are a number of great films and documentaries that you can show at work or recommend colleagues watch at home (Netflix for example) in order to help inspire them. The obvious ones are *Blue Planet 2* and *A Plastic Ocean*, or you could show *End of the Line*, *Cowspiracy*, *Chasing Coral*, *Plastic Paradise*, *Straws*, *Pump*, *Albatross* or *Bag It*, and mostly recently *War on Plastic*, a short series by the BBC.

Information

There are many websites and Facebook pages available, listed in Appendix V. But there are websites such as the United Nations Sustainable Goals, our own GECCO page, made specifically for Early Years educators, and Just One Ocean, Surfers Against Sewage, War on Waste, Eco-Schools, Real Nappy pages, and many more where you can ask questions and share best practice – well worth some computer search time.

Meetings

With the directors widely on board from their individual perspectives, you might want to discuss the issues further in supervision one-to-one meetings and use an action plan or meeting record form to record titles of discussions and agreed actions. Like all good business people, ensure actions are **SMART** (specific, measurable, achievable, realistic and timely), but let's add another **S** and make them sustainable too!

With strategies very broadly seeded, meet with your **operations team**, area managers, senior managers, managers for training and development, health and safety, and maintenance.

Area managers largely support managers with preparation and compliance for inspections, as well as with the quality of childcare in line with our ethos and our own pedagogy. Our organisations aren't inspected on sustainability – and area managers pushed back, expressing fear that a focus on sustainability would distract them from their main job. It wasn't because they were against the idea, but their jobs already took all their time and more, so it was hard for them to fit everything in. And they are right, of course: their first focus must be the children and the quality of teaching for the children, and communications with parents. We had to look at what they might do less of in order to accommodate the new focus, so we decided to decrease auditing responsibilities – something which they mostly didn't enjoy anyway but which had crept in inexorably over the years! A win–win compromise.

Very recently I discovered the work of John Siraj-Blatchford and Lynnette Brock on Education for Sustainable Citizenship in Early Childhood, work that brings sustainability into the quality arena and supports children's progression with schemas and schemes. This combination of quality with sustainability with free flow for children is a very exciting approach and I will be excited to see how this evolves.

I found that just by **wandering around the buildings and watching** people at work, with my sustainability hat on, that I was able to identify a significant number of things that we needed to improve. I saw windows open with heating and air conditioning on! Lots of lights on when they didn't need to be; lots of single-use plastic still in use, even on a Forest School trip I saw someone use water bottles long after I thought I'd stopped them. I missed a lot of things on the first visits, such as plastic toothbrushes, and nappy sacks, so I hope the list in Appendix VI will help others to jump some of the delays we incurred.

I discovered that much more support was needed for those in leadership roles. **Nursery managers** were often used to doing things a certain way and they had a full-time job caring for and educating the children in their care, not to mention some having to cope with high staff turnover, a lack of recruits, lots of basic training to run, as well as their management roles. I found some of our leaders had just not managed to reflect on new procedures or practices and their administrators were still placing orders on their instructions for single-use plastic. This was a similar pushback in practice to the concerns expressed by the operations team, but without words – worse actually, in practice.

I included a **regular agenda item** on sustainability on all managers' monthly meetings going forward to give a structure and time for group reflection and to share good practice. In this way each manager, and therefore each nursery, would progress at a rate suitable for them, their colleagues, children and parents. I wanted to hear their objections and blockers as well as what had gone well. These were open and frank discussions so that the issues could be acknowledged, science presented if required, and, ideally, solutions discussed ready for implementation.

However, several managers turned out to be **already passionate** about sustainability. I found I had an experienced vegan, for example, who contributed disproportionately with great ideas and went on to lead her nursery to being the first 'plastic-free' day nursery in the UK – thank you Barbara Chaitoff! Others also signed up to local and national initiatives and awards systems, which totally delighted me.

Pilot changes

Sometimes you may want to pilot a change, such as electric hand driers, or wormeries or soap blocks, because you may have concerns as to whether it is going to work for you, so it's an idea to trial certain things before cascading throughout the entire company to avoid making avoidable mistakes.

Green conference

You may have staff conferences and could either include sustainability as one item or have the whole day on the subject. Make it optional if you can; it helps assess commitment. There is a company that produces **eco-games** (such as eco Snakes and Ladders and Twister) that you can rent or buy, which can help bring the subject to people in a more accessible, enjoyable way. We found a blend of active learning and discussion, as well as formal PowerPoint-based presentations and play, to work well.

Figure 2.1 Tops Day Nurseries HR Director Charlotte Percival and managers playing an eco-game of snakes and ladders

Nursery champions

With the huge workload on managers in early years settings, you might want to consider appointing champions from within each setting to help lead each location towards more sustainability. Much of the work will be around changing daily practice, turning lights off, doing the composting, identifying any maintenance issues, supervising water butts and policing the banned items from entering the building (for example plastic bags, balloons, glitter). We turned to the health and safety (H&S) representatives as we felt the environment would fit neatly into their job descriptions, so asked them to be **environment, health and safety reps**. This might work for you too. We also had them attend a conference once a year so any and all additional information could be provided to them fairly easily. H&S was well managed within the organisation and we were in the process of trying to become almost less H&S aware, seeking to promote the benefits of risks (not hazards) rather than the increased protection/'cotton-wooling' of the previous decade. This choice of delegation was good in theory, but we didn't do it as well as we could have; we didn't provide enough support after the first conference and left them far too much to do it on their own. It really is a huge job to change the culture of an early years setting from being health and safety oriented into one with embedded eco-sustainability, even for one such as ours where Tops' forest school ethos, physical risks, and loose parts play were already part of the offering (more on all those later).

Sustainability awards

In the first year of our new mission, we initiated a new award at our annual awards night for the most eco-friendly sustainable nursery, marking them against a range of measures such as their electricity bills, their gardening efforts and their initiatives. This went down well and was reported widely in the local press. However, in the second year, we didn't allocate enough time for the marking and measuring and learned that we would need to set aside more consideration for this going forward, and improve the desk-based reporting to inform it.

Regional business and national awards

We also looked at applying for regional business and national awards instead (more about awards later) in order to show colleagues that our actions were worthy of respect externally, which in turn they could be proud of with their own families as well as colleagues. Photos of the awards being given were popular with family and friends of the colleagues who won, as well as with the local press, and we even had a positive comment from our bankers – always useful to have support from financiers.

Paperwork changes

Alongside each change, and overall, a huge bank of paperwork needed to be changed to reflect the new purpose of the organisation, from policies, procedures, the business plans, job descriptions, inductions, marketing plans and the website – each department would have a list to work through, and I expected that to take a year, and of course learn more as they are updated further. We wrote a brand new document on our corporate social environmental responsibility (CSER), which helped clarify our own thinking as well as provide a further opportunity to structure communications with all stakeholders.

Induction

We have a five-year plan PowerPoint presentation, given to all managers and deputy managers on their appointment, whether an internal promotion or new recruit, and the sustainability section was replicated and adapted for induction for unqualified and qualified recruits as well by the training team. This helped with providing a repeated and clear vision, mission and objectives. A suitable, frequent, repeated stream of communication was, and still is, necessary to make a cultural change.

Walk the talk

As the company leader I have to walk the talk and to make sure I am seen to be doing this, and anyone in the position of leading a move to sustainability has to be very aware that what they do shows more than what they say. It would be appalling if I was to walk into a nursery with a single-use coffee cup in my hand, or carrying water in a single-use plastic bottle, or putting wastes in the wrong bin, so I absolutely do not. Some decisions were a sacrifice for me, like losing my glittery finger nails (yes, that's mostly plastic) and becoming a vegan was and still is hard for me, so I 'flex' that on occasion. I do still fly on holidays and to conferences, but I try to compensate when I do so (more of that later on). So my practice is far from perfect, and therefore it's only fair that I don't expect perfection from others either, but do stop to admire those being more sustainable than I am. I think we have to draw up the lines we are going to stick to and do so, and then apply some pragmatism to those areas where we feel we need to or want to.

In a talk by the creator of Weconomics, I discovered that another name they had coined for the chief executive officer (CEO) of a company was communication executive officer, and indeed communication is a significant part of getting the vision out.

Feedback

Feedback needs to be shared with colleagues, to show them their efforts are being successful, or less so, so that we can adapt accordingly and continuously improve. The types of information we share with colleagues include savings made and what they are then spent on. Perhaps savings on electricity bills could be spent on improving resources, or staff events. We share investments made in saving energy such as when we replace an old diesel or petrol vehicle with renting a new electric one. We have a **league table** to compare settings' achievements, for example on their carbon footprint (electricity, gas, petrol, diesel); for the number of 3-year-olds still in nappies; for the number of colour and black and white photocopies. Some of the managers are quite competitive with each other, so this works well to motivate them to improve.

Feedback needs some effort to **communicate**. You can encourage colleagues to take photos and share them on Facebook, share blogs to put on the website, and we send emails as relevant to all staff. We also use a periodic staff newsletter and a private Facebook group to share good practice, including anything relating to sustainability. We also run competition questions on Facebook with small prizes for the one drawn out of the hat of the correct answers. Be as creative as you can be to inspire and encourage and the team will come with you ... or at least a good proportion of them will.

Video

I also engaged the video production company that do our nursery videos to create a video of the sustainability vision for the company. This was internally circulated and then put on our website. We also commissioned an animation of the sustainability vision, which added a bit of fun to the message.

Practical demonstrations

Practical demonstrations that are first completed at managers' meetings are cascaded to nursery colleagues through their meetings or on the floor, until they become **standard daily practice**. So we might make eco-baby wipes (with no plastic in them) or start up a wormery, or put together an eco-egg for their washing machines, or pot up some plants. These are fun and yet worthwhile activities that show we really are doing things and actually making changes towards sustainability that are visibly cascaded through each nursery.

Finding meaning in their work

Colleagues want to finding meaning in their work – which one would expect them to find in our sector while working with children. Adding in a further purpose of sustainability, in order for those children to have better lives when they are adults, can be added in logically and purposefully. This purpose of a sustainable education for children is not someone's part-time job, but at the heart of what the organisation does. This purpose can drive innovation; colleagues take the purpose to heart and find activities and resources that are innovative and unique and can be shared with pride, which is great for self-esteem and respect for all.

Helping colleagues financially through introducing sustainability is of huge bonofit to all involved. Some such discoveries have been: the laundry dryer balls and eggs that save on electricity as well as chemicals, and have an added bonus

Figure 2.2 Tops Day Nurseries colleague trialling one of the electric bikes

of being hypoallergenic; the electric bikes that we managed to provide free of charge to colleagues thanks to our commercial director spotting a local authority green grant initiative; finding sustainable energy suppliers which offered free LED light bulbs, draught excluders and home energy assessments for colleagues' homes; another that provided free 'water hippos' to put in your water tank to reduce water usage; and drain filters to catch waste oil before it blocked drains. We are genuinely helping colleagues to benefit as well as saving the planet – a win-win situation.

I was delighted that some colleagues agreed to join me in a **charity** that we set up alongside the company to further our sustainability ambitions. We named it

GECCO. GECCO was initially co-funded by screenings of the sustainability film *A Plastic Ocean*,[6] and also by the company – I hope it will be further funded from the proceeds of this book. It has received grants and donations to help fund its work. The new cloth nappy initiative has been fortunate to attract funding from a charity auction, enabling parents to try out real nappies instead of single-use plastic nappies for free. I felt a charity would be best placed to share the good practice and information we had discovered with the wider community, both in the UK and internationally. GECCO allows us to give people the option to engage if they want to, wherever they are. Volunteer work and engaging in something positive and bigger than oneself and one's work is very much part of the sustainable economy model and corporate social environmental responsibility (CSER).

Conclusion

Any cultural change involving everyone in an organisation is a challenge that needs a lot of reflection and planning to succeed. I found this particular change is very much part of a journey, and it keeps evolving as we learn more, notice more, and others do the same and share things. So before you start, begin with the end in mind and ensure your sustainability vision is clear so you can communicate it effectively to colleagues. Engaging your colleagues' heads and hearts is a top priority when making a cultural change – reflect on how best to do this with your team. Communication needs to be clear, and repeated often, using all the methods at your disposal. Measure where you are and celebrate improvements, and don't forget to role-model what you want the behaviour to look like. Good luck!

Notes

1. World Commission on Environment and Development. (1987). *Our Common Future: Report of the World Commission on Environment and Development.* Available from: http://un-documents.net/ocf-02.htm.
2. See www.davidmarquet.com/.
3. World Economic Forum. (2018). *Annual Report 2017–2018* [online]. Available from: www.weforum.org/reports/annual-report-2017-2018.
4. Pfau, B. (2016). What do millennials really want at work? The same things the rest of us do. *Harvard Business Review* [online]. Available from: https://hbr.org.
5. Pledger Weeks, K. (2017). Every generation wants meaningful work – but thinks other age groups are in it for the money. *Harvard Business Review* [online]. Available from: https://hbr.org.
6. *A Plastic Ocean: We Need a Wave of Change*, 2016 [documentary]. Directed by Craig Leeson. UK.

3 | Pedagogy

Introduction

I don't doubt that we can all include sustainability in our pedagogy, so this chapter looks at some of the key ideologies in the world currently and shares some thoughts on how sustainability can be integrated. It introduces a new concept from SchemaPlay called 'Education for Sustainable Citizenship in Early Years' by John Siraj-Blatchford and Lynnette Brock, which you may not have heard of.

First, you might consider where you stand yourself, and what your impact might be when you start to include sustainability in your decisions and actions.

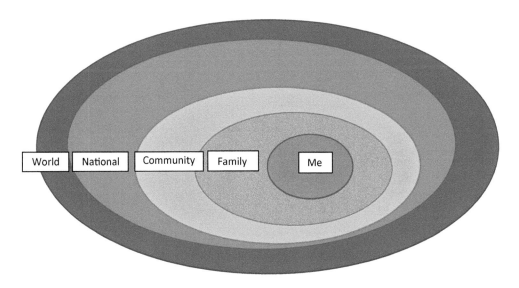

Figure 3.1 Spheres of influence

How does sustainability fit with your pedagogy?

We need to provide a learning environment for young children that meets their needs and aspirations without compromising those of future generations. The adults need to role-model and lead practice to consider sustainability, but to do so we need to learn, alongside the children, how to sustain the world's resources into the future. This hasn't been something society has been particularly concerned about until recently, but the tide has changed.

Sustainability is either specifically referred to within our national curriculum, such as in Australia, New Zealand and Scotland; or it could be worked into it more discretely, such as in England; or you may not have a national curriculum at all. You may be working from international curricula, or specific ideologies such as Montessori, Steiner, Forest School or Reggio, or you may have developed your own unique blend to suit you, your colleagues, the children and their families. Ultimately, it doesn't matter where you're coming from. Sustainability is a journey; one where we learn, we adapt our behaviour, we maybe make some mistakes, we do things differently, we learn from others, we work together. We learn something new and revisit previous practices.

Activities in nurseries are likely to be part of the basic or continuous provision; enhanced provision or adult-linked or -led; but could also be child-, parent- or community-led. No matter what the activity, display or set-up, reflection on the sustainability of the resources used and role-modelling of values by adults is important if we want our children to inherit and sustain the world. The benefits of any risks you choose to allow or enable are as important to consider as with any activity you do, no change when they are sustainable. You might consider if the risk benefits justify the activity, i.e. are they sustainable, both immediately and longer term?

Reflective practice

Reflective practice is commonplace in our sector already; we just have one more aspect to reflect on as we go forward. Every time you set up an activity, reflect on it, or pack it away is an opportunity to consider how sustainable that activity was. You might ask yourself questions about where the resources came from, what is happening to the resources now the children have finished with them, has there been any impact or even improvement in the environment or quality of life through the activity? Was the activity in line, or did it promote, or damage your own sustainability targets?

Your reflections, whether written, photographic, or in your head, are likely to find that your sustainable pedagogy has supported healthy eating; consolidated links with parents, schools, and the community; and provided numerous educational opportunities on a whole range of concepts, from what materials are made of to what they are used for and how to recycle them. These will tie in with a child's knowledge and understanding of the world, but also with their personal, emotional and social development; communication and language; and physical development (the EYFS prime areas) as well as the other interconnecting specific areas of literacy, mathematics and expressive arts and design that are broadly similar the world over.

It is up to us, managers and colleagues, to reflect on the sustainability of our pedagogy, and always question what we are doing. Sometimes things creep in undetected and regular reflection is needed to check how sustainable activities are and whether they also could be improved as we learn more.

Characteristics of effective learning (COEL)

Working through these sustainable activities and provocations will mean children are able to develop all of the characteristics of effective learning (COEL):

- Playing and exploring – children investigate and experience things, and try things out for themselves.

- Active learning – children concentrate and keep on trying if they encounter difficulties, and enjoy their achievements.

- Creating and thinking critically – children develop their own ideas, make links between ideas, and develop strategies for doing things. They also engage in sustained shared thinking.

Characteristics of effective teaching and learning can be encouraged and supported by using sustainable items. Children can learn actively, concentrate and persevere, and celebrate their achievements just as well if not better within a sustainable setting as in one that is not concerned with the environment.

Contextual Interconnected Web

The Liverpool John Moores University project (Boyd 2017)[1] produced a Contextual Interconnected Web as part of its sustainability project, which helps us picture the influences and considerations in place, arguably relevant no matter what your pedagogy. They have also cross-referenced sustainable choices to the British values of democracy, rule of law, individual liberty and mutual respect/tolerance for those with different faiths and beliefs. British values do link well with the three pillars identified in 1987[2] of economic, environmental and social/cultural development – colloquially people, planet and profit.

The United Nations Convention on the Rights of the Child[3]

This was published in 1989 and says amongst the many articles (54 of them) that all adults should do what is best for children and that government has a responsibility to make sure children's rights are protected, as well as to create an environment where children can grow and reach their potential. Article 29 states that a child's education should help them learn to protect the environment. Children need to investigate and experience things, but they can only do that if adults provide an appropriate environment for them to explore.

Respectful Childcare

Your nurseries may include Respectful Childcare, as described by Janet Lansbury,[4] Magda Gerber[5] and others, whereby infants and children are understood to be unique, capable human beings with natural abilities to learn without being taught. However, while we can most certainly trust our children to develop their own natural abilities without active tuition, it perhaps isn't yet completely natural for them to practise sustainability without specific guidance because children do not understand the impact of their actions on the wider world. They cannot understand what they don't yet have knowledge of.

Loose parts play

Loose parts play was first proposed by architect Simon Nicholson in the 1970s.[6] He believed that loose parts in our environment could empower our creativity – a pedagogy that has been influential in early years settings. The loose parts are freely accessible to children and adults just replenish or change them. The loose parts can be natural or synthetic: for example, stones, stumps, sand, gravel, fabric, twigs, wood, pallets, balls, buckets, baskets, crates boxes, logs, flowers, rope, tyres, shells or seedpods. Children may also pick up items on their excursions. The main provider of the parts is the adult, so it is important to be conscious of the sustainability of each item that they offer. Given the list above, I think this should not be difficult at all!

Figure 3.2 Using wood and metal resources instead of plastic

Communication Friendly Spaces

Another excellent ideology to engage with is Elizabeth Jarman's Communication Friendly Spaces.[7] These are areas that act as the best possible environment for children to learn and develop, and communicate with each other, and with adults. These spaces aid children in being creative, and thinking critically through developing their own ideas and making links between concepts. They are supported in developing critical thinking strategies, and all resources can, of course, be fully sustainable.

Resources for treasure baskets and heuristic play

Elinor Goldschmied developed treasure baskets for babies who can sit up and also the heuristic play approach for toddlers. Her ideas are still helping early years colleagues to provide the rich and nurturing environment that children need if they are to thrive mentally, emotionally and physically. Sally Featherstone,[8] Penny Tassoni, Sarah Davies and many others subsequently developed the ideas on resourcing such baskets, for both indoors and outdoors. The focus has been on resourcing such baskets with natural items and re-using items from the kitchen and the home, so this fits beautifully with sustainability, please see Chapter 13 for more information on assessing items.

Dr Laura Jana[9] **asks us to respect the needs of the toddler brain**; we must nurture the skills today that will shape your child's tomorrow. She argues for the need to lay out a strategic plan for cultivating the skills our children will need to succeed. Her straddling of the business world with teaching in early years is brilliant and can be complemented through our knowledge of the damage we are doing to the environment through use of non-sustainable practices. What is the point of equipping our children for a world that we will have destroyed?

Continuous provision

Alistair Bryce-Clegg's excellent books, such as *Continuous Provision in the Early Years*,[10] list suggestions for malleable materials for continuous provision, such as: putty, jelly, clay, ice, salt dough, snow, compost, soap flakes, tapioca, shaving foam, custard, couscous, porridge, beans and mud. With our sustainability hat on, we need to further consider how sustainable each of these items is. In some cases, we may need to approach the activity differently, such as purchasing or acquiring the ingredients in a more sustainable way, e.g. using out-of-date food items to reduce food waste rather than purchasing edible food. Purchasing is covered in Chapters 12 and 13 in some detail.

Provision enhanced by an adult

Quite often you will have set up an activity or a provocation and will then watch to see where the children take it. You might have brought some rather dried out plants in and left the watering can out in the rain the night before for the children to find; you might put a pile of 'rubbish' in the middle of the room with bins close by; you might have a story book to read to them about a turtle having a close escape from a plastic bag. You can set your creativity free and try things out to capture their fascination and, once fascinated, you will have the opportunity to reflect out loud and to teach.

Rewards

Many settings prefer intrinsic rewards, but many use a combination of both intrinsic and extrinsic. Undoubtedly, it is extremely satisfying to grow and eat your own food and to appreciate beautiful flowers you have grown – these are thoroughly sustainable activities.

But do you use stickers as part of a reward system? If you do, avoid the plastic/ vinyl stickers and use paper versions instead. No one needs plastic stickers that last for 400 years and clog up washing machines and drains. Instead, opt for paper stickers that are home compostable. They're not as easy to find, but I assure you they do exist. Try Graphic Monster,[11] for example.

Routines

You will have routines within every day that give you the opportunity to discuss, answer questions and ask questions about sustainability, such as when cleaning up, brushing teeth, preparing food, gardening or caring for pets. You won't know all the answers, but every question could lead you towards another small change. For example, are your cleaning materials toxic? What is the toothpaste made of? Where does this fruit come from? Is the pet food sustainably sourced? The answers may well lead you towards more sustainable practice going forward, as this is a journey that each service can undertake in line with their own pedagogy. My hope is that we share this information and learn from each other.

Child-led

Once educators are comfortable with the sustainability ethos, they will find it increasingly natural to engage in eco-friendly activities that the children have inspired. They may be making models with recycled items from home; they might run out of cress for their sandwiches and be interested in growing some; they might want to build dens – what with? They might start re-arranging some crates into a shop. The creativity of children is phenomenal; we just need to respond with sustainability as part of our armoury.

Parent-led

Some activities will have been inspired by something a parent or family member said, or by an event in the community. Does someone have a birthday coming up? Maybe a child has been taken to the farm over the weekend. Almost everything the children and their families have done, or are planning to do, can be considered from a sustainability perspective. Share your thoughts and discussions.

This is a huge cultural change from the way we have been approaching things, so it definitely helps to have the parents in full support. If parents understand why we are considering sustainability, it will exponentially improve your influence on saving the planet and give our colleagues the chance to make an impact. Some parents may still be using balloons for events and memorials, plastic wipes for cleaning hands, and single-use plastic cutlery for parties, and we have the opportunity to educate them.

Community-led

Look out for opportunities for you and the children to engage in activities, such as a carnival or a beach clean. It goes without saying: approach them with sustainable practice in your head; re-use, recycle, and repurpose. Enjoy the beach clean, taking the opportunities as they arise to discuss why there is rubbish on the beach and nurdles in the sand – what would happen if you left it? And what should you do with the rubbish you pick up?

Education for sustainable citizenship in early childhood[12]

In 2016/17 a new model was piloted in Kent County Council in the UK using a model that was developed to support children in recognising the need for the limited resources of the planet to be:
distributed fairly, and in understanding our interdependence with nature and other cultures and communities. The perspective has been developed in a decade of collaboration with colleagues engaged in early childhood education and care (ECEC) around the world and in a UNESCO-commissioned review of the progress that was made in the Blatchford and Pramling-Samuelsson, 2015). It is consistent with the 2030 UN Agenda for Sustainable Development, the UNESCO Global Action Programme on Education for Sustainable Development, and the Education for Sustainable Development Goals: Learning Objectives (UNESCO, 2017).[13]
The booklet describes a project involving six preschools in developing training materials for education for sustainable citizenship (ESC). SchemaPlay provided them with support in auditing the provisions and setting targets for development and training for staff, working with a key person in each setting to support the educational progress of target children using the EYFS.

I was fascinated to read about the project that the children did with lemurs, visiting their nearby wildlife park to learn and experience the endangered lemurs living there. The children learned about caring for the natural world and, very importantly, learned that they could take action to protect it: they were enabled to work with radio-telemetry tracking equipment, created campaign posters to share in their community, and played hide and seek games pretending to be lemurs and trackers. I loved the very positive presentation of the project; it's an optimistic and celebratory approach that emphasises the importance of providing positive role models, and promoting a model of 'sustainable citizenship' where individuals accept responsibility and take pride in their day-to-day sustainable actions as part of a global movement towards sustainability.

This approach avoids traumatising children with climate catastrophes and terrible consequences of the behaviour of early generations, which can only cause fear – as we know, this is not conducive to learning at all. The approach also combines a free-flow approach, using schemas and schemes to better support children's development, thereby combining an emphasis on quality of provision with sustainability.

Conclusion

No matter what your current or proposed pedagogy might be in your day nursery, setting, service or establishment, sustainability can be integrated into it. Doing so can and should enhance the quality of teaching and learning, and the quality of children's play, therefore supporting the main aims of education in the early years. We should not wait for governments or external organisations to legislate or enforce the inclusion of sustainability into our practice; the responsible thing to do is to include sustainability as soon as we can practically do so, in a way that works for your own community, both now and well into the future.

Notes

1. Boyd, D., Hirst, N., Sageidet, B., Browder, J., Grogan, L. and Hughes, F. (2017). A critical analysis of concepts associated with sustainability in early childhood curriculum frameworks across five national contexts. *International Journal of Early Childhood*. 49 (3), 333–351.
2. World Commission on Environment and Development. (1987). *Our Common Future: Report of the World Commission on Environment and Development*. Available from: http://un-documents.net/ocf-02.htm.
3. United Nations. (1989). *Convention on the Rights of the Child.*
4. Lansbury, J. (2014). *Elevating Child Care: A guide to respectful parenting*. UK: CreateSpace Independent Publishing Platform.
5. Gerber, M. (2003). *Dear Parent: Caring for infants with respect*. 2nd edn. US: Resources for Infant Educarers.
6. Nicholson, S. (1971). Theory of loose parts: How not to cheat children. *Landscape Architecture*. 62 (1), 30–34.

7. Jarman, E. (2009). *The communication friendly spaces approach: Improving speaking, listening, emotional well-being and general engagement.* Elizabeth Jarman Limited.

8. Featherstone, S. (2013). *Treasure baskets and heuristic play.* UK: Featherstone Education.

9. Jana, L. (2017). *The toddler brain: Nurture the skills today that will shape your child's tomorrow.* USA: Da Capo Lifelong Books.

10. Bryce-Clegg, A. (2013). *Continuous provision in the early years: Practitioners' guides.* UK: Featherstone Education.

11. Graphic Monster. (2017). *Custom paper stickers* [online]. Available from: www.graphicmonster.co.uk/custom-paper-stickers-49-c.asp.

12. Siraj-Blatchford and Brock. (2017) Education for sustainable citizenship in early childhood. Dorset, UK: Minuteman Press.

13. http://en.unesco.org/gap; http://unesco.org/images/0024/002472/247444e.pdf.

4 Plastics, and their alternatives

Introduction

We have used 'plastic' in our early childhood settings for virtually everything, from baby bottles to bibs, uniform, cling film, gloves, slides, toys, furniture, computers and transport. It is everywhere. Plastics have revolutionised the world but have now become a major environmental pollutant.

This chapter is about what plastic is, why there is a problem with plastic pollution and what we can do about it in our early years sector.

What is plastic?

The term *plastic* was originally used to describe anything that could be moulded, such as clay, or even our personalities.

Plastic is now also a term used to describe products that often have very different qualities. They look and act differently and it can be very confusing. For example: nail varnish is plastic, but so is chewing gum; car tyres are mostly plastic, and of course straws, plastic bottles, cling film, parts of TVs, bags, etc., can be made of plastic. These examples aren't made from the same base ingredients, though. Plastic can be made from cellulose, oil, vegetable oil, shale gas, corn starch, plant starch, and even chicken feathers. The different plastics take different times to biodegrade, from weeks to hundreds of years or perhaps not at all. There are even some which are compostable in our back yards in a few short months, and break down into harmless chemicals, in which case they are not an environmental pollutant after all.

You can smell plastic, particularly when there is a lot in one room, like in some toy shops. Apparently the smell is the residual of what makes up the plastic, other substances used during the manufacturing process and sometimes fragrance added to the plastic to cover the smell.

Some biodegradable plastics are oil-derived plastics with a degrading initiator added to make them fall apart (degrade) more quickly. Unlike compostable plastics, they don't always break down into harmless substances and may leave behind a toxic residue.

On an atomic level, plastics are made from single units (monomers) combined in a variety of ways in a process called polymerisation. This is why plastics are also called polymers (poly = many, mer = part), and you often find the word *poly* used in the name, e.g. polystyrene.

Natural polymers occur in nature, including silk, wool, DNA, cellulose, starch and proteins.

Synthetic polymers, such as plastic, are made by scientists and engineers. They are extracted from natural resources, but even though the base material may be a natural product, the polymers derived from it are not. To make synthetic polymers, the monomers are joined together, using heat and/or pressure and a catalyst (additional chemical to help the process along). Different combinations of monomers result in different products and there are hundreds of different kinds of plastic available.

Currently, nearly all plastics (millions of tons each year) are made from **ethane**. Most ethane is derived from oil but it can also be from coal, gas, and plants.

Most oil-derived plastics are resistant to chemicals, micro-organisms and water. They don't rot. They might even last forever. The two main types of plastic to look for are PET and PLA.

PET plastic does not biodegrade. The vast majority of the world's microbes and bacteria do not recognise this man-made material and so will not assist in decomposition. We find PET in nappies, sanitary protection, seatbelts, carpets, fabrics, clear containers, and a whole lot more. It can be recycled if collected

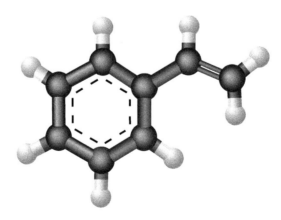

Figure 4.1 Chemistry of plastic

appropriately and if it can be separated from other products, and then made into more similar products.

PLA is a plastic derived from polylactic acid, which is a certified compostable plastic.

What is the problem with plastic?

Plastic has been manufactured and made into products all over the world without much thought as to what happens when that product reaches the end of its useful life. Sometimes its life is just one use, like a balloon, or a straw, so it becomes waste very quickly indeed, and yet it's a product that can last a lot longer than a human lifespan. We don't even know how long it will last because it hasn't been around long enough yet for it disintegrate. Landfills that have been partly dug up have had plastics in them come up looking as intact as the day they went in, which might have been 50 years ago.

People don't know what to do with their waste plastic. Some of it could be shredded or melted and recycled, or it could be burned instead of oil (which could contribute to climate change), but it doesn't make the same grade of plastic as the first time. Unlike glass if sorted into colours or types, plastic gradually becomes less and less useful, ending up as black plastic, which can only be burnt.

Only a small percentage of the plastic we use goes into our own recycling bins (far more does where there are bottle recycling facilities like there are in Germany), so it can end up in landfill with our general waste. Even if it is put into the recycling, a lot of recycling is not actually recycled; it is shipped off to anywhere who will take it. In the past it has been sent to China, currently some of it is going to Malaysia, but sadly these countries also cannot cope with the volume of recycling, so a lot is dumped in a pile somewhere, perhaps in a jungle, where it causes pollution on the land, contributing to destroying habitats for animals that are already endangered. The plastic blows into the waterways, and into the sea. Even worse, some countries blatantly just dump tons of rubbish from their trucks straight into the sea, every day. On Earth Day 2018 the top 20 countries ranked by 'Mass of Mismanaged Plastic Waste' was published by the Earth Day Network, showing the worst are all in the Far East, topped by China, then Indonesia, Philippines, Vietnam, Sri Lanka and Thailand, but the US was also on the list. The data used was actually for 2015 so may not be fully accurate now, but the fact is that sending our waste to the Far East is not acceptable if it's just dumped into the environment.

According to the journal *Science* in 2015,[1] up to 13 million tonnes of plastic enters the ocean each year, a figure too huge to imagine – basically one truckload per minute. The result is plastic in every part of the ocean. Even in the very deepest parts of the ocean, 11km deep, samples taken in 2019 showed that every creature living in those dark waters had plastic in its body. It has got everywhere. Every filter-feeding shell fish tested recently in the UK had plastic in it. Every fish-eating human being has probably got plastic in them already; scientists have already found it in human excrement.

Even while the plastic is still in use it can be toxic because some additives are actually toxic and can leach from the plastic into the substance contained within it, such as a food or drink. An example of an additive is bisphenol A (BPA), which was added to plastic to make it clear and shatterproof. BPA was banned from plastic baby bottles back in 2010 by the EU and from baby bottles and cups in 2012 in the US. BPA had been identified as mimicking the endocrine system so that the body is confused and the hormone balance thrown out, which can cause infertility. Some additives are known carcinogens. Scientists on *A Plastic Ocean* pointed out that we only know about BPA because of a scientific study; this does not mean that other additives are safe, just that scientists haven't investigated them yet.

Plastic floating around in the sea is a bit like a sponge for bacteria and other chemicals, so when whales, dolphins, fish, turtles and birds eat the plastic, they can become sick from those as well as having their stomachs blocked with bits of plastic, effectively and painfully starving them to death. And if that's not bad enough, they could also get caught up in plastic that prevents them feeding or breathing, and again innocent creatures suffer a painful, horrible death.

Plastic made from oil, which is also used for other processes, will eventually run out – it's not sustainable by definition. Some oil is in unspoilt areas such as the Arctic and Norway, which currently have drilling bans in place, but I presume they will be under increasing pressure to release these reserves as oil reserves that are more accessible run out. It will also be increasingly valuable.

Plastic pollution

The world is suffering from a plastic pollution crisis and countries all over the world are beginning to react, if very slowly. Many large and powerful companies depend on selling their plastic products for their survival and the employment of their staff, so politicians are giving manufacturers, distributors and retailers time to change. There is currently no slowing down of plastic being made, and being wasted. Crow's top 10 plastics and resin manufacturers state the largest manufacturer is Dow Chemicals, with global sales of $49 billion and employing nearly 50,000 people worldwide. The following nine on the list are all multi-billion-dollar companies too, each with thousands of employees. They make the plastic for similarly huge companies, such as Nestle, Unilever, Coca-Cola, Pepsi and Procter & Gamble, who are all beginning to make the right noises about replacing plastic and also engaging with US-based recycling specialist TerraCycle. A good example of their efforts is the Fairy Ocean Plastic Bottle, which is made from 10 per cent ocean plastic and 90 per cent post-consumer recycled plastic. Proctor & Gamble says it has already met its zero waste goals in 19 countries, including the UK, Germany and Indonesia, but I would challenge how representative those zero waste goals are. P&G are the manufacturers of most of the world's plastic, 'single-use' nappies, and they certainly aren't recycling those other than in one pilot factory in Italy, i.e. close to 100 per cent that are not zero waste, so what is their goal, 1 per cent zero waste?

What can we do in our nurseries to reduce our dependency on plastic, particularly single-use plastics?

First, do not use single-use plastic as if it were re-useable to try and save waste. This is because they aren't designed for that. For example, single-use water bottles can leach toxins into the water you are about to drink if they get warm, like in the car.

The first step to eliminating single-use plastic is to identify where it is being used. I started by observing the daily routines in the nurseries so that I could see what plastic was being used, and then I researched whether these were necessary and if there were alternatives. Below is a list of what I initially found, although the journey continues to both spot and replace plastic. Because there were so many, I've listed them in alphabetical order:

Aprons

We were using single-use plastic aprons for food service, nappy changing, plus some messy activities. This really isn't necessary. Any experienced nursery practitioner knows when a baby boy is about to spray the area and what to do to minimise the mess, and it is very unusual for a nappy to leak in nursery as they are changed frequently. We do have cloth aprons for food service that just go in the wash after meals, and we also have vinyl, wipe down aprons that can be used whenever a colleague feels that they need it. This has increased our laundry, but we believe it's a better decision than continuing with single-use aprons – and within a few months it also saves money.

Balloons

We were using balloons to attract potential new children at fetes and open days. They often carried them away tied to their wrists initially as they were filled with helium, and when helium became expensive because it was increasingly rare, we put the balloons on sticks. Once identified, we stopped buying them and used bubble-blowing machines and paper windmills instead. There are numerous fascinating items that a child might carry around and take home to provide a marketing edge for your service. We also used balloons within the nurseries for moulding papier-mâché to create landscapes for our children to paint and explore. We haven't found an inflatable replacement, so now we just use cardboard or mud/clay.

Cleaning materials in plastic containers

Some nurseries were using large numbers of plastic bottles for a variety of cleaning liquids. Our current improvement is to use large containers of concentrated fluids, and re-use the smaller ones, and send the large ones back to the manufacturer to be topped up. There's very little waste. There are other alternatives, such as powdered products in cardboard boxes. We also discovered we could make our own – see Chapter 11 for more on this.

For safety reasons, we are not allowed to re-use a bottle for a different chemical, but products we make ourselves can go into plastic spray bottles such as the ones you can buy in a garden centre. We label them ourselves and, provided the contents are not toxic (e.g. white vinegar), we haven't had a problem with inspectors.

This is still a work in progress, and more companies are coming on board supplying more sustainable and non-toxic cleaning materials, so we continue to research this area.

Cling film

Cling film is of course made of plastic. It keeps perishables fresh for longer, doesn't require a drawer full of clips, is lightweight and easy to store. There are concerns about using it in a microwave: if you heat it, it may release phthalates, which are hormone disrupters. It is an unsustainable single-use plastic, made from non-renewable oil. It can also often be a problem to dispose of due to contamination from food, so it usually has to go into the general waste bin, where it is likely to end up in landfill, unless you have a waste company that burns the general waste.

In the past we have also used cling film for a range of play activities, from storing our play dough and clay to putting paint in it so the children can experience feeling the squidgy paint without getting paint on their hands or clothes, and we have even stretched it over frames and painted directly onto it. It's a very versatile plastic and we are sorry to say goodbye to it – perhaps one day someone will invent a way of recycling it so we can use it again.

There are a range of alternatives, depending on the use it is being put to. For covering a plate of food, the simplest thing is to put another plate or a plate cover on top. This does require a bit of investment, and can be a drain on storage, as they are rather a bit bigger than an average plate. Glass jars with lids are perfect for storing leftovers in the fridge. You can buy Mason jars and sometimes find them in charity shops or car boot sales. Re-useable silicon food bags are also being promoted as alternatives for people who prefer not to use plastic. If the food is on a tray and you don't have a glass or metal lid already, you might use aluminium foil, or a plastic tray you use for serving.

Part-opened containers can be resealed by wrapping them in beeswax wraps, which are becoming increasingly popular, although many vegans object to the use of bee-made products. You can either buy some readymade or make your own. To make your own, cut cotton fabric (bed sheet thickness with a very tight weave) to size, using pinking shears if you want a patterned edge, pop it onto some parchment paper and sprinkle the fabric with beeswax beads or grated beeswax. Let it melt in the oven for 10 minutes, brush the wax around to ensure all the edges and corners have been saturated. Then peel the fabric up and wave it around for a few seconds; leave it to dry properly on a hanger or drying rack. There are quite a few videos on YouTube if you'd like to see it or check the ingredients/quantities. Commercial wraps tend to add pine resin and jojoba oil to make them more resistant to washing and re-using, and you may be able to make them this way yourself, although we haven't tried yet! To use the wrap, you put it over your container and seal with the warmth from your hands. The main problem we've found with beeswax wraps is you can't wash them in the dishwasher, washing machine or in hot water, as the wax comes off. You need to wash them in cool water with a very mild natural soap. They won't last indefinitely, but you can always refurbish them as and when needed. We trialled beeswax wrapped but stopped using them in our nurseries.

Cutlery and crockery

We only used single-use plastic cutlery for parties, where we were catering for more than our usual number of children. This was an easy swap – we just bought more metal cutlery, which we were already using on a day-to-day basis anyway. Over the years, this will save us money and the time and effort required to purchase new sets of disposable cutlery, although there was an initial outlay. We mostly use ceramic/china crockery now. The occasional one is broken, but generally they've been a huge success and the children learn how to handle things that will break if you drop them.

Children's birthday parties at home often use dozens of plastic-coated paper plates, cups, bowls, cutlery, banners, badges, candle holders, etc., but schools and PTAs as well as some nurseries are beginning to offer to loan or rent birthday party hampers, with all the colourful party paraphernalia, but to come back afterwards, having been cleaned, for re-use. This saves parents a lot of money and everyone else a lot of waste. There are home compostable alternatives on the market now as well, made from compressed leaves, for example.

Gloves

We were using single-use plastic gloves for food service, nappy changing, applying suncream, and clearing up bodily waste. We simply stopped using them – mostly! If a member of staff has a problem with their skin integrity or a particularly mucky job to do, they can still use plastic gloves if they want to, but at worse use just one glove – on the hand doing the dirty work – that would halve your plastic glove bill.

As a routine, though, we came to the conclusion that if the local hospital felt it was unnecessary to use gloves when handling blood during blood donation services, and colleagues were using suitable handwashing before and after contact, then we didn't need to use gloves either. We also noted that silver service waiting staff in five-star hotels do not wear gloves, so why should we need them for food service? We did some research, checked with Ofsted (UK) inspectors, and then asked the nursery colleagues to stop wearing gloves.

For washing up, we still use heavy-duty plastic gloves that last for a few months, because the water is too hot to do the washing unprotected. There has been some objection to the removal of single-use gloves by some colleagues, generally those trained 20 or so years ago who felt that, after wearing gloves for decades, this constituted best practice.

Glitter

On the run up to Christmas, I noticed that the children were using glitter for their craft, mixed in with sand, in the water trays, making reindeer food for Father Christmas, etc., and had a horrified, eureka moment when I realised I was looking at microplastic. I love glitter: it's pretty, makes quite ordinary craft look amazing, it's certainly Christmassy, and we had been getting through kilos of the stuff in all our nurseries. Some glues have glitter in them already; you can also have glitter makeup and glitter in nail polish.

After some research, I discovered that, at less than 3mm in size, glitter passes straight through water filters and ends up in the sea and on the sea bed, where it can be eaten by shell fish, corals and small fish, which in turn are eaten by bigger fish, which human fish-eaters consume. Glitter is usually made of plastic with added chemicals for colour, which can be toxic. It can cause huge damage if it lands in a child's eye, and it certainly won't do us any good if we eat it. Like microbeads in facial scrubs, it needs to be banned. I decided to ask my colleagues to stop ordering glitter and did a blog on it, which the press caught on to. It went viral worldwide – a large chain of childcare centres stopping glitter just before Christmas! Can you imagine? We had numerous emails and Facebook messages of support from our own parents, with just a few dissenters internationally. My colleagues and I, and the parents, were interviewed by TV and radio stations. As a result, many other day nurseries and some schools have followed suit and we are immensely proud to have made a reflection that has affected so many others. One nursery banning glitter wouldn't have much impact on the state of our oceans, but if many nurseries and schools stop, we will have a significant, positive effect.

I was approached by a company offering to sell us eco-glitter, but it turned out that it was still 10 per cent plastic and the certificates they had awarded themselves were either defunct (expired in 2014 and were for marine plastic) or pure greenwash, such as about being biodegradable and commercially compostable. That's not to discount the fact that those who do buy the eco-glitter will be making a much better choice than a 100 per cent plastic product that might take 500 years to degrade. In the glitter aftermath, we have found that the children do not actively ask for glitter, and we have discovered new ways to add sparkle and colour to their materials by using natural petals and minerals.

Glue

Most nurseries in the UK use PVA glue, which stands for polyvinyl acetate. This is a mix of petroleum-based, synthesised chemicals with no natural ingredients.

The advantages of PVA are that it does not yellow over time, it remains flexible, will not break down, dries clear, does not give off any harmful fumes, will not affect the PH balance of anything it comes into contact with, and is non-toxic unless you ingest it. Most nurseries use PVA in abundance, for obvious reasons. However, it is easy to make a non-toxic, white glue using all-purpose flour, water and a pinch of salt. The only challenge then is how to get flour that is past its sell by date so you don't demand more food than you need to eat – and it would be a problem for those with gluten intolerance. We recently made a connection with a company prepared to let us have flour and other food products whose packaging had been split or compromised, to use for play – so that is a promising step forward.

Liquid soap in plastic pumps

We had a look at the many plastic containers that we were throwing away each week and realised that quite a few had hand soap in them. If you are using liquid soap, you would save by buying it in much larger containers and decanting into re-usable small pumps. There is more on this in the hygiene section.

Nappies and wipes are covered in detail in Chapter 5.

Paint

Children's paint can contain toxins, chemicals and plastics, so when I visited some Australian nurseries recently, some large containers of paint which were marked non-toxic and eco-friendly caught my eye. On investigation, I discovered there are various suppliers of more natural paint that is made using mineral earth and clay. They leave out preservatives, heavy metal toxins, solvents, synthetics, additives and fillers, and given that some of it invariably ends up in small children's mouths, this seems like a great idea. Naturalearthpaint.com[2] also advertise that they have gold certified Green America awards, and their paint can be used on wood, stone, fabric, glass, paper and more. Australia would appear to be ahead of the UK on this, but we are certainly investigating our options – I have contacted our usual supplier to see what they can offer. Australian companies also offer natural face paints and natural vegetable, fruit and herb dyes for eggs. There is more information on paint in Chapter 6.

Plastic bags and nappy sacks

Plastic carrier bags had been banned for decades in day nurseries, due to risk of suffocation. Big plastic bags are replaced easily with rucksacks, swimming bags and cloth bags. For wet/soiled clothes and soiled nappies we now supply branded, washable, re-useable wet bags that are popped into the washing machine along with the soiled items, so that we can forbid any type of plastic bag coming into the nursery

Shoe covers

Our under-12-month rooms are shoe-free zones. The concern is that outdoor messes could be walked into the room where babies are playing on the floor. In the past, we have used shoe covers made of plastic that you might get away with using a couple of times before holes appear. Socks are a bit of a problem if you slip, and bare feet can be an issue if you have athlete's foot, verrucas or perhaps dirty feet from walking outside bare foot. It's easy enough for colleagues to wear indoor shoes or slippers, so we have stopped providing plastic covers. Visitors just slip their shoes off before coming in. With everything else babies put in their mouths, were we being overprotective anyway?

Straws

We used these for drinking, for blowing bubbles through, for construction, and for threading. We easily found replacement straws made of paper and cardboard, although they do fall apart after a while. We also found metal straws but were concerned about the possibility of injury if a child were to fall with one. Metal straws also need washing, but are dishwasher safe and often come with a tiny brush specially designed for cleaning them. As the straws are so narrow, there is also the possibility that something could get stuck inside it that we couldn't see. Although this is a risk with all straws, whatever they are made from, in the past they would have just gone into the bin after one use

Little boxes of milk and juice are often supplied with straws attached in the UK. In Sweden, when travelling overnight on trains, you are supplied with little boxes of water which do not come with straws. Our 1-year-old had no trouble drinking out of them once we tore off the corner, so no need for plastic straws.

All kinds of alternatives are now available as well as paper, including pasta (a problem for gluten-free people), grass and bamboo.

Toothbrushes

We use toothbrushes for teeth cleaning, but also for some craft activities, and generally they are plastic and brightly coloured. Those used for toothbrushing were thrown out every three months, whether we needed to or not. Reflecting on this from a sustainability point of view, we decided to research alternatives to plastic and consider whether we really needed to change brushes so often. We found bamboo brushes through a local supplier but sourced in China, and we decided to do some training with the nursery practitioners so that brushes were only thrown out when they needed to be rather than on a regular cycle. Our normal supplier was not able to supply non-plastic toothbrushes, but we found an eco-supplier who could, although we had to buy a thousand at a time to make it worthwhile importing them. The cost of the bamboo brushes, including importation, was similar to our plastic ones, and we achieved savings by reducing the turnover time.

The new bamboo toothbrushes are plain but they do have our name engraved on them, and we are able to write the children's names on them with a sharpie, which we couldn't do on the plastic ones. They work well. It is worth paying attention to what the bristles on 'eco' toothbrushes are made from – it turned out that ours contained 10 per cent home compostable plastic, which we have yet to test. There is also the option to have boar bristles, which would have been a problem for any vegetarian, vegan or Muslim families, so I'm glad we didn't turn out to have those! There is more information on toothbrushes Chapter 11.

You can also source bamboo paint brushes.

Toys

As most childcare settings, we had enormous quantities of plastic toys, from cars, dolls, home corner equipment such as microwaves, hoovers, irons, buggies, to stickle bricks, Lego, doll houses, musical instruments … the list is actually endless. We were also given box loads of plastic toys from parents clearing out playrooms, particularly after Christmas. Several years ago, we made a decision to start replacing our plastic resources with more open-ended ones. In general, we don't buy plastic toys any more (see Chapter 13) and we give away plastic toys that we are gifted. The nurseries now look very different from even three to five years ago, and they certainly smell much fresher too. Most of our resources now are wood, metal, wool, glass, cotton, hessian, stone, shells, sand, water, clay, and even feathers, fir cones, leaves, flowers and grass.

We do have some plastic toys left which we have no intention of getting rid of, such as Lego, Duplo and stickle bricks, but we are looking forward to the Lego company making their product more sustainable, as they announced recently, so that when we come to purchase new products we can consider those.

Our table-sized touch-screen computer is largely plastic, but we will not be replacing that now that so many families have tablets, computers and touch screens at home.

We still have a few plastic dolls, as cloth dolls don't seem to be as popular, long-lasting or as easy to undress.

Wherever possible, we opt for the real thing – ideally a small version if there is one, such as pots and pans, and travel irons with plugs removed. Key suppliers and also Ikea have started to rise to the challenge and offer small-sized real items: kitchen dressers, musical instruments, wooden rings and even natural, varnished slices of wood and bags of selected stones. Of course, these are at a premium price compared with sourcing them (stones!) yourself.

The other big disadvantage of much of the plastic range is that they are made in China. The moulds may have been made in the UK but there are no manufacturers that could make the products even at 400 per cent of the cost of making them in China. We were told that one of the main reasons for this was because there is every kind of plastic engineer in quite a compact area of China, so the whole process is very efficient.

I still have concerns about transporting across the ocean; not because of the cost, but because of the noise pollution to marine creatures. There is currently no tax that includes this particular cost to the planet. A monetary cost to reflect the cost to the environment is sometimes the only thing that will deter manufacturers from importing and exporting across the globe.

Uniform

We were very excited to learn that we might be able to buy some uniform fleeces that were made from recycled plastic until we discovered that when we washed those uniforms the microfibres would wash off the clothes, go through the washing machine filters, and into the water supply, to make plastic soup! We made contact with an eco-cotton supplier of uniform only to discover that it was twice the price and used a huge amount of water to make the cotton. We looked at bamboo cloth for uniform, but it was three times the price, and needed an awful lot of ironing to get it looking presentable for the next day. Unfortunately, we are having to continue using our original suppliers for sports shirts, tabards, tunics and fleeces, but have returned to organic cotton for t-shirts. To counteract this, we are looking into improved filters for our washing machines that can catch microfibres before they enter our environment.

Recycled plastic can't usually be used for toys

Manufacturers are beginning to make items from recycled plastic, and we have managed to source recycled fencing panels, which are more expensive than wood panels but last for very much longer. However, a note of warning: one manufacturer I talked with explained that when they recycle plastics, they don't know exactly what is in the plastic, what has been added to it, or what it has been coloured with, so when they have chopped it up, melted it down and reconstituted it, it is not quality-controlled like virgin plastic. This means that it does not comply with the EU Toy Safety Directive, which is why you don't generally find toys made of recycled plastic. An eco-toy might instead be packaged in sustainable packaging, or made of recycled cardboard, sustainable wood, and coloured with natural dyes. I did find one recycled plastic toy boat, but it was made specifically from American milk bottles – a specific and identified plastic source.

Conclusion

Plastic is far better used for essentials, perhaps medical equipment, where it can't be replaced and has to last, rather than for single use in a nursery. We can replace virtually all single-use plastic with something that doesn't last as long, and doesn't cause plastic pollution. Those we can't replace we can just manage without. In time our scientists and entrepreneurs will work out what to do with plastic once it's no longer fit for purpose, and the politicians will put carrots and sticks in place to make us use plastic for what it is truly needed for, and not for what it isn't. According to the Ethical Corporation,[3] in 2019 we are only 9 per cent of the way to a circular economy, so we have to 'stop extracting, stop wasting, optimise what we already have and recycle more and better'.

Finally, although we've made many changes at a strategic level, sometimes I will see some single-use plastic in use. Usually its old stock which we might as well use, but spot-checking invoices for a while after making replacements in order to avoid any single-use plastic starting to creep in to your nursery again might be a good idea based on my experience.

Notes

1. Jambeck, J.R., Geyer, R., Wilcox, C., Siegler, T.R., Perryman, M., Andrady, A., Narayan, R., and Law, K.L. (2015). Plastic waste inputs from land into the ocean. *Science*. 347 (6223), 768–771. doi: 10.1126/science.1260352.
2. Natural Earth Paint; eco-friendly paint kits. (2018). www.naturalearthpaint.com.
3. www.ethicalcorp.com.

5 | Nappies and wet wipes

Introduction

Single-use, 'disposable' nappies make up the single biggest waste product that most nurseries generate. Every baby and toddler in nappies uses a nappy every three to four hours, creating a ton of waste each! And typically it costs three times as much to dispose of them as it did to buy them. Wet wipes flushed down toilets cause enormous sewer blockages, costing the communities significant inconvenience and cost, and damaging the environment. This chapter discusses the ways that adults working in the early years sector can make more sustainable choices regarding nappy changing frequency, potty training, different types of nappies, laundry, and wet wipes.

Background

Previous generations used terry nappies, washed and re-used them, but the single-use plastic nappies have been very convenient. Originally sold to use for travel and emergencies, they have become a routine part of childcare in many countries. Hospitals, midwives, and day nurseries usually only use 'disposable' nappies. The fact that they aren't disposable and they actually take around 400 years to break down into microplastic in landfill, and possibly never if they end up in the sea, has escaped our notice, and decades of parents have now only used single-use nappies.

However, we are becoming more aware of the problem. According to Veolia,[1] about 8 million disposable nappies are thrown away each day in the UK, which accounts for 3–4 per cent of all household waste. That is 3–4 per cent in every household, whether they have children still in nappies or not! The UK gets through around 3 billion nappies, weighing about 700,000 tonnes, and costing about £100 million per year in disposal, and that's just one small country.

Most local authorities, politicians and regulators (e.g. Ofsted) are doing nothing or very little to encourage parents or early years staff to train children to use pants in a timely manner, nor to wear re-useable nappies. There are exceptions to this, such as the Welsh local council that decided to impose an additional waste collection tax on those families still throwing nappies in the waste for children over the age of 4, unless they had diagnosed, related special needs. But this did meet with resistance – perhaps as most local people did not understand the necessity for doing anything about nappy waste. A few councils have also introduced financial incentives to parents buying some cloth/real nappies, recognising that this kind of investment can produce a financial and environmental return.

What can we do to be more sustainable in our early years services?

Potty training

The age that children stop using nappies has been increasing over the last 20 years from around 18 months to 2 years then to 3–3½ years old. There are increasing numbers of 4–5-year-olds who are also still in 'pull-up nappies' or not reliably toilet trained and are therefore being turned away from school, which is extremely inconvenient for working parents, and can be humiliating and damaging to self-esteem for both parents and children.

A good place to start is to check whether you have any 3-year-olds still in nappies in your setting. There may be some children who have special needs, such as developmental delay or physical bladder/bowel control issues, or perhaps they were very premature, so obviously there needs to be flexibility, and consideration for emotional upheaval also. There is also a cultural element to the age of children being toilet trained – some countries teach children more effectively than others and children can be out of nappies even before 18 months, because they are popped on a potty as soon as they can sit. I'm not suggesting one or the other, but we found that monitoring the average age in nurseries and comparing them against each other helped indicate where staff needed training on potty training, and where all was within our expectations.

The last thing that we want to do is to cause parents to feel guilty about delayed toilet training success, because it is hard enough to be a parent already. Instead, there are practical things that day nursery colleagues can do to help, but before we did that we looked at re-training staff. We found that potty training was barely taught on many early years courses preparing colleagues to work in the sector, the ethos being just watch for signs that children are ready and go from there, there's no hurry. But actually this became so laidback that children were still not potty trained ready for school, so redressing the balance is essential.

We found a system that enabled us to re-teach colleagues and support parents at the same time, as well as making it fun and causing no pressure or unhappiness in the children. The Potty Training Academy offered us a website, books, videos, stories, puppets, stickers and great suggestions and tips that helped us to reduce the average age of children coming out of nappies. We also have a plaque on our wall advertising that our nurseries are potty training academies, to encourage parents to also take the initiative and ask for support with potty training. Using the key worker system, where members of staff form a bond with parents and are able to discuss this subject openly and supportively, and giving the benefit of their experience and expertise to the parents, can only help get children out of nappies easily, effectively, happily – and ideally when they are closer to 2 than to 3.

Frequency of nappy changes

How often are you changing the babies' nappies? Modern nappies can last all night, yet we sometimes change them every two hours in a day nursery. Obviously they need changing immediately if soiled, and you need to change a child with a sore bottom more often, but you might be over-changing, causing more

Figure 5.1 Potty Academy books and resources

work, more cost, more disruption to children's play and more expense, so perhaps it is worth some reflection and changing to three to four hours if you are on a two-hour schedule?

Nappy choices

Single-use plastic/cellulose nappies

'Disposable' nappies are not sustainable; they are waste after only one use by definition. They are made of oil, wood pulp and chemicals, and the process uses a lot of water and energy too – using up a massive amount of resource. They are then often wrapped in a nappy sack to keep the smell contained, then put into a bin liner in a nappy bin for the rest of the day, and then thrown into general waste, where they often go to landfill. Many calculations on the sustainability of nappies miss all the extra wrapping after use. In a nursery in the UK the nappies should go into a yellow bin to be incinerated, which might at least contribute to energy production, but this is not mandatory. Single-use nappies are not currently recycled anywhere in the world, apart from in one pilot factory that has recently opened in Italy. The problems have been the poo – bacteria, and the difficulties caused by the combination of materials used. Most adults are unaware that it costs **so** much to dispose of 'disposable nappies' – at least three times what it cost to make them – yet the manufacturers contribute nothing to this (at the time of writing).

A key problem is that we throw single-use nappies away together with the poo and urine from the baby in them (contra to the small print on the nappy packaging!), so if they go to landfill they also form a bacterial problem that leaches into the environment because the sewage system designed to treat poo properly is bypassed. The plastic and the poo are a major environmental hazard that most parents and colleagues in the early years sector may not be aware of. They also come in plastic packaging, which also goes to waste, and they are bulky, requiring regular shopping or delivery trips, all adding to their carbon impact.

Biodegradable nappies

Biodegradable nappies sound good, and you have to pay extra for them. Advertisements may say they biodegrade in only 50 years instead of 400 years, but this would almost certainly be in a commercial biodegrading facility. If you use biodegrading nappies, are they separated and sent to a commercial biodegrading machine? If not, they will be going to general waste/landfill or be incinerated.

If your nappies are going to be incinerated, there is little point in buying biodegradable nappies – why pay the extra cost just to burn them?

Biodegradation happens with sunlight, heat and oxygen. There might be some of this in general waste, but as the nappies are covered with more rubbish it gets darker and there's less oxygen, so they may never biodegrade, much like plastic nappies. If nappies get into the water where its cold and there's little oxygen, they are still going to kill fish, birds and whales long before they disintegrate. Maybe they are useful as a stage to go through, but my personal opinion is that most biodegradable adverts are 'greenwash' – just to sell the product rather than an actual improvement in sustainability.

Nappies made from renewable sources/chemical free

At least these nappies do not use as much of our non-renewable supplies, and care is being taken to source the materials, energy and water more responsibly. Some companies might deliver them using electric vehicles. If made with plants and not turned into a plant-based plastic, they might biodegrade more quickly too. These are a better option, I feel, than the plastic single-use nappies, but perhaps as emergency back-up if you can't do the laundry of re-usable nappies? Watch out for development in this area. Perhaps they will become home-compostable one day, which is the gold standard to ask for in single-use products.

Washable, re-usable, cloth nappies

Despite the fact that we use water and energy to wash these nappies, they are the most sustainable option by far, all things considered. You need to follow the temperature instructions on the nappy, but in general should not use a wash temperature of more than 60 degrees, and preferably use 40 degrees for most of the time because modern nappies made of bamboo and microfibre cannot be boil-washed as they fall apart. You don't iron them, and ideally hang them out to dry on a line in the sun rather than tumble dry. You cannot use a low water eco-setting on the washing machine as they need lots of water to clean them properly.

If you do use a tumble dryer, it needs to be on a low temperature or you may damage the nappy fabric. It's much more preferable to hang them up to dry but sometimes they get a bit scratchy and that can be turned around with a couple of minutes in a dryer or a really good hand rub. The sun has an anti-bacterial, anti-smell effect, which is very helpful too.

The Scandinavians use drying cupboards which use less power than tumble dryers. You should also buy your power from a renewable supplier or use solar panels to avoid contributing to climate change through burning fossil fuels for the energy to dry them.

Cloth nappies are made from a range of fabrics these days, all of which need an outer, waterproof layer to stop the contents from escaping. The outer is usually plastic-based, but there are also natural wool waterproof layers which just need oiling to maintain their effectiveness. Some nappies are all in one; the liner and nappy are integrated into one easy-to-put-on nappy, much like the 'disposables' we mostly use, but you can also buy two-part nappies and change the inner more often and retain the outer for re-use with the next nappy or two. The two-part nappies dry more quickly but take a little longer to put on. Fastening a cloth nappy is either Velcro, poppers, or 'nippers', which are very easy-to-fit clips (plastic) and replace the old-fashioned large and sharp nappy safety pins.

Microfibre

This modern material is light, dries very quickly, and is relatively cheap, but it is made of plastic, so uses up oil. They don't biodegrade and will leach microplastics into the water when washed. They also aren't as absorbent when squashed, e.g. when carrying the baby, or when the baby is in a car seat or wearing tight-fitting clothes, they might leak a little. Still, they are a better choice than using a nappy once as you can use these again and again; they are particularly durable and often have very cute designs. Watch out for improvements in fabrics to stop plastic microfibres escaping into the drains, and improvements to washing machines to stop this also. I'm hoping a university will do some research on how much microplastic is escaping from different manufacturers' nappies to help inform our purchase decisions.

Bamboo

Bamboo is a very fast-growing plant, it doesn't need any fertiliser and self-regenerates from its own roots. Bamboo can be made into a super soft, very absorbent nappy, it uses a lot less water to make than cotton, but it is slightly less hard wearing than cotton. Bamboo doesn't grow in the UK, so it will have been grown somewhere else and imported (extra cost and noise to the environment, therefore). There are further sustainability issues with bamboo as it can made into fabric using toxic chemicals. Look for the brand name TENCEL. This uses a process to recapture and re-use 99 per cent of the chemicals, and it won the 'European Award for the Environment', so this is a good choice. The material is sewn into shaped nappies that are as easy to put on as a disposable, but you wash them instead of binning them. Although not perfect, this is arguably the best choice to make currently; however, it does take longer to dry than microfibre so those in wetter climates might still prefer a microfibre nappy. Bamboo nappies need washing at 40 or 60 degrees.

Cotton

Traditional nappy squares or terry nappies are made of cotton. It's relatively cheap and robust. Cotton uses a lot of water when growing, which is a disadvantage, and also it doesn't grow in the UK so will be imported. You might want to look for organic cotton as that is grown without pesticides. There are nicely shaped cotton nappies too now, easy to put on, with Velcro or poppers, or tags, so much easier than the old-fashioned nappy pins. The traditional terry nappies can be boil-washed, whereas the others cannot, but boiling is expensive.

Hemp

Hemp is very absorbent, which makes it popular for a nappy booster (extra pads you can put into any cloth nappy to make them more absorbent), but it does take a while to dry. Hemp is grown using no pesticides, very little water, requires a relatively small amount of land and produces double the yield of cotton, making it one of the most environmentally friendly fabrics currently available. It may also be grown locally to you. It also doesn't irritate the skin and is hypoallergenic – great stuff. It's a shame there isn't more of it available – yet.

Liners

When you use a cloth nappy it is normal to use a liner to collect the solids and make them easier to flush down the toilet – either with a shower head, shaking or with a nappy knife or spoon. Liners can be disposable or washable. Bamboo liners are more absorbent but also take longer to dry. In a nursery you might want to use a disposable one and put it and the poo into the yellow bin for incineration, but it would be much better to put the poo down the toilet – IF you have one available and staff willing to do it! Liners should not be flushed down a toilet, because if they don't block your own toilet they may well block drainage further down the line, just like wet wipes. Even if the packaging says flushable, don't do it!

Storage

Many parents build up a stash of cloth nappies, buying and selling them on to suit their baby and their style. Each baby will need 20–30 nappies at home and enthusiasts may build up quite a library. Nurseries need about four nappies per baby in nappies for a full day, and would wash daily. Back-ups would be essential in case the washing machine broke down or you had a power cut.

20–30 nappies is about the same amount of space as two large packets of single-use nappies, so you do need a large hamper, shelving or drawers for them.

With 20 babies in a nursery, 80 nappies, picture eight large packs of single-use nappies you would need to store, which probably isn't very different from storing 20 baskets of nappies for each baby/toddler.

The second-hand value for nappies is very good, so the investment, which could be £250 or more, can be partly recovered, on top of the savings from not buying 6500 single-use nappies. Mixing different brands and types of nappies can help to fit all babies, but may also confuse adults as there are differing ways of fitting the various nappies – but there are some excellent YouTube videos that can be watched to help you teach colleagues.

Real cloth nappies in nurseries

Very few nurseries accept babies in cloth nappies, but this is changing as more is understood about modern cloth nappies. Nappies don't need to soak in buckets of diluted bleach all day anymore – this just isn't done at all! All of our nurseries are delighted to welcome children in cloth nappies because this is so much more sustainable and actually totally doable!

At nursery you need to try out/choose a model of operation or maybe a combination to suit:

1. Parents supply the re-usable nappies and take them away to wash at the end of the day. Just store as you always have in the past, basket or box per baby/child, and return in a wet bag without tipping the poo out.

2. Nursery supplies re-usable nappies while at nursery, changing them on arrival and changing them back into parent-provided nappy at the end of the day. Launders nursery nappies.

3. Nursery supplies the re-usable nappies but gives them to parents to take away and wash at the end of the day and return (risk of non-return, so you need a lot of spares). Parents can use whatever they wish at home, but need to bring the baby back in a re-usable nappy.

4. Nursery supplies the nappies and does the laundry.

   a. Nappies are individual per child, washed after two to three days, keeping in a wet bag, and having tipped poo out before storage ideally. Laundry as described for parents. You will need extra washing machines – several small ones are better than one commercial one. A sluice would be useful or a shower head by a toilet to rinse poo into the toilet. For part-time children this is a problem, as you may be washing one or two nappies in a load, and it takes a while, which isn't time or cost effective. You will need a housekeeper to do the laundry.

b. Nappies are communal. All stored together, a risk assessment is required for transfer of disease and infections. You will need to put nappies into a bacteria-neutralising soak, such as the one made by Biovation, if you want to wash nappies from different babies in the same wash. Your environmental health officer may require you to use a hot wash (cotton, which you can't do with microfibre or bamboo nappies, so nappies would have to be cotton). A sluice or shower spray by the toilet would be very useful. Bigger loads are possible, so you could use a commercial machine. You will need a housekeeper to do the laundry.

Nurseries providing their own re-useable nappies for children are few and far between, I think, because the sector is still not very familiar with either why or how to use them, but also because the laundry is a challenge. Staff time is needed for loading, unloading, hanging up and folding the nappies, so you really need a couple of machines, approximately one washing machine for every 12 babies, and probably an extra pair of hands too. You may be lucky to have a nappy laundry service, which would be of great benefit if you have large numbers of babies and toddlers, but this will mean stocking probably twice the nappies and will add significantly to your costs due to the transport between nursery and launderette – unless it's very local.

Financially, for a nursery, using re-usable nappies versus disposables is pretty neutral. Although you save a lot of money over a year making the swap to re-usables from disposables normally, it's the cost of extra washing machines, a sluice, and a housekeeper that takes the savings away again.

Wet bag use

These are wonderful inventions, coming in different sizes. Ideally, you put the poo into a toilet, then wrap the nappy up and pop it into the wet bag. At the end of the day the bag is turned inside out into the washing machine, or into a larger wet bag, or a dry bucket with a lid or a wet bucket with a soak in it, with a lid, until there are enough to run a load. Nappies can be stored for two to three days before washing but would normally be done daily or as there is enough for a load in a day nursery. Washable nappies don't smell like single-use nappies do because the poo has been removed and there isn't the chemical interaction you get in disposables. Wet bags are much better than plastic nappy sacks, which are one use. Wet bags can also be used for wet clothes to return to parents. They may well be made of plastic – but they aren't one use, and you can expect them to last for many children, saving a lot of single-use plastic bags.

Working with parents

Increasing numbers of eco-minded parents are using real nappies and we are starting to see parents choose our nurseries because we welcome their children in real nappies, and because we know how to use them or are happy to learn. It may give you a competitive edge to offer real nappy support in your nursery, and in the future it could be a real disadvantage if you don't.

If you have staff who are parents of children not yet potty trained, you have a huge opportunity. If you can persuade the member of staff to try out real nappies, perhaps provide them with a hamper of them, they will be the expertise for parents to draw on. Perhaps you can lend the money for the purchase to help incentivise staff back to work? Or perhaps engage with a company or charity who can loan or rent them to staff who cannot afford the initial investment?

Many nappy distributors, including the national online companies, sell trial packs for parents to try or return, and there are also nappy libraries all over the country where you can often try out a range of nappies for free also.

We have gone one step further, and provided a hamper of real nappies for parents to try for a couple of weeks, because parents can experience for themselves how easy they are to use, how attractive and economic they are, on top of being more sustainable, and therefore we hope that they are more likely to want to make the change.

Of course a change to real nappies does not have to be for every single nappy. Parents and staff could start with just swapping one for one – that already saves about 90 nappies from the bin – and can we can still opt to keep a few single-use nappies available for occasional emergencies, or travelling for example. The general culture should be to use cloth nappies for everyday normal use because this is the responsible, sustainable thing to do to help protect the environment for our children.

Baby/wet wipes

Every time we change a nappy we wipe the baby's skin, perhaps with cotton wool and water, but perhaps with a commercial wet wipe. In a nursery the wet wipe, covered in poo and urine, is usually popped into the nappy and put into the nappy bin for incineration later. At home it probably goes into general waste.

London has announced several times the major problems with wipes causing blockages in drains and gutters, and flushing into the River Thames, where other solids combined to make huge balls of unsightly and unhealthy waste. These cost a lot of money and unpleasant time to cut them up and take them elsewhere for disposal

Wet wipe fabric – spunlace

The fabric that wet wipes are made of is called spunlace. It is highly unlikely you will find that listed in the ingredients on a baby wipe wrapper, as they only list the contents of the liquid they are soaked in!

Spunlace is a composite of different fibres, which nearly always contains polyester and polypropylene to increase strength. The fibres are bonded together by chemical, mechanical, heat or solvent treatment. Other ingredients are usually viscose (made from wood pulp or bamboo pulp), wood pulp or cotton.

This means that spunlace will not biodegrade nor compost, and therefore must not go down any toilets (it will likely block the toilet, the pipes, or the sewage plant). They should not go to landfill or into the water as they will contaminate the environment for hundreds of years.

Wet wipes used for wiping down tables, first aid, computer screens, etc., are also all made of spunlace.

Wet wipe liquid

Some wrappers highlighted how pure and healthy the ingredients were, but referring to the wet part of the wipe, not the cloth. There are also a number of irritants and chemicals in some commercially bought baby wipes which can aggravate delicate skin. Some have a warning that includes possible allergies, immunotoxicity, organ system toxicity, hazard warnings of 5 or even 7 out of 10, and moisturiser that contained alcohol, preservatives and irritants. There are some purer ones around that are actually 99 per cent water but, of course, they cost more!

Having reflected on the ingredients, we thought we'd rather use something a lot more natural. After conducting our own research, we came up with a recipe for making our own baby wipes – no irritants and no plastics. At one of our monthly managers' meetings, we demonstrated the method, gave notice to our suppliers and stopped buying any more commercial baby wipes.

DIY wet wipes

- 1 roll of heavy duty paper towels (use good quality, such as Bounty, because cheap paper towels do not work for wipes; they just disintegrate)

- 1.25-litre sealable container (old wipes containers, Tupperware, clip boxes, old plastic coffee containers or empty gallon plastic ice cream buckets all work, as long as they don't leak when you turn them upside down)

- 1¾ cups boiled water (or distilled) – cooled but still warm – (can just use regular water if you use them in less than a week like we do)

- 1 tablespoon of pure aloe vera – check the ingredients as some brands are not pure

- 1 tablespoon of pure witch hazel extract (optional)

- 1 teaspoon of liquid Castile soap (we use Dr Bronner's or Bio-Origins)

- 10 drops grapefruit seed extract or 2 capsules of vitamin E (optional)

- 1 teaspoon of olive oil (optional)

- 6 drops of essential oils such as lavender or orange or tea tree (optional but do not use tea tree for babies under 6 months)

1. Cut the roll of paper towels in half using a sharp knife.

2. If using a plastic shoe box or old wipe container, accordion-fold the towels into the container. If using a Rubbermaid #6 container (I highly recommend), place the towels cut side down in container.

3. In bowl or quart-size jar, mix the water, aloe, witch hazel, Castile soap, GSE/vitamin E and oil, and stir.

4. Add essential oils if desired and stir.

5. Pour over paper towels in container and let absorb – this takes about 5–10 minutes.

6. Turn the container upside down to make sure wipes are well soaked.

Pull the cardboard roll out from the inside. This should also pull the innermost wipe out and start them for you. Depending on the brand of paper towels you use, you might have to experiment with the amount of water.

Use as you would regular wipes, and smile, knowing you are not causing the children or the environment any problems!

If you want to take some in the buggy, car, or handbag, just decant half a dozen into a smaller, water tight tub or Tupperware-type box.

Note: If you have children with extremely sensitive skin, you may need to leave out the essential oils or use calendula or chamomile instead.

Re-usable DIY wipes

You can also make re-usable ones. Just cut up old tea towels or t-shirts into 8×8 inch squares. Fold them into old wipes containers and pour the same mixture (above) onto them or spray on each wipe with a spray bottle before using. These are an even cheaper option, but you do need to keep them individual to each child

Figure 5.2 Making our own wet wipes (1)

Figure 5.3 Making our own wet wipes (2)

to avoid cross-contamination. Commercial re-usable wipes (small flannels really) are also easy to purchase from cloth nappy distributors.

We have found the cost to be compatible with retail wipes, but if you get a good discount for wholesale baby wipes, those will still be much cheaper. Moving to DIY wipes will be a cost, not a financial saving, at this time.

Conclusion

Every decision in sustainability is likely to be less than perfect, but there can be no doubt that we need to use a lot less single-use plastic 'disposable' nappies! This is a big cultural change and we can expect a lot of objections, from parents and staff. The bottom line is that re-usable nappies are a lot cheaper over a year for parents, despite the laundry, and a lot better for the environment, but they are a bit more work – although not as much as you might expect, at least per change. Can we stop using single-use nappies altogether? I think we can, but maybe keep some single-use nappies for emergencies (as originally intended). Don't expect to make the change overnight as it will take time to convert staff and parents. But use of real nappies instead of single-use, even one per day, can make a huge difference to the waste disposal bill overall, plastic waste pollution and use of fossil fuels.

The government could help the move to re-usable nappies by making the manufacturers foot the bill for getting rid of the disposable nappies after use. I expect the manufacturers would pass that on by putting up the price of 'disposable' nappies, i.e. for parents, which may not be a vote winner, although it would reduce the cost to the local authorities largely dealing with the waste, which would reduce council tax for everyone – and that would be popular!

I am hoping that the UK will ban wet wipes that contain plastic. The *Evening Standard* newspaper[2] announced in May 2018 that the Environment Secretary was intending to do this, but we will see. There is no need to wait for politicians to act first; we can make this change straight away. However, if plastic single-use wet wipes do get banned, perhaps the manufacturers will take the opportunity for more of them to start making sustainable wet wipes that don't clog the drains, are made without plastic, and save us the time and effort of making them ourselves!

Notes

1. Veolia. (n.d.). Real nappies: The facts! [online]. *Veolia*. Available from: www.veolia. co.uk/westberkshire/waste-minimisation/waste-minimisation/real-nappies-facts.
2. Morrison, J. (2018). Wet wipes to be banned in UK as part of drive to cut plastic waste. *Evening Standard*, 8 May.

6 Play activities

Play activities for our children need to be carefully considered from an eco-sustainable perspective. It is helpful to have a set of criteria to work through when setting up activities, or thinking about purchasing new materials.

This chapter describes a set of criteria, and then considers a range of 10 activities against those criteria to establish how sustainable, or not, they are, and reflects further on how they can be made more sustainable. The same simple format can then be used to assess your own activities as required.

Set of criteria

1. Does the activity use any existing resources?

2. Are the resources recycled from elsewhere, e.g. scrap store, car boot, passed down, donated?

3. If new, what are they made of?

   ▪ Virgin non-replaceable minerals such as plastic made entirely from oil?

   ▪ Virgin replaceable materials, certified as sustainable, such as FFC wood?

   ▪ A blend of virgin and recycled materials, such as some plastics – what percentage is the blend?

   ▪ From a mineral dug from the ground that damages the landscape or the seascape (and the creatures living in that land/water)?

   ▪ Has the material been imported and transported to you, or is it local?

4. How have the materials been transported – diesel, petrol, or electricity from renewable sources? Using transport that is already in place or a specially implemented system?

5. Will they last for years and be a good investment, or is it single-use?

6. How much care will you need to take of them, and can you do this with the children?

7. Will the item(s) need painting or varnishing?

8. When they reach the end of their life, can you return them to the manufacturers, or will they go to recycling, landfill or incineration? If they escape into the air, environment or water, will they damage the environment?

If you have established that some of the process is not sustainable, has the manufacturer or distributor done anything to compensate for the damage, such as using the quarry holes for water sports, paying a third party to fund sustainable activities or scientific research to benefit the environment? Is there anything you can do to offset the damage?

With this criteria in place, we can reflect on some of the learning and play activities within our nurseries and we can then decide how to proceed. It may be that we decide to stop offering a particular activity altogether, because it clearly isn't sustainable, such as playing with balloons in the garden. On the other hand, it may be that we can find a way to continue an activity by making a sustainable change, such an alternative item, or using a different supplier, or finding a way to re-use, maintain or repair resources or products.

There may be a number of different ways we could proceed, but we must also remember to be pragmatic and not jump in too deep, too quickly. It is important to work with suppliers rather than against them, and consider the local community, as well as our budgets. We make the best decisions we can at the time, but must remember to regularly review practices to see if there is new information available, new scientific discoveries, or new resource alternatives. At the point, we can make a new decision ... and another one at the next review ... and another one ... until we get to the best we possibly can.

Below, I'm going to reflect on 10 different activities that we offer as part of our continuous provision, available to children all of the time. They are each well suited to our settings and provide good learning opportunities for our children. With the sustainability criteria in mind, you may find that some of these aren't appropriate within your settings, which is to be expected given different locations, suppliers and priorities of your day nursery:

- sand play

- water play

- paint

- chalk

- paper

- glue

- digital table/computers

- home corner

- craft activities

- construction, e.g. Lego, blocks, loose parts

- musical instruments

- treasure baskets for babies' tummy time.

Sand

Sand is made mostly from rock, broken down by weathering processes. Also, some sea sand is created by parrotfish who munch up coral to get to the algae inside – the coral is then excreted as fine sand. It's a reasonably plentiful resource. Digging it up can cause damage to the landscape or under the sea, so it's a good idea to ask where it comes from and how far it has been brought. Sand can last for years as long as you can find a way to clean it. One of my nurseries in Somerset, UK, once tried to throw away an entire outside sandpit of sand – they filled their general waste bin and the waste collectors refused to take the bin because it was too heavy, so they had to take it all out again, bag it up, and pay even more for a man and a van to take it away! This was definitely learning the

Table 6.1 Sand

Activity	Renewable?	Land/sea damage?	Local?	Investment that could last for years?	Care?	Paint or varnish?	End of life?
Sand	No, but there is lots available and it does renew while there are parrotfish and stones to grind.	Yes	Can be	Yes	Yes	No	Depends on disposal method

hard way, so I hope I can help prevent this happening again by sharing with you. How much better would it have been to clean the sand and re-use it? Sand itself is not a good environment for bacteria, so it is reasonably safe for children to play in. However, there's no doubt that sand outside, particularly if uncovered, can be used as an animal toilet, so it needs checking daily and cleaning periodically. Even inside, children could inadvertently add contaminants that may need cleaning out. You need to risk-assess your sand depending on its location and covering and decide how often to clean it.

To clean sand: On a sunny day, use a kitty litter scooper if you see any larger 'nasties' you want to remove. You could also sieve it. We're told by the Royal Society for the Prevention of Accidents[1] that play sand will need to be regularly disinfected. One method is to fill a large plastic watering can or sprayer with a sustainable bleach alternative, thoroughly soak the sand and allow the cleaned sand to sit for about 15 minutes and repeat until the area has been covered. Make sure to stir it around with a rake or stick/spoon to allow the wet sand to dry out. And of course, ensure the sand is reasonably dry before children continue to play in it.

Bleach itself is a nasty product. Its harmful effects can include irritation to the eyes, respiratory system, and throat, as well as severe allergic reaction with skin contact. It's not compatible with health, nor with sustainability. So what else can we use?

The sun itself is a disinfectant, and so is hot boiling water. You could use white vinegar and melaleuca (tea tree oil), or combine baking soda and vinegar. Or even hydrogen peroxide and lemon. Just make sure to never mix them all together! Vinegar and hydrogen peroxide creates paracetic acid, which is very irritating to skin, eyes and nose. There are loads of recipes online if you search for alternatives to bleach.

We have started to use 9 parts water and 1 part white vinegar because it is easy to make, is harmless to children and works wonderfully well. In a spray bottle or watering can, mix the water and white vinegar, add a few drops of tea tree (although not for sand infants will play with) or lavender and use as above.[2]

Water

In the UK, we usually have a plentiful supply of water, and it comes through our taps fit to drink, although some has fluoride in. You may filter this out for drinking, but it is certainly fit to play with, so we are incredibly lucky. This isn't the case in many other countries. Water is a very precious resource and we must be sensitive to that fact, and not waste water unnecessarily. Water can cost more than oil in the desert. Even in the UK, we occasionally have a garden hose ban in

Table 6.2 Water

Activity	Renewable?	Land/sea damage?	Local?	Investment that could last for years?	Care?	Paint or varnish?	End of life?
Water	Yes	No	Yes	n/a	No	No	OK

a dry summer. In many countries, there is water rationing and taps are only on for a few hours a day, or worse, people have to walk to wells for water. Water that we collect in rain butts is often not fit to drink because it has sat in a stagnant container outside, sometimes in warm conditions, so bacteria and bugs are a hazard. We avoid this risk by not drinking it, or playing in it where children could put it in their mouths, but it is fine for welly boot play and most useful for watering the garden. All we need to do is clean the water containers and toys periodically, according to our risk assessments. It would be best to clean these with a natural cleaner such as the sand cleaners above.

Paint

Until recently, we generally bought our powder paint and ready-mixed paint from our usual early years supplier. I looked up the COSHH information, which included: wear dust masks, avoid contact with skin and eyes, provide ventilation where dust is formed, on combustion emits toxic fumes of carbon dioxide (which means we don't want it going into general waste or being incinerated). There was no data on aspiration, potential health effects, reproductive toxicity, etc. It also stated that Brian Clegg powder paints had *not* been approved for children under 36 months! But it does conform to all relevant parts of the European Toy Safety regulations (EN71).

I then looked up the finger paint, which is 'safe for children as it has a lick deterrent designed to prevent licking and swallowing of the paint'[3] – denatonium benzoate. They are wheat- and gluten-free, and comply with regulation EN71 but, worryingly, they also might cause temporary irritation, coughing or wheezing.

Table 6.3 Paint

Activity	Renewable?	Land/sea damage?	Local?	Investment that could last for years?	Care?	Paint or varnish?	End of life?
Paint	Depends on source, but lots available	Yes, if minerals mined	Can be	Yes	Yes	No	OK

There is no available data on ecological information, and I was very disappointed to see the same product safety data sheet was used for standard, fluorescent and glitter finger paint, with no consideration for what the glitter is made of! We need to ask our suppliers about sustainability, and expect them to provide data sheets, and make it clear that our decisions are based not only on price and availability, but on impact to the planet. Until writing this book, there had been areas of our resourcing that I hadn't investigated. For instance, I just took it for granted that our paint was fine. It wasn't until I recently visited Australia and saw 'eco-paint' written on the front of their powder paint containers that I started to query ours. I also discovered that Australians and Americans are way ahead of the British in this aspect!

Eco-paints are made with organic fruit and vegetable pigments, with no harsh chemicals that might go into curious mouths. There's no need for the bitterest substance on earth – denatonium benzoate – to discourage children putting it in their mouths then. Although, the eco-paints I looked at aren't recommended for children under 12 months because of the natural fruit acid; the same can be said for many of the paints we are using in our settings.

OkoNorm paints are all ethically made in Germany, from chalk and natural food colouring. They market them as appealing to 'green parents, Montessori nurseries and Waldorf Steiner educators',[4] but I think they're a great choice for any childcare provider who is looking for a natural paint.

You can also buy Natural Earth paints, which are made with earth rather than chalk, and mix 1:1 with water for a range of beautiful colours. However, this may be a double-edged sword because, once the earth is used, it is gone. They are also far more expensive than commercial paint.

It's also worth bearing in mind that paint does not have to be purchased commercially. It can be made from a vast array of materials, which may be more sustainable, and may well be healthier … although not necessarily more economic!

Here are some possible recipes:

- 4 tbsp bicarbonate soda, 2 tbsp white vinegar, 1/2 tsp light corn syrup, 2 tbsp corn flour, food colouring.

- Use dried out marker pens and soak them in water in a jam jar.

- 1 tbsp self-raising flour, icing gels, 1 tbsp salt, and a little water for puffy paint – but see if you can use flour that is going out of date rather than using food grade flour.

One of the methods you could use is to mix chalk – white Kaolin or cosmetic clay – with herbs. You can use any herb, as long as it's powdered and coloured. Things that have worked well are turmeric for orange, ground mustard seed for yellow, spirulina for dark green, beetroot for red, bilberry fruit for purple, activated charcoal for black and arrowroot for white. Using herbs and chalk in equal parts, you then need to add a liquid. If you use water, the paint will last about a week in the fridge. If you use glycerine, make sure to get food grade glycerine and it will last a month if kept in an airtight container. Glycerine can sometimes make the paint too runny to use on anything other than a flat surface and all these colours can stain hands and clothes.

It's common for childcare providers to use shaving foam with colouring as a substitute to paint. Shaving foam is pretty toxic stuff, especially to the marine environment, as it contains sodium lauryl sulphate. Most of it ends up down the sink. Aerosols in general contain a propellant, such as butane (made from petroleum oil) and propane (made from natural gas). Neither of these are sustainable.

Chalk

So how sustainable is chalk? Chalk is made from calcium carbonate, which occurs naturally in limestone. The limestone/chalk is quarried, crushed and ground to fine particles, then mixed with water and/or formed into sticks, baked slowly, cooled, cut to size and boxed. Once the limestone is quarried and used, it is gone ... definitely not renewable. However, there is plenty of it around at the moment and it's mined in the UK, so is reasonably local for us on the south coast. After use, it will either be dust and swept up to go into general waste or it will be on paper and might go through the recycling system as a contaminant. If it is washed down the drain, it will do no harm – that we know of.

Paper/card/cardboard

We get through a lot of paper every day working with children. The best thing to do is use second-hand paper – paper that's been printed on one side and no longer needed, paper from the scrap store, or from companies who don't use it, or scrap donated by parents. This is completely sustainable and you can put the paper in the recycling after use.

Table 6.4 Chalk

Activity	Renewable?	Land/sea damage?	Local?	Investment that could last for years?	Care?	Paint or varnish?	End of life?
Chalk	No, but lots of it	Yes	Can be	No	No	No	OK

Table 6.5 Paper/card/cardboard

Activity	Renewable?	Land/sea damage?	Local?	Investment that could last for years?	Care?	Paint or varnish?	End of life?
Paper	Yes, if responsibly sourced	Yes	Can be	Yes, for books, art or just one use	No	No	OK

Paper is made from wood, a resource that is renewable, provided the wood is grown using responsible forestry practices. Nowadays, most wood is grown responsibly, but it's worth looking out for the FSC mark. It is important that we recycle our paper, or we can also compost it in the garden.

Another thing to consider about your paper's source is how far it is being shipped to you. If it has travelled hundreds or thousands of miles, this obviously negates the sustainability of paper! Provided you have the storage, it is well worth having it delivered in large quantities every so often rather than small, frequent deliveries. This not only often reduces cost, but will reduce the vehicle trips and resulting emissions.

Laminating is not at all sustainable. Laminating takes time, money, and makes paper non-biodegradable. Instead of laminating children's work, try pressing flowers, drying out leaves, or even coating them in beeswax. Unfortunately, you may have to compromise for posters in the kitchen, as those need to be wipe-clean, but it's worth considering how to reduce your laminating.

Glue

PVA is a white glue, which is an emulsion of polyvinyl acetate in water. It isn't toxic to humans unless it is burned, so it's a type of plastic. It could be described as biodegradable, but then so is just about anything, it just takes a very, very long time to biodegrade, so it's not a sustainable product. Some glues give off volatile organic compounds (VOCs), which may include greenhouse gases, ozone-depleting substances and chemicals involved in the creation of smog and other

Table 6.6 Glue

Activity	Renewable?	Land/sea damage?	Local?	Investment that could last for years?	Care?	Paint or varnish?	End of life?
PVA glue	No	Drilling for oil	Can be	No	No	No	X

gases that are hazardous to human health, but PVA is usually fine. It's a very useful product, sticks most things, is a good consistency, and is cheap, but there are sustainable alternatives on offer.

Flour and water makes a glue paste that works for children sticking paper, just about, but it won't stick anything heavier like cardboard or fabrics. Also, in-date flour is a food, so that's not sustainable either – but you could try and source out-of-date or nearly out-of-date flour. On the same basis, we ignored recipes with milk powder, which is even worse in sustainability terms!

A more effective glue recipe is water, corn syrup and vinegar, boiled. Stir corn starch into the boiling mixture and continue to boil for one minute. Allow it to cool and store it in a sealed container. There are many recipes on the internet, such as on ThoughtCo[5] and SnappyLiving,[6] to make your own glue. There are waterproof glues without milk, but with gelatine (which can be made from cows or seaweed); super glue made using gum arabic and glycerine; library paste (with flour, sugar, alum, water and optional clove oil); and lickable stamp glue (with white vinegar, gelatine, sugar and mint extract).

Home corner

Every home corner is a perfect opportunity to either celebrate sustainability or to wreck it. A home corner normally includes a number of small units to support children working through what happens in a kitchen. For example, there might be equipment to play at cooking and cleaning, such as a little oven, hob, sink, microwave, kettle, iron and ironing board, cutlery and crockery, pots, pans, and food, chairs and a little table, tablecloth, vase of flowers, and whatever else your imaginative colleagues and the children can introduce. In years gone by, we would buy a plastic kitchen with plastic accessories and plastic food. Now, good practice is to re-use items from home, such as old kettles and microwaves and irons, with the plug and wire cut off. We raid our own cupboards, and those of our families and friends, and we hunt through car boot sales, jumble sales and charity shops for real little teapots, silver jugs, cutlery, crockery, pots and pans in steel and copper, fashion jewellery, trays, fabrics, pictures, wood tables and

Table 6.7 Home corner

Activity	Renewable?	Land/sea damage?	Local?	Investment that could last for years?	Care?	Paint or varnish?	End of life?
Home corner	Depends on resource	Depends on resource	Can be	Yes	Yes	Yes	OK

sideboards, and any item that might fascinate a child. Rather than a catalogue and money, we need time and imagination to resource our home corners. This means that we create an outstanding, sustainable play area that we can be proud of. Many settings also use real food in their home corners that the children can eat or use and explore.

Craft activities

This is just a very small sample of the types of items that we can, and do, use for collage, decorating, craft, sorting, and generally playing with. The important things are what each of these resources are made of and where they come from. Anything that has been used once (or more) already, whether for the same or a different purpose, can be considered sustainable. For example, buttons off a shirt, even if they are made from plastic, are a better idea than buying new ones.

Buying new shells is a risk unless they are from a sustainable source or washed up on a beach as we must not encourage anyone to go fishing for shells that are still on living creatures. Feathers are the same; we wouldn't want anyone to kill a bird just so we could play with the feathers, nor pluck a bird for its feathers, but feathers found or second-hand are good. Although, you might want to risk-assess a feather found on the floor for bacteria and possibly spray it with a cleaner. Glitter is highly unsustainable, as it is a microplastic that ends up

Table 6.8 Craft activities

Activity	Renewable?	Land/sea damage?	Local?	Investment that could last for years?	Care?	Paint or varnish?	End of life?
Shells	Yes	Can be	?	Yes	No	No	OK
Buttons (plastic, wood, glass)	Can be	Can be	?	Yes	No	No	OK
Feathers	Can be	Can be	?	Yes	Possibly	No	Ok
Glitter	No	No	?	No	No	No	X
Pompoms – wool	Yes	No	?	Yes	No	No	Yes
Stickers (plastic)	No	Yes	?	No	No	No	X
Fabrics, ribbon	Can be	No	?	Can be	No	No	OK
Pine cones	Yes	No	Yes	No	No	No	Yes
Conkers	Yes	No	Yes	No	No	No	Yes

washing down the drain or blowing away or going into landfill. There is a new product being offered under the guise of 'eco' glitter. While these may seem like a good substitute, we need to make sure they are truly plastic-free, and need to know what minerals or metals have been used to make the glitter instead. Claims of being biodegradable need to specify how long this eco-glitter takes to completely break down, otherwise it's just another example of greenwash. Stickers are normally plastic coated so won't biodegrade properly for decades, although it is possible to buy paper stickers (mentioned in Chapter 13). Wool and fabrics that are second-hand are again great, and wool is one of the least offensive animal products as it is generally harmlessly sheared off and renews annually. Fabric and ribbon could be made of nylon, rayon, or polyester (oil-based), in which case buying new is not sustainable. However, if it's cotton or bamboo, it is at least renewable – although they both use a lot of water and labour in production.

Pine cones and conkers, and indeed anything else that falls off a tree or plant, should be treasured and hoarded. They are great to play with and are a totally sustainable play activity resource. Although, you may want to do a risk assessment for poisons if you're not fauna-savvy. Ideally, collect these resources with the children, as it's a great activity in itself – not to mention rather time-consuming if you do it by yourself!

Modelling clay

Clay does not need much processing when it comes out of the ground in order to play with it. It usually needs cleaning and tiny rocks and lumps are removed, and sometimes sand is added to create the workable clay that we like to play with. The only further cost is to package it and transport it to the day nursery. Sometimes companies add plastic into clay – avoid that by checking the ingredients.

You can buy coloured clay such as Ailefo Modelling Clay, which is of course far more expensive as they've added natural dyes from fruits and vegetables, but no perfume or parabens. The company warns that the colour can transfer onto furniture but can be removed from hands with water and soap, which is probably slightly better than food colouring used in products.

Table 6.9 Modelling clay

Activity	Renewable?	Land/sea damage?	Local?	Investment that could last for years?	Care?	Paint or varnish?	End of life?
Clay	No, but lots of it	Yes	Can be	No	No	No	OK

A warning about playing with clay, though, is to not wash hands in the sink as you could cause a major blockage problem in the drains. Wash hands in a bucket of water: the clay will settle to the bottom, and then the water can be poured off the top (outside). You might even re-use the slurry clay left in the bottom of the bucket again.

There are endless resources available for play activities such as construction, music and treasure baskets. I've categorised some of the most common materials here, for ease, but really, they're limited only by your imagination ... and possibly your budget!

Construction

Table 6.10 Construction

Activity	Renewable?	Land/sea damage?	Local	Investment that could last for years?	Care?	Paint or varnish?	End of life?
Lego, Duplo	No	Yes	?	Yes	No	No	X
Wood blocks	Yes	No	?	Yes	Yes	Yes	Yes
Loose parts	Yes	No	Yes	No	No	No	?
Octagons	No	Yes	?	Yes	No	No	X

Musical instruments

Table 6.11 Musical instruments

Activity	Renewable?	Land/sea damage?	Local?	Investment that could last for years?	Care?	Paint or varnish?	End of life?
Wooden	Yes	No	?	Yes	Yes	Yes	OK
Plastic	No	Yes	?	Yes	No	No	?
Coconuts	Yes	No	Not usually	Yes	No	No	Yes
Gourds	Yes	No	?	No	No	No	Yes

Treasure baskets

As with most resources, if the items for construction, musical instruments and treasure baskets are sourced second-hand, they are sustainable. If you are buying new, they are sustainable if the product they are made of is produced sustainably, e.g. anything made from FFC wood is sustainable, anything made from plastic is not. This is why manufacturers are starting to look for other materials to use. Of course, they are still selling the plastic toys and equipment because it is a cheap material to produce, and therefore is easier to sell at a lower price. While consumers continue to consider price before all things, we can continue to expect unsustainable resources on the market. Often, though, this is a pragmatic decision. There is no denying that plastic is an amazingly versatile material, resilient and durable, and often things can be made from plastic that would be totally unaffordable from any other material. It also can last for decades or longer, so can be considered an investment. I am not seeking to ban plastic or to live a plastic-free life; however, I am making a conscious decision on whether I think the lack of sustainability in the product is worth the children's learning opportunities from it, or staff functionality, or convenience. This has to be an individual decision made at each nursery based on its ethos and its budget. I was almost totally unaware of the unsustainability of plastic until very recently, but now I know what can happen to our environment through demanding it, I am a lot more circumspect on whether I buy it or, more often, don't buy it at all.

Table 6.12 Treasure baskets

Activity	Renewable?	Land/sea damage?	Local?	Investment that could last for years?	Care?	Paint or varnish?	End of life?
Metal whisks	Yes	Yes	?	Yes	Yes	Yes	OK
Natural sponges, loofas	Yes	No	?	No	No	No	Yes
Wooden spoons	Yes	No	?	No	No	No	Yes
Poaching pan	No	Yes	?	Yes	No	No	Yes

Books

There are hundreds of beautiful story books and fact books that we can share with children to help teach them about sustainability, which will generate discussions, understanding and actions to help look after their world. Here are just a few examples of some books we use in our nurseries. When I've visited nurseries in other countries, as well as our own, I've also found that parents and local people have also written books that work with their local culture, and children and their educators can also write their own books, which are always brilliant. There are more books listed in Appendix VII for anyone wishing to get some ideas. There are hundreds and hundreds available at local libraries, or even at our fingertips with an internet search.

Duffy's Lucky Escape[7] by Ellie Jackson and Liz Oldman is an engaging story about a sea turtle and her encounter with plastic in the sea. It is beautifully illustrated and has prompted many discussions and activities in the nurseries.

Not for Me, Please: I Choose to Act Green[8] by Maria Godsey and Christoph Kellner is a story about a little boy called Luke who sees the damage caused to the environment and decides he can change his ways to protect the world.

Lola's Beach Clean-Up[9] by Melaina Gasbarrino is a story about a little girl who lives on a beautiful island and rallies her friends together to clean up their beach.

What a Waste by Jess French is about rubbish, recycling and protecting our planet.

My Green Day and *10 Things I Can Do to Help My World* by Melanie Walsh are lovely pop-up books suitable for 1- and 2-year-olds also, with very clear images and very few words.

The Adventures of a Plastic Bottle is a nice story about recycling.

One Plastic Bag by Isatou Ceesay is about the Recycling Woman of Gambia, bringing some multicultural images that might be relevant to children in your setting.

A Planet Full of Plastic by Neal Layton is suitable for slightly older children. It has hand-drawn illustrations rather than the real photographs we prefer, but it's lots of fun. And there is some real science in this one that I think could inspire our children to consider becoming environmentalists and engineers one day to help clear up the mess.

Computer games

There are a number of computer games that teach sustainability. One of the most popular games on our digital table is a sorting game where the children move images of items such as plastic spades, bikes, bottles and food into the appropriate recycling container. They love playing the game and become amazingly adept at discerning what is metal, plastic, glass, or organic. Obviously, this is best followed up by doing the real thing in the nursery and at home, but they just love playing it by itself as well.

There are also quite a few resources available on YouTube. Some great videos that we use are:

- **Sustainability**: told as a children's fairy tale with a beautiful montage.[10]
- **Teach kids sustainability**: what does it mean to be green?[11]

Reduce, re-use and recycle to enjoy a better life[12]

As with the computer games, it is important to engage the children in discussions about sustainability. Activities themselves can be a fantastic gateway to this discussion, but they don't mean much to a toddler without being placed in the real world for them. Can a small child see a link between a craft activity where they make their own guitars out of boxes and elastic bands, and the need to re-use and recycle? Maybe. But that understanding can definitely be helped along by us. Here are some great examples of activities that can start a sustainability conversation:

- cutting up brown bananas for composting
- telling the story of the three little pigs with props (bricks, sticks and straw)
- upcycling plastic bottles into an igloo
- going bug hunting
- crafts and collage with sweetie wrappers
- using an old-fashioned set of scales to weigh stones and pine cones
- loose parts play
- constructing a climbing pile of tyres
- silver goblets and copper pots in a home corner
- making paints.

In order to lead children on the path to sustainability, we must make sure to appropriately role-model. We must show them what to do, and how to do it, and perhaps most importantly, explain why we need to. Of course, it's important to make these discussions fun, otherwise the children won't want to listen.

Introducing activities as part of the everyday routine, such as reading stories about sustainability, can help minimise the chance that children will view it as a distraction from their fun times. Circle time, or at the table after lunch, are also fantastic places for striking up these conversations. Actually, any time, any place, anywhere, as appropriate, is good.

Conclusion

Every activity we do has some impact on the environment, but we can choose more of those activities with less impact and consider whether we want to continue to offer those that we now know are damaging. We can start a dialogue with our suppliers to show that we care about where our products come from and how sustainable they are, and use our spending power to show that this is important to us. We know that research and science is being updated and developed all the time, so the decisions we make today may not be the best decisions going forward. But that is okay, because this is a journey of learning and sharing good practice with colleagues and parents. And we can teach children about sustainability while they play.

Notes

1. Sand Play in Children's Play Areas. (2016). Royal Society for Prevention of Accidents [online]. Available at: www.rospa.com/play-safety/advice/sand-play/.
2. Original recipe from www.sustainablebabysteps.com/natural-household-cleaners.html.
3. Finger Paint. (n.d.). The Consortium Care. Available at: www.theconsortiumcare. co.uk/finger-paint.
4. OkoNorm Finger Paints 4 Primary Colours, available from www.babipur.co.uk/ natural-wooden-toys/art-crafts/okonorm-finger-paints-primary-colours.html.
5. Helmenstine, A. (2017). *5 Ways to Make Glue.* ThoughtCo. Available on www.thought co.com/homemade-glue-recipes-607826.
6. 11 Homemade Glue Recipes. (n.d.). SnappyLiving. Available from: https://snappyliving. com/11-recipes-to-make-your-own-glue/.
7. Jackson, E. (2017). *Duffy's Lucky Escape.*
8. Godsey, M. (2018). *Not for me, please!: I choose to act green.* CreateSpace Independent Publishing Platform.
9. Gasbarrino, M. (2017). *Lola's Beach Clean-Up.*
10. Sustainability: A Children's Fairy Tale with Beautiful Montage. (2013). Worldfrom-aboveHD. Available from: www.youtube.com/watch?v=fKWQuU0sHPw.
11. Teach Kids Sustainability: What Does it Mean to be Green? (2010). Lisa Gottfried. Available from: www.youtube.com/watch?v=lieN18OTlME.
12. Reduce, Reuse and Recycle, to enjoy a better life. (2017). Happy Learning English. Available from: www.youtube.com/watch?v=OasbYWF4_S8.

7 Children's gardening

Introduction

This chapter discusses the benefits of gardening and offers practical guidance on how to get started. It considers the equipment you need, spaces and containers for gardening, and information about the types of plants you can grow. There are also suggestions for planting activities to do with children and some ideas on community involvement.

Why do some gardening?

Growing food, herbs and flowers for a purpose is a wonderfully sustainable and fulfilling activity in which children and colleagues can engage. Gardening can be done both inside and outside, and on any balconies or patios. The link between putting time and effort into gardening, watching plants grow, and then eating, smelling or touching the results is a vital one. It grounds us in our environment and connects us with our planet. The seven areas of learning of the Early Years Foundation Stage in the UK (communication and language; physical development; personal, social and emotional development; literacy; mathematics; understanding the world; and expressive arts and design) can all be supported with gardening activities. Opportunities to develop the characteristics of effective learning (COEL) of playing and exploring, active learning, creating, and thinking critically are also well supported with gardening.

All of our nurseries grow some basic fruits, vegetables and herbs in their gardens with the children. It becomes part of the daily routine of looking after and respecting their environments, as well as enhancing their environments both inside and outside. Children at our nurseries take the products of their gardening home to share with their parents, with photographic records in their development records, as the food grown is often eaten in situ and the flower petals may end up in 'perfume potion'.

Recent research presented at the World Forum in Macao showed that children absolutely adore flowers. Australian researchers asked children what they wanted most in their gardens at nursery; the answer: 'flowers'. They especially enjoy picking flowers and using them in their play. *Psychology Today* published an article by Lorette Breuning, PhD, stating that 'flowers make you happy by triggering your happy brain chemicals'.[1] Flowers trigger dopamine because our brains sense something special is coming; they trigger oxytocin because of the link between flowers and relationships; serotonin is triggered when you experience a sense of pride in growing or admiring flowers; and children trigger endorphins if they are exerting themselves in the digging and harvesting.

I heard a beautiful story recently from Odstock Day Nursery in Wiltshire, UK, where some children transported cut roses that had been left in their 'forest' by an adult. The little group of girls and boys replanted them one at time, very carefully, in a ring in the sand pit. If was, of course, 'Ring a Roses' from the song, a completely child-initiated and collaboratively completed activity by the children.

With dozens of children in a nursery, adults need to plant a lot of the same flowers and consider layouts that prevent one or two children running through them all and flattening them, and to cope with a lot of picking flowers.

It's not just plants that help children; it's also the microorganisms in the potting soil. Getting those little hands dirty is really good for children, helping them build their immune systems.

Plants in hospitals have been found to make patients more positive, have lower blood pressure and reduced stress levels. Researchers such as Dr Charles R Hall of Texas, Dr Bonnie L Grant, Certified Urban Agriculturist have written about the advantages from their perspectives.[2] There has even been the suggestion that time with plants may make people smarter by allowing them to stay alert, and reducing mental fatigue. We have also seen that our nursery children sleep longer and deeper outside, which is great for their intelligence, mental and general development. Most Scandinavian parents take their babies outside in their prams, even in the winter and in freezing temperatures, so that they can benefit from the fresh air.

Getting started

It is an enormous help if you have just one member of staff who is keen on gardening – or at least on being outside! If not, you could see if there are any parents who can help or call for volunteers from the community. You could also incorporate learning some basics about gardening into your team meetings. We have a staff meeting once a month, and this is an opportunity to spend 10 minutes doing a practical gardening activity.

If your service lacks any plants at all, start with just one type of plant, then grow lots of them, before learning about and progressing to another plant. In time your children will have gardens inside, outside and in between.

National children's gardening week occurs in the spring in many countries, raising awareness of gardening and encouraging people to take part. This might be a useful trigger to engage parents and colleagues.

The UK children's gardening week site has a video on how to grow a pot plant. Even the most non-green-fingered person can enjoy some gardening with the tutorial, which provides guidance all the way from choosing the plant, to filling it with compost, digging a hole through to planting.

Don't accept 'but I don't have green fingers' as an excuse. Knowledge and a bit of persistence, trial and error will overcome all. Plus, adults will derive the same benefits as the children, so there will be smiles and job satisfaction all around in time.

Figure 7.1 Gardening with the children at Tops, Parkstone

What you'll need

Equipment for gardening

You need small watering cans and water sprayers to look after pot plants. Child-sized forks and trowels as well as old spoons are very useful too!

If you have a condensing tumble dryer that produces water, you could use that water for watering, as we do. However, it's worth using a filter in the washing machine to make sure plastics from clothing such as Nylon aren't getting into the water – something like the Cora Ball™ or a built-in filter in the washing machine itself.

Every garden should have a water butt, so the children can water their plants from that – just make sure the lid is locked onto the butt so there is no chance a child could climb in. Children who like to transport will enjoy moving the water from butt to plants in their watering cans, and will happily engage in this for some time, which is great for their physical strength, coordination and persistence. This water is free and without added chemicals such as chlorine and fluoride. If your water butt has run out, the children will need access to an outside tap to water the plants.

You don't really need gloves – let the children get earth on their hands – but you might want welly boots and aprons depending on the weather and conditions.

Buying fully grown plants will not be cheap, so developing a potting shed area and a greenhouse somewhere in your garden would be a great investment if you have space.

Figure 7.2 Simple gardening tools for children made of metal and wood

Space for planting outside

It isn't necessary to have a large outside area to carry out gardening activities. A raised bed or bit of wild earth outside, or even a patio, is enough to get started. Plants can also be grown in old furniture, recycled buckets, tin and enamel containers, butler sinks, ceramic pots, tyres, plastic bottles and glass bottles, to name a few. Upcycle donations from parents and other items you find with the children's decorations. You and the children can be as creative as you like.

If your setting doesn't have any space for gardening, you could take on a vegetable patch or allotment nearby, and make regular trips to do your gardening. Gardening is also an excellent way to engage with the community, such as with different generations. For example, some of our nursery children do gardening activities with residents of local care homes. There are also companies and charities that will sponsor gardening activities in schools and early years settings, paying for compost, seeds, pots, and equipment, such as the Rotary Clubs, Lions Clubs, Round Table, Greggs Foundation Environmental Grants and The Co-operative Community Fund. Also, see Foodforlife[1] to learn about engaging with farmers' markets.

Compost

You need to use different compost depending on what you are growing, what has been grown in the soil before (if anything) and what you plan to grow. Some plants need more acidic or more alkaline compost; some need more drainage than others. See below for more detail.

The Dos

Do choose a specialist compost for the task in hand. This will ensure you create the optimum growing conditions, whether inside or outside.

Do check out your garden soil pH balance before you get planting and, depending on the results, for example, you may need to mix in lime soil improver to get you started.

Do use any leftover compost and dig into your existing soil around your garden as a soil improver.

Do pot up your existing and new plants in fresh compost each year to minimise pests and diseases being carried over. This will also provide new nutrients that will have been used up.

Always water in your plants (even if the ground is moist) to remove air pockets and ensure the roots are in contact with the soil.

The don'ts

Don't sow seeds in standard compost. For best results use a specialist seed compost that provides optimum root growth and contains plant food to help them develop.

Don't be put off from growing fruit and vegetables by lack of space. You can achieve healthy crops in pots, hanging baskets and grow bags, even in the smallest of areas.

Don't forget that some acid-loving plants such as azalea, camellia or rhododendron will require an ericaceous compost with a lower pH (more acidic).

Don't assume that there are enough nutrients in your garden soil to use for potting up containers and baskets. It may contain unwanted weeds, pests and diseases, and the soil won't hold as much water as potting compost would, so your plants may suffer.

Don't forget that decorative barks not only look great on beds and borders, but they suppress weeds and help retain valuable moisture too. Some plants need more or less drainage, so you may need pottery shards or gravel underneath the compost. Just check the plant's needs on the internet or at a plant nursery.

Don't forget to follow the compost label instructions.

www.lovethegarden.com/advice/gardening/flowers-shrubs/complete-guide-choosing-right-compost

Broadly speaking, there are five different types of compost:

Peat-based compost

There are many formulations of peat-based composts available to the gardener. These are made from a base of peat blended with other ingredients such as fertiliser, sand and/or grit, vermiculite or perlite, wetting agents and lime. The exact formulation will depend on the intended use of the compost.

Loam-based compost

Loam-based composts are soil-based growing media made from a mixture of loam, sand or grit and peat, with increasing amounts of plant foods added. It contains the smallest amount of nutrients as this encourages the best germination and growth of tiny roots and shoots. For example, John Innes No. 1 Compost contains slightly more nutrients and is for transplanting seedlings. John Innes No. 2 Compost is for when you are potting up small plants, and John Innes No. 3 Compost has the most nutrients, as this is designed for final planting up of plants ready for display or cropping.

Peat-free compost

Peat-free compost can be made from several different base ingredients, such as wood fibre, composted bark, coir, and green compost.

Specialist composts are then produced using one of the above as a base, to which other ingredients are added depending on what they are to be used for. These come under the following headings, which also have an explanation of what they consist of and where they are used:

Organic compost

Organic composts contain a mixture of materials, e.g. peat, expanded wood fibres and composted bark in varying proportions. They are enriched with naturally occurring nutrients, derived from plants and animals, to feed plants for differing periods depending on the organic compost purchased. Some feed for up to three months. In addition, composts may be certified as organic by organisations such as the Organic Farmers and Growers Association.

All/multipurpose compost

This is a compost that can be used in various parts of your garden, from beds and borders, to pots, containers and hanging baskets. They come in different blends of ingredients. For example, some contain varying plant foods that will feed your plants anywhere from six weeks up to six months; others will limit the amount of watering you need to do, by absorbing water then storing and releasing it as and when the plant requires. You can get peat-free compost. Peat itself though is an increasingly scarce resource, taking hundreds of years to become peat, so use it very sparingly if at all.

Do add your own home- or garden-made compost (see more information on this in Chapter 15).

What to grow

Next you need to choose what to grow. It's best to grow non-toxic, air-cleaning plants inside and to think about where they will be kept. Different plants prefer different environments, so you'll need to consider the amount of shade, sunlight, drafts, etc., and choose your plants accordingly.

Outside, grow whatever thrives locally, as you have a better chance of success in terms of soil type and climate than if you try to grow something that isn't indigenous. This also offers opportunities for teaching children and colleagues the names of local plants, which is part of their culture.

At our nurseries in the UK our most popular vegetables to grow are tomatoes (which you can do in a grow bag on a patio if you have limited garden space), carrots, spring onions, runner beans, onions and peppers.

Plants that clean air

Introduction

Toxic air is an increasingly serious problem for us and for our children. UNICEF made the issue their top priority for 2019. Air inside is often even worse than the air on the roadside, where diesel cars, particularly old ones, are mostly to blame.

The toxic air gets into our homes and nurseries from the roads, but is added to by aerosols, cleaning chemicals, formaldehyde in some furniture, chemicals in paint and carpets, and it isn't flushed out well due to our insulated, closed-window homes.

Research at NASA identified plants that were able to remove ammonia, benzene, formaldehyde and xylene from indoor air. Some are edible too, so if children do decide to try eating them, you don't need to worry. 'Sick building syndrome' causes headaches, dizziness, nausea, eye, ear and nose irritations.

However, there are many common houseplants that cause illness or even death, if eaten in high enough quantities or rubbed against. It is important to risk-assess each plant and decide whether or where to grow what. How likely is it that the children will dig up that daffodil bulb and eat it without you getting to them first? Usually plants like ivy are bitter and irritate the mouth and tongue, so children are highly unlikely to eat enough to cause serious effects. If you have pets in the nursery, you can never assume that plants safe for humans are safe for the animals, so you need to check all over again!

The following are the 14 common house plants that are poisonous: most result in a skin reaction or upset stomach, but some may cause a shock reaction or life-threatening symptoms (www.thebump.com/a/poisonous-plants-for-kids):

 1. Philodendron

 2. Pothos – pointed, heart-shaped leaves

 3. English Ivy

 4. Easter Lily

 5. Oleander

 6. Daffodil bulbs

 7. Leopard Lily (flecks of white and yellow in the leaves)

 8. Peace Lily

 9. Mistletoe – berries

10. Holly – berries

11. Caladium (elephant ear) – pink, red, white on the heart-shaped leaves

12. Azalea (outside)

13. Morning Glory (LSD in the seeds)

14. Foxglove – extremely toxic – causes heart to slow down.

Living plants kept indoors are known to be great for cleaning carbon dioxide and pollution from the air, and providing oxygen for us to breathe. I strongly recommend you include living plants in every child's working environment (don't forget the staff room and parent areas), and if you already have a couple, add some more! Plants that are good for freshening air but are not toxic for children or cats and dogs include:

- *spider plants*, with the further advantage that they produce baby spider plants that you can detach and re-plant (Figure 7.3)

- *ferns*, which are also natural humidifiers (Figure 7.4)

- *gerbera daisies* – they need partial to full sun and the soil must not get wet or their roots rot; they are lovely colours. How about a real one of these in the centre of the table for lunch rather than the imitation ones that often get used? (Figure 7.5)

Figure 7.3 Spider plant

Figure 7.4 Fern

Figure 7.5 Gerbera daisy

■ *dragon tree* – prefers semi-shade (Figure 7.6)

■ *prayer plant* – the leaves curl at night, which is rather fun; it only grows to 12 inches; and semi-shade or semi-sun suit it best (Figure 7.7)

■ *red emerald philodendron* – a 'vining' plant that benefits from a water-absorbing pole to help water it and support it to grow upwards (Figure 7.8)

■ *Christmas cactus* (Figure 7.9)

■ *coleus* (Figure 7.10)

■ *African violet* (Figure 7.11).

Figure 7.6 Dragon tree

Figure 7.7 Prayer plant

Figure 7.8 Red emerald philodendron

Figure 7.9 Christmas cactus

Figure 7.10 Coleus

Figure 7.11 African violet

Plants to encourage insects – butterflies and bees.

Another idea to consider is to grow plants that sustain local insects, such as butterflies and bees. The colourful nasturtium flowers are very attractive to butterflies. The butterflies lay their larva on the flowers, which grows into caterpillars, which then eat the nasturtiums. Children can collect the caterpillars, put them in a caterpillar house and feed them the nasturtium leaves until they turn into a cocoon. They will be able to watch them develop into butterflies, whereupon they are released back to the nasturtium bed, and a very sustainable and informative cycle occurs. If children happen to try eating the nasturtiums, this isn't a problem. Indeed, Michelin chefs sometimes use them as edible decorations for their food presentations. You can buy the butterfly growing stations from catalogues rather than do it yourself, of course.

We were able to buy very reasonable bee and insect houses from a local international supermarket, which had been made from sustainable wood, and could be hung easily from a fence post using the short length of rope already attached. Bees have been observed forming mini hives projecting from the front to winter over in. We can help this along by putting some insulating wrap over the hives in the winter to help protect them from the cold and sustain them into the following year. Without the bees, many plants will not pollinate and this is an important message to share with the children, along with the opportunity to role-model not being afraid of bees. I am actually frightened of bees, but when you have children you need to at least pretend not to be scared – and with practice perhaps you won't be! We don't actually do bee-keeping in our nurseries because of the risk of allergic reactions from bee stings, but that isn't to say that others couldn't do this if risk-assessed appropriately, and with staff confident to learn to do this.

Mushrooms

We also had some success with growing mushrooms indoors with a pack bought from a company recycling their coffee grounds. Mushrooms can be grown in nurseries – and of course eat them either raw or cooked. It's really easy as all you have to do is spray them several times a day with a water spray and the mushrooms grow, and grow quickly.

Figure 7.12 Growing mushrooms from coffee grounds

Other activities that you can do with the children

▨ Plan a window box of herbs.

▨ Write letters in salad by filling a tray with earth and sowing salad seeds in the shape of a name.

▨ Paste the photograph of a child's or an adult's face onto a pot and grow some grass, mustard and cress (sprouted seeds) hair. All these grow quickly, which helps smaller children engage more easily.

▨ Grow your own pizza toppings. Outline a planting area in a big circle with stones, divide the circle into slices and grow pizza toppings such as tomatoes, peppers, basil, rocket, spinach and rainbow chard. This kind of activity blends really well with doing healthy cooking activities with the children too.

In settings where younger children may be prone to digging out the small plants, try an edible hanging basket. Plant the vegetables/herbs together and bring them down to touch, smell and water under close supervision – then hoist them just out of reach. It's a great way to bring colour and fresh-growing plants inside without the risk of early destruction under eager fingers.

Figure 7.13 Children's gardening at Tops, Musgrove Park Hospital, Taunton

Plant care

You will need to check what light and watering each plant prefers, but generally watering inside plants twice a week is sufficient. Many plants like spraying as well as the earth watering and some plants like their base soaking for an hour or two rather than watering from on top. Hanging baskets outside may need watering every morning and evening. If plants grow well, they will need repotting periodically – check the instructions, or with a gardener!

Help from the community

Many large banks and insurance companies include a community and socially responsible aspect to their company's purpose. As part of that, they often encourage staff to volunteer time as part of their community involvement and are very interested in contributing to joint gardening initiatives. We have also had plants and planters donated. We can sell them the advantages to human health if they are not already aware and there is mutual benefit to association with these companies.

Conclusion

Every childcare setting would benefit enormously from having gardening activities, inside and outside, in all weathers. There is lots of assistance available if you or your colleagues are not knowledgeable already. Perhaps target one new seasonal activity at a time, enabling colleagues and children to learn together, and in a couple of years the environment will be transformed into a much healthier learning atmosphere for children and adults.

There are many websites and plant selling sites that help with advice, such as:

- https://dengarden.com/gardening/Non-Toxic-House-Plants-For-Homes-Children-Cats-and-Dogs

- www.apartmenttherapy.com/keeping-your-pets-safe-10-nontoxic-house-plants-aspca-137830

- https://royalvistavets.com/toxic-non-toxic-indoor-plants

- https://farmfoodfamily.com/non-toxic-houseplants

- https://greatist.com/connect/houseplants-that-clean-air

- www.healthline.com/health/air-purifying-plants

- www.tipsbulletin.com/plants-that-clean-the-air

- www.garden365.com/wp-content/uploads/2014/03/Best-Air-cleaning-plants-.jpg

Note

1. Food for Life. (2018). *School Farmers Markets.* Soil Association. Available from: www. foodforlife.org.uk/schools/what-can-you-do/school-farmers-markets.

8 The natural world and pets

Introduction

One of the issues we currently face is the dramatic biodiversity damage that humans have caused. We build towns and cities, make roads and car parks, dig into land and under the sea, damage corals, burn and cut forests down, desertify large areas, make land and sea radioactive, produce new organisms, genetically engineer and transport foreign species that may over take local nature, and as a result we have decimated the planet. There can be little debate that there is a very serious biodiversity crisis. Some refer to what is happening now as the sixth extinction crisis, the Anthropocene, after the five known extinction waves in geological history. Although others say that this is overstating the importance of humans, and the planet will survive after us, but humans, however, won't.

Exactly how much damage humans have done is very difficult to ascertain, but scientists estimate we could have lost between about 2 million and 100 million different species. Various universities worldwide, and charities such as the World Wildlife Fund, are working hard to understand what is happening and what can be done to change this. We think we understand what we are doing, but really, we're just experimenting. The effects of our experiments and our actions can be dramatic and life-threatening. What if plankton growth in the sea drops further because of global warming? What if the Gulf Stream stops altogether, or if El Nino changes behaviour? What if climate change causes droughts, floods, sea temperature rises and hurricanes? What if a super-contagious organism becomes super-antibiotic-resistant? Are some of these things happening already and could this get much worse?

Recently, Greta Thunberg and students around the world have started striking on Fridays to try and make adults do something about the climate change crisis.

This chapter discusses the types of activities that colleagues in the early years sector can do to teach young children about care and respect for animals and the natural world in general. The role of colleagues is vital as they are in a position to inspire interest, questions and discussions. Adults can role-model caring for and learning about animals and insects in their environment, within the building or garden, and also through visits to other places where animals live locally, whether in parks, fields or conservation projects. The children can be inspired to appreciate, respect and understand something of the importance of living creatures at this very early age, which we know is formative of how they will behave as adults.

The role of colleagues in pet husbandry

I once heard a criticism of a day nursery from a parent along the lines of, 'Well, if they can't keep the goldfish in a clean bowl, how can they care for small children in a building?' This is a good point. Whatever additional animals we choose to have in our centres, they have to be looked after really well as a micro view of how we look after all the animals on the planet. How we look after pets has to be a good example of how it's done. It's much better not to have them if colleagues do not have the time and commitment to do this well.

So your first consideration is, who wants to be in charge of the new animal? And are they truly capable of doing this, or what support will they need to fulfil this important role? Plus, what will happen if they are ill, on holiday or if they leave the organisation? You need several people who are keen to take responsibility before taking the big step of having your own pet in your day nursery.

Many colleagues may not have had pets as children, and even if they had, they might not have done it well! Others may be keen initially but may change their mind after cleaning cages out a few times. So some research on which animals to consider, what habitat they would need, the budget (not forgetting vet bills, food and toys), what they need to eat, to sleep, to be happy, and to do the research properly before purchase, is essential. A risk assessment will also need to be completed for the planned introduction, taking into account specific children as appropriate as well.

Choosing a pet

Small animals

Pets in a day nursery need to be big enough to withstand a little uncoordinated treatment because the under-5s are not always in total control of their bodies. Anything really small like mice, hamsters, gerbils, chicks, and the young of bigger animals are easily injured accidentally. Supervision will need to be close, and one-to-one – do you have the staff for that? You might consider that having a baby animal without its mother is inappropriate, as it hardly shows respect for the bond between mother and baby, so either have both, or opt not to do this. There might be a compromise available for adult small animals, such as allowing them to go free in an exercise ball or larger enclosure to protect them from rough handling.

Guinea pigs and rabbits are a better size for the under-5s. Guinea pigs are vocal, which is fun; they will squeak with delight when their food is brought but also squeak in fear, and they also have a low rumbling sound when they are content, all of which can help teach empathy. Rabbits can be house-trained and allowed to roam around relatively freely, both inside and outside. It is, however, important to ensure that they are kept securely, especially at night, or you might suffer a loss from foxes or other predators in your locality.

Larger animals

Anything bigger than these are increasingly safe from the children, but the children can be at risk from them. A dog or cat could certainly cause serious injury to a child, and even the most placid of animals must be supervised. Even animals that have been calm and tolerant for many years can become less so as they age, or become unwell, and whereas they may once have put up with a toddler pulling on their coats, they might suddenly lose patience and snap, so we need to be alert. We have been obliged to 'retire' older animals back to a home without little hands to annoy them in respect to both dog and small children. Some settings have pot-bellied pigs, goats, llamas, ponies, and all kinds of bigger pets, usually inspired through an interest of the owner or teachers at the setting.

More than one pet?

Most animals need company in order to be happy, a few prefer to be alone most of the time, and some will fight with others of the same sex so cannot be kept together as they mature. It is not fair to keep a sociable animal alone with just humans for company, so your research will have indicated whether you need to have a pair or more. And watch out – you don't want to end up breeding dozens of rabbits, or gerbils, or guinea pigs, by accident.

These are some pets and experiences we have had in our nurseries:

African snails

We enjoy having African snails in the nursery because they breed when they are happy and fed properly. Then all the rooms can have them, children can take them home, and you can give them away to the other nurseries in the area. They grow very large for a snail. They are easy to feed. A big warning though: African snails must not be let out into British gardens because they are an aggressive and invasive species that do not belong in Britain – the hint is in the name. You will have to destroy the eggs quickly if you do not want to breed them. Your preference should be for local animals and insects, ideally, just in case any escape.

Snakes and worms

We have only had snakes to visit because the safer constrictors, like corn snakes, eat pinkies (baby mice), which is unpleasant for children to witness and it is illegal in the UK to show children a snake feeding if its food is alive rather than dead. Pet shops, though, may be prepared to bring snakes and spiders and other reptiles to visit to give children the opportunity to experience looking and maybe touching them at close hand. Some snakes and reptiles feed on crickets (live), so again you'd be better avoiding this for such young children.

Worms on the other hand are vegetarians, and having a wormery is a great idea (covered in Chapter 15).

Goldfish

Goldfish are easy to look after and pretty. The children find them calming and like feeding them. It is also fun to make the tank interesting, with little shipwrecks or toy mermaids, coloured stones, etc., as well as having the correct oxygenating equipment for the tank. The tank needs to be heavy enough or fixed down so that children cannot pull it over, and it needs a lid to prevent toys being dropped in and damaging the fish.

Chickens and ducks

Chickens and ducks are great for watching the lifecycle from eggs to chicks/ducklings to grown hens/ducks. The best way to do this is with wild ducks nesting nearby if you have a pond or river, but some settings have hen coops in their grounds. A mother hen communicates with her chicks while they are still in the eggs, turning them and warming them, so fertilised eggs should not be separated from the mother hen or duck. Mother hens are famous for their mothering instincts, so who are we to artificially stop this? There are companies than rent out incubators together with fertilised eggs for children to watch the chicks to emerge, and then give them back once they start growing up into chickens rather than fluffy little yellow balls. We used to pay for this service until it was pointed out that we were bringing orphan chicks into the world, which is a bit sad, and that returning them to the farm was something that needed to be checked if we wanted to be sure that they were going to live free-range, happy lives and not be crushed, literally. However, this has to be a decision for each nursery to make in the light of knowledge and the local community's expectations as well as the inspection regime.

Day nurseries can offer hens a good life in large, safe areas outside, with a roost at night to protect them from the foxes and no pressure to produce eggs, but you need planning permission to have cockerels and you can't have several because they fight, so you need to work out what to do with males early on!

In the UK, we are allowed to cook and eat the unfertilised eggs from our chickens, but I understand that in parts of Australia this isn't allowed under their health and safety regulations. You would need to check with your local inspectorate.

Spiders and insects

The children will naturally come into contact with spiders and insects in the environment inside and particularly outside, so you don't need to keep insects – unless you have a colleague on the team who has a passion for something particular and wants to keep some at the setting to share this with the children.

However, I have seen staff bring in caterpillars that they found on the marigolds outside. They put them into a tank with a lid and air holes, or you could just use a jam jar with some netting across the top, together with some fresh marigold leaves. The children were able to watch them eat, then go into cocoons and then come out into butterflies, and then release them back into the marigolds outside for the cycle to run again – a wonderful activity. There are some suppliers that sell containers with everything ready. There are some poisonous caterpillars around, so don't touch caterpillars unless you know what you are doing or you could end up with a nasty rash (back to the risk assessment and identification guides).

Some organisations will bring in large spiders for the children to see and handle. It is worth looking them up if your children and/or staff have a fascination for them, or you might want to consider this to help with overcoming fears.

Other opportunities to connect with animals outside

Insects

Outside in the garden, we have the opportunity to watch insects. Many staff do not know their names nor their habits, so it is an opportunity for everyone to learn. Some of the children may go on to develop hobbies or professions as scientists, which can all start in a nursery garden studying the bugs they find in the bug hotel, or in the flower beds, or under logs and bricks, or in the trees and bushes. We are hearing reports of huge decreases in bug and bird populations. In Germany, for example, although there weren't many studies done in the past, they are showing a drop of 70 per cent in the last 10 years in the weight of bugs caught in a light trap. Bee numbers are also dropping dangerously; the use of farmed fields to grow livestock feed is destroying bee habitats, and the use of pesticides and herbicides is killing off bugs. With the loss of bugs we lose the birds that feed on them, too, and there is serious concern for the drop in song birds around the country. Humans have already killed virtually all species of animal that weigh over 50kg. The remaining land-based ones are all endangered and many water-based animals are also rapidly decreasing in numbers. In the nurseries we can help with bug hotels, keeping areas of the garden wild, and growing plants that support butterflies, bees and birds. We can also provide a watering station or bird bath.

Bats

One of our nurseries is in an old church and on a bat migration route, so the children have the opportunity to study the bats around sunset using a 'bat detector'. These are small pieces of electronic equipment that can translate the bat's echolocation calls into audible sounds so that you can listen to the bats as they hunt. The Bats Conservation Trust and the Woodland Trust have information and volunteers that can support a project on bats if you and the children are interested.

Birds

Any nursery can support birds through placing appropriate nesting boxes in their gardens, or on their walls, and tiny cameras can be placed inside so that the children can watch the eggs hatching into baby birds, and parents feeding their chicks. The RSPB and the British Bird Lovers provide tips and activities that can support you and the children to develop an interest in local birds. Providing water and feeders for birds is an easy way to attract them into your garden.

Ponds

Ponds are great places to watch natural life. They do pose a risk from small children falling in them, but are safer than rivers! Tadpoles are an annual favourite in some of our nurseries. Staff can use a sieve to collect some spawn and put them in a tank for the children to watch them turn into frogs or toads. There are some things to be aware of, though: don't put the tank on the windowsill in direct sunlight as the water will get too hot and they will die; do put some weed in for the tadpoles to feed on; and do make sure you have large stones for the tadpoles to climb onto when they turn into frogs or toads or they will drown. And then return them all to the pond that they came from. We recently found we had collected some mosquito larvae as well by accident – and you don't want that hatching into the nursery!

Visits to see animals

My preference is to visit animals where they occur locally, but you may be in a city where there are very few opportunities. However, consider if there may be birds of prey in a local church spire. You may have a conservation project that links with where their home was, perhaps many thousands of miles away, such as the lemur project in Kent or Monkey World in Dorset. Some nurseries are on or near farms or zoos, or make trips to go and visit the animals there.

Sadly some creatures are only prevented from complete extinction by being kept in captivity because their habitat has been ruined by farming, logging or climate change, so the only chance the children have to see them is in zoos, oceanariums or aviaries. Even giraffes and koalas have joined the endangered list recently.

At child-friendly farms or rare breeding establishments, the children can often feed lambs, and experience goats, pigs and other medium-sized farm animals close up. The association between stroking them and killing/eating them is a difficult one, as children will not associate sausages and bacon with farm animals unless they are taught this. Not all colleagues will be comfortable with this subject, and particularly not if they are vegetarians or vegans – there are significantly increasing numbers of these now. Wool from sheep is a bit easier to discuss, as is honey from bees, but even then we want to teach respect and care of sheep and bees, and avoid anywhere not demonstrating the same.

Ponies and horses can be observed wild in some areas in the UK, such as the New Forest, but cannot be approached as they can bite or kick. Visits to stables can be very enjoyable and informative experiences for the children, although rides are not always possible for the very young due to the insurance restrictions on the stables.

Oceanariums containing fish, reptiles and mammals are wonderful for teaching children, but there has to be a limit to stop us causing cruelty to the animals and many countries now understand this. The Canadians now have laws in place to ban cetaceans, dolphins and whales from being kept in tanks or pools, now that we understand these animals' needs more than we did in the past. There has been international condemnation of Sea World, travel agents and others who use cetaceans in their shows or to sell holidays. We used to think that if we fed cetaceans well that they would be okay in captivity, but sadly they are not. They need the open ocean, the company of their pod; they are highly intelligent creatures requiring far more stimulation than we can give them in captivity. They should not be kept in a space equivalent to a bath to us: it's cruel and their lives are short and miserable.

Looking after animals

Bedding

Children can associate with the need for animals to have beds and bedding, perhaps a bedroom, so this is an interesting topic to research and discuss when looking after an animal. We can talk with the children about sleeping, and being warm and safe and dark to help them sleep. But that some animals like to sleep during the day, some children like to have night lights, some like comforters – and that is all a great learning experience to encourage empathy with animals.

One of the useful things about some small animals is that their bedding can be shredded paper as well as straw and hay, so this is another way of re-using stuff again before it goes to waste.

Cleaning

Cleaning out the used bedding, and floors of cages, is not a pleasant task, so some reflection on who will do this, when, and whether any protective wear is necessary is required. It's likely this will fall to the adults rather than the children, and if there are animal droppings on the waste it probably needs to be in the waste bin rather than in the garden for composting. Cleaning out bird cages can carry a significant health risk for lung disease, which is one of the reasons why I haven't suggested caged birds as an option for a childcare setting. The other main reason for not having birds is that they should be able to fly – can you manage that kind of space in your setting?

Food

New pet owners will need to look up what their pets require on the internet or at the pet shop, which is part of the fun and learning undertaken when engaging in the care of any animal. Going to the pet shop to choose the pet and buying the food is a trip that many children will enjoy very much, and you might run a project around this process. Food for some animals is costly, and there may be storage to consider, so this is another area you will need to research and reflect on before taking on new animals. Overfeeding by children able to access the food too easily, and underfeeding by adults forgetting to add the feeding to the daily routine are both risks to counter. Some animals will be happy to eat our waste, such as parts of vegetables that we don't eat, including vegetables the nursery has grown themselves. It's a wonderful thing for the children to be able to share in harvesting the vegetables, or even dandelion leaves, and then feeding the animals.

Environment

Animals in cages are at risk of being very bored. The cage needs to be as large as possible, but at least to the minimum size that your research will tell you is suitable for each one. The children will enjoy finding out what the animals need to do and would like to do and providing appropriate items, such as chew sticks, tunnels, ramps, balls, digging areas, even toys. This is another great opportunity for discussion, and learning empathy.

Weekends and holidays

Some pets will need to be looked after every day – leaving enough food and water for the weekend won't be enough for the more human-oriented pets. Who is going to pop into the nursery to look after the animals, or take pets home for weekends or holidays?

Figure 8.1 Caring for rabbits at Tops Day Nurseries

Dealing with concerns and challenges

Sickness and death of an animal

It is inevitable that anyone having animals in their settings will need to cope with a pet being unwell and occasional deaths. Someone will need to take the pet to the vet and there could be some significant bills to pay or a hard decision to make. Hard though it is to watch children grieve over the loss of a pet, it is the best way to prepare our children for the inevitable, worse losses that occur in everyone's lives. Children will learn that the pain does ease in time, and that it is okay to laugh and have fun sometimes, even in the midst of grief. So I would recommend that you don't try and sneakily replace animals that die with duplicates. You will probably be found out, which leads to loss of trust and children missing out on the opportunity to learn about life and death and to develop some resilience.

Allergies

Dogs and cats can cause issues with allergies, and that could prevent some children from accessing our service. There are animals that are less likely to cause allergies, such as poodles, which don't shed hair like most dogs as their coat is wool. Watch out also for fleas: the animals will need to be treated. Some children and adults are allergic to a flea bite, which will cause nasty wounds and swelling, and could even raise a fever. Children can also be allergic to some insects, bees for example. You may want to reflect on your first aid provision in the setting and the permissions from parents – are you able to keep an anti-histamine to adminis-ter to children and to adults should a severe allergic reaction occur? This issue must be included in the risk assessments you would have done for any animal or insect in the setting.

Fear

Some parents and children are frightened of some animals and/or insects. Adults may have been attacked by an animal when young themselves, and this fear is communicated to children very easily. It's important to identify when there is a family fear so that children can be introduced gently to animals and reassured. You might meet with the family to discuss the educational benefits and social benefits of having animals. Looking after animals is a wonderful opportunity to break a cycle of unnecessary fear and to confront fear with being brave, support-ing the resilience that children need to develop.

At the same time children need to be taught how to approach a strange animal safely so that they do not unwittingly put themselves in danger. Children need to always ask the animal's owner if it's alright to approach the animal, and then approach slowly and calmly, put hands out to be smelled before attempting to stroke, and avoid eye contact to start with as animals consider this to be aggressive. Certain animals need specific handling, but confident, calm and gentle handling, with good role-modelling and supervision, will work.

Cultural attitudes

It is important to consider different cultural attitudes towards animals. Some cultures consider animals such as dogs and cats to be dirty and they are not allowed inside. If you decide to introduce one, you will need to consider this – because families could withdraw their children, disrupting their bonding to staff in the nursery as well as the financial sustainability. On the other hand, you might have some success in sharing the British love of these animals.

You may also have staff from cultures which dislike animals in homes, and you risk losing a member of staff who is good in all other areas because they would feel uncomfortable having animals in the workplace.

Some cultures will eat some animals but not others, and this will also likely affect how they treat those animals when they meet them in homes, streets or in the environment elsewhere.

It is therefore important to check your families' and colleagues' opinions on introducing animals to the workplace before you do so. Ask what animals they like/don't like, and perhaps ask for volunteers to help with their care at the same time. A Survey Monkey-type questionnaire, informal one-to-one discussions or meetings will yield the information you need.

With good information you can make the best decisions for you and for all involved with your service, including any animals.

Forest School, nature-based, Beach School and similar

The practice and ethos of outdoor learning is increasingly popular in early years settings across the world. Learning with nature has been part of Western European education since the eighteenth century; Rousseau, Froebel, McMillan, and Montessori all referred to learning about nature, and learning with the senses. Forest Schools originated in Scandinavia in the 1950s and were intended to expose children to the natural world. By the 1980s, they had become an important part of the preschool programme in Sweden. Bridgwater College in Somerset were recognised as the pioneers of the British Forest School movement in 1993, and more can be found on their website.[3]

Other nurseries, such as our own Tops Day Nurseries, have developed their own versions of the Scandinavian Forest Schools, or the Bridgewater College adapted version for the UK. Some nurseries are Beach Schools, and there are a number of day nurseries around the UK that spend all (or nearly all) day outside, virtually no matter the weather – 'there is no bad weather, just bad clothes.' With regards to sustainability, learning through outside play may cause some impact on the local environment, such as when children pick flowers, make dens, make smelly trails, or maybe dam bits of stream. We have begun to see some Forest Schools stopped from using sensitive or delicate areas in the South of England due to damaging impact. Efforts have to be made to not overpopulate sensitive areas in case the effects aren't temporary, because the opportunities for lifelong learning and love of the environment that grows in the children and the colleagues leading these activities are priceless.

What is a concern, though, are the unsustainable resources often listed in the handbooks and websites for Forest Schools, such as wet wipes and single-use water bottles. Often, however, these same handbooks will suggest amazing, sustainable ideas, such as solar showers hung from a branch, recycling of old net curtains and head scarves, use of leaves, twigs, branches, and mud, and generally creating resources with natural materials. Nurseries utilising these freely available guides may find it easy to slip into bad habits without assessing sustainability, assuming that everything 'Forest School' is by definition sustainable, when it may not be.

Colleagues and children also identify plants and animals, learn to make and respect fire, and learn to use tools such as scissors, knives, mallets, peelers, loppers, secateurs, saws, hand and even battery-powered drills. Activities such as cooking on the fire using local fruits and vegetables, sweet chestnuts or baking potatoes, and making bannock, chapattis and nettle soup are worthwhile, significant learning experiences for the children that are also sustainable.

There are dozens of craft activities that can be practised in the Forest School environment using the natural materials found in combination with resources taken along, such as hessian, thread, pipe cleaners, card, clipboards and paperclips. I refer you to *100 Ideas for Early Years Practitioners: Forest School* by Tracey Maciver[4] and *A Practical Guide to Nature-Based Practice* by Niki Buchan,[5] which illustrates and celebrates the nature-based early years practice that has emerged within Australia and New Zealand.

Conclusion

Caring for living creatures both inside and outside the nursery gives children an understanding about what animals, birds, insects and fish need for survival, and also gives us the opportunity to discuss their importance. This role-modelling and discussion will help the next generation develop empathy, knowledge, interest and curiosity, and then use these skills when it is their turn to look after the environment and all living creatures within it.

Notes

1. Breuning, L.G. (2017). Why flowers makes us happy: How flowers stimulate dopamine, serotonin, and oxytocin. *Psychology Today*. 21 June. [Online] www.psychologytoday.com/us/blog/your-neurochemical-self/201706/why-flowers-make-us-happy.
2. www.bioadvanced.com/articles/5-benefits-houseplants and www.ambius.com/blog/health-benefits-of-plants-in-hospitals/.
3. www.forestschoolassociation.org.
4. Maciver, T. (2018). *100 Ideas for Early Years Practitioners: Forest School*. Bloomsbury Education.
5. Buchan, N. (2017). *A Practical Guide to Nature-Based Practice*. Featherstone.

9 Electronic equipment

Electronic equipment is part of our children's lives and most early years settings will now have some – although not all, as there is furious debate over their addictive use versus their educational use, which I won't discuss here. Technology supports projects and research, with some programmes being particularly useful for mathematics, science and technology, and literacy, as well as being able to show real images of animals and the outside world.

Nursery managers, administrators, book-keepers, etc., are all likely to use computers, printers, scanners, and cameras at some point. Made of plastic and metal, they certainly make an impact, but these days one cannot run a business without them.

Figure 9.1 Digital table

Assuming that your setting does have some electronic equipment, this chapter looks at what you might have and how sustainable it is, both in use and at end of life.

Tablets

You may find, as we did, that using tablets to track children's development saves time, paper, cutting up photographs, glue, and also enables efficient tracking of development by cohort, which supports quality lesson planning and maximises our impact on the children's opportunities. Tablets can also be used to track accidents, registers, communications with parents and can form a very useful tool for professionals that enables them to spend more time with children and yet also have more data with which to inform their decisions. So we use a lot of tablets – at least one per room. To help them last longer we put strong rubber bumpers and screen protectors on them, but their charge ports damage easily and a charging bank is a better solution if you can afford it. The longer a piece of electronic equipment lasts, the more sustainable it is, but if it's getting slower and slower, it will be costing your colleagues time. You probably need to pension off your equipment every three years, but it has become indispensable to have it.

Phones – fixed, portable and mobile

Managers use phones to communicate with each other's offices, and communicate with parents by phone, email, WhatsApp, Facebook, Twitter and Instagram. They can also photograph faults for maintenance, meter readings and can have a host of other programs to suit their service. They are vital for communication in emergencies, and even for general operations, so we have to have them, but they seem to go obsolete quickly, and need replacing roughly every three years.

Computers

Most nursery offices have at least one tower computer, keyboard, mouse and screen. There might also be a laptop or two around, and maybe a projector for staff meetings and for projecting images for the children. We may have a nursery camera that we can link to the computer, either directly or using a card reader. This equipment is vital for the operation of the business, for communicating, for tracking enquiries, book-keeping, and basically we can't easily manage a nursery

Table 9.1 Technology

Activity	Renewable?	Land/ under sea damage?	Local?	Investment that could last for years?	Care?	Paint or varnish?	End of life?
Computers Printers Mobile phones Tablets	No	Yes	?	No	Yes	n/a	A challenge!

without one. Yet it also becomes obsolete within a few years and has to be replaced. Most nurseries do not have TVs anymore, but some may have the old enormous screens rather than flat screens – recycle these as soon as you can as they use a huge amount of electricity.

Tops Day Nurseries provide table top 'tower' computers and one large digital table for each 3–4-year-old room, and colleagues use tablets to track children's development. However, they cannot be said to be a sustainable activity.

Second screens

We observed that nursery administrators were often having to look at two things at once, so were printing documents to check against what was on the screen. By purchasing a second screen, we were able to reduce the amount of copying by enough to pay for the screen in just a few months. Our administrators were very happy to have a second screen on their desks, as was I! Unfortunately, this also means a second screen that will need to be sent for recycling in due course. Screens need to be turned off at the end of use as the sleep mode still uses energy.

What to do at the end of life

Computers are made from plastics and metals, and are not built to last, so they use up resources, cause damage where the raw materials are mined, they incur running costs of electricity (try to ensure that this is renewable energy), and disposing of them every couple of years can be disastrous, even scandalous, when it's dumped in vulnerable developing world countries, and risky in terms of data protection if hard drives are not wiped correctly.

Older computers can be turned over to children to play with while still working, and then to take apart when they stop working – but do risk-assess them if they are taking them apart as some of the components may have heavy metals, batteries, and sharp edges that could pose too much of a risk without very focused supervision. Some items may not be able to be taken apart, as many electronics nowadays are designed to be impossible to self-repair.

One of the biggest challenges with computers is what to do when they stop working effectively. Repair shops will often tell us that they cannot be repaired easily because they are now obsolete – generally two to five years after purchase. The current system is such that computer manufacturing companies continually produce new, innovative models that they need consumers to buy. After all, we all want more and more memory, technology to make it all more transportable, more facilities ... don't we?

If we could only get the manufacturers to take the technology back when we are finished with it, take responsibility for the machines, and take them apart/rebuild, recycle or upcycle. They could then sell us the same materials made into something smarter all over again. We really should all be renting computers, phones, white goods, tablets, etc., and giving them back at the end of their life, instead of throwing it all into a waste recycling area where the company has no idea what is in the materials or how to separate it in order to recycle the components. Companies are beginning to consider this model, and indeed we have printer companies already doing this, but it's important that consumers ask about this in order to encourage manufacturers to continue to develop in this direction.

A recent scandal emerged that a lot of European and American computers that had been sent in good faith to be recycled in African countries were actually being dumped in fields in Uganda. The equipment destroys the landscape and potentially pollutes it as well: landfill without the hole in which it's usually hidden. Rich developed countries should be ashamed of themselves for taking advantage of poorer countries or allowing unscrupulous traders to do this on our behalf.

The computer waste company that we use sent us this document, which I think makes interesting reading for UK residents, and I hope that all countries either have something similar or develop something similar:

WEEE Directive

In January 2007, the Waste Electrical and Electronic Equipment (WEEE) Directive was introduced into the UK law by the Waste Electronic and Electrical Equipment Regulations 2006. The main aim of this is to encourage people to re-use and recycle equipment. This in turn reduces the total electrical and electronic equipment being produced. This law allows recyclers to help prolong the life of electrical equipment instead of simply throwing it away and causing harm to the environment. Every year in the UK, the general public dispose over 1.2 million tonnes of electrical waste. Our overall aim is to reduce this figure.

WEEE is the fastest growing waste stream in the UK. In order to transport and recycle WEEE waste legally, you must be licensed by the Environment Agency. All companies that offer the service we provide must hold a Waste Carriers License and an environmental permit or exemption. All WEEE waste that gets collected should be recycled in accordance with guidance on Best Available Treatment, Recovery and Recycling Techniques (BATRRT) and treatment of Waste Electrical and Electronic Equipment (WEEE). This ensures that everything is done to the optimum efficiency and everything possible has been done to prolong the life of equipment.

When collecting and recycling any WEEE waste, it must be accompanied by a Waste Transfer Note stating how many items of each variety have been collected and a rough weight. If in the case that items with glass displays or acid lead batteries are present, a Hazardous Waste Consignment Note must be provided with the correct EWC Codes. In association with the Hazardous Waste Consignment Note.

Just a word of warning: make sure you do demand proof that hard drives in computers and printers have been wiped or destroyed before they are recycled, particularly with the new data privacy acts (GDPR) in the UK. You'll often have to pay for this privilege, but it is definitely a must-do. I hadn't realised that, when you send documents to a printer, they are saved/buffered to print; or when you scan documents into a printer, they are stored on a hard drive – so a printer is liable to hackers and information theft just like computers are.

Printers

Most computers are or can be linked to printers. The printers use paper, but also ink in cartridges, and power. The big companies like Xerox and Epson are aware of our increased focus on green printing and sustainable ink. According to Cartridge World:

Each year in the UK, 45 million non-biodegradable printer cartridges are binned and end up in landfill sites. Some of the plastics used to manufacture cartridges can take up to 1,000 years to decompose, leaving more than enough time for their toxic chemicals to spread into the soil and pollute the environment.[1]

Cartridge World promise that their ink and laser printer cartridges are remanufactured, which creates 46 per cent less CO_2 than a new cartridge. They cite independent studies to evidence this if you check out their Think Green website (www.cartridgeworld.co.uk/environment/think-green).

There are some printer companies already renting out printers to businesses, much like TVs and video players were in the 1970s. You may have moved away from renting or leasing, as you can often end up paying many times over for a printer compared with buying one. If companies could make the difference between renting and purchasing much smaller, and if tax law was amended to make leasing equipment less onerous, we might see a swing back to renting IT equipment. Computers use a fair amount of energy and should have energy-saving modes during the day, but also we need to make sure they are switched off overnight or when they are going to be out of use for any period. Part of the energy-saving mode during the day will help keep your data safe, as you should program in a password in order to re-open the desktop so that casual people passing through the office do not have access to private information.

Power

Electricity should be bought from a renewable energy supplier, and try to take advantage of your own solar power, as well as solar or wind-up charging of batteries and phones if at all possible.

Ink

The ink in photocopiers today uses dry toner powder, which is made of tiny plastic particles. The plastic comes from fossil fuels. They have to be heated up until they melt – which uses energy. The melted plastic then limits the recyclability of the paper. Without doubt, the whole process puts stress on the environment. Scientists and innovators are working hard to increase the amount of sustainable materials in ink and to reduce energy consumption, but this is still ongoing.

There was a scare a few years ago about ink toners being toxic, but these days print ink is made from water, ethylene glycol and alcohol, so drinking it would make you sick but wouldn't be life-threatening. And the powder toner would only irritate your lungs if you inhaled a huge amount of it. Printer toner is not listed as a known or probable carcinogen.

Quantity of copying, black and white versus colour

The fewer photocopies you create, the better for your budget as well as from a sustainability point of view. We started recording the number of photocopies in each nursery every month, and also whether they were using black and white or colour. Colour copying is five times the price of black and white. Our first target was to reduce colour copying down to under 20 per cent, which we achieved.

The second target was to reduce the number of copies in total, and that has also come down by 20 per cent, saving a significant amount of money as well as resources. We did this by using electronic systems a lot more, such as welcome packs to parents and colleagues, and by thinking twice whenever we went to print things, by using competitive tables to compare nurseries against each other, and even awarding prizes for successful nursery teams. We also turned the automatic setting to 'ink saving' and black and white rather than the top quality/colour, so it was a conscious effort to print in a more deluxe mode, with periodic checks to ensure it stayed this way.

Packaging

Computers, printers, tablets and phones are all delivered in packaging, which can often be extensive in order to protect the goods. Distributors are beginning to look at more sustainable packaging of their machines and sharing deliveries, but given the high value of their products and their vulnerability to damage in transit, they may be slower to arrange more sustainable packaging than those distributing less vulnerable products – and they are being incredibly slow! We started taking photographs of this when it occurred and emailing them to the distributors complaining about the waste of resource, particularly when they used plastic bubbles rather than the more sustainable cardboard and paper. Some big boxes are good to have, though – the children love playing in them and making them into spaceships, boats, buses, or whatever their imaginations can dream of!

Batteries

Batteries are needed for our technological toys and some office equipment. They are made of metal and plastic, and chemicals such as nickel and cadmium, both of which are extremely toxic and can cause damage to humans and the environment. Some also contain acid, some lead and some mercury, so they are pretty awful. In the UK, the Early Years Foundation Stage requires some technology to be available in settings, which in many case means toys or equipment that use electricity via the mains or batteries. Some innovative entrepreneurs are trying to make them more sustainable, but the best answer at the moment is to try to avoid using them and use wind-up or solar-powered items, such as wind-up torches and solar phone chargers. Nurseries have to assess their own culture against these conflicting ideals. Batteries are particularly damaging if they end up in landfill. They are classed as hazardous waste and must be recycled by experts – certainly never thrown in a general waste bin. Even rechargeable batteries will

Figure 9.2 Recycling batteries

eventually fail to hold a charge and will need recycling. We collect batteries in the nurseries in secure boxes and send them by internal mail (next person going takes them by hand) to our office, where we box them up ready for collection. We don't like keeping batteries in the nurseries for any longer than essential, particularly the very small camera and watch batteries, as they pose a swallowing hazard. There are methods for recycling most types of batteries, so there should be national recycling schemes in every country.

In conclusion, electronic equipment or information technology is a part of the modern world, and it's down to every owner/manager, together with their customers/parents, to decide to what degree they use it, and enable children to use it. We can reduce our impact by buying good quality to last, if that's an option; printing less; and by considering carefully what will happen to equipment at the end of its life when we buy it. Don't leave working out what will happen to it until it dies, and never just put an old computer in the bin or skip – it needs to be properly recycled, as per the WEEE Directive.

Note

1. Cartridge World. (2018). *Cartridge World Environmental Awareness* [online]. Available from: www.cartridgeworld.co.uk/environment/think-green.

10 Building design

Environments that we provide for young children need to be inspiring and motivating, but they could be provided in a humble, portable cabin, out in the forest, or in a state-of-the-art modern skyscraper. Most likely, you and your children will be located in buildings such as community halls, houses, former shops, pubs or churches. Repurposing an old building is a sustainable action by definition. Retrofitting it with energy-reducing technology (adding solar panels, insulating, double glazing, for example) can make the whole even more sustainable. However, some older buildings may be expensive and difficult to retrofit, or impossible to get planning permission for due to their historic importance. You need to do your sums to work out what the most sustainable and pragmatic approach could be and to get the appropriate permissions. This chapter discusses new-builds, and choices for materials, insulation, roofs, flooring, windows, heating, lighting, waste water and paint in your setting.

New-builds

Designing a new-build is a good investment in terms of the opportunity to reduce your regular energy bills. Retrofitting can be subject to planning permission, building regulations and additional cost, making the appeal of the new-build more attractive. You may have read about the German Passivhaus buildings,[1] which are designed to use hardly any heating through super insulation, or the Passive Solar House, which is designed to use the sun to do all the work. Technology is developing all the time. There are multiple international shows demonstrating ever-improving window technology, ventilation, and heat-recovery systems.

We have been involved in the design, build, and then utilisation of several new-builds and have some experiences to share that may be of assistance to you. But first, why should we choose green building materials?

Building stock accounts for around 57 per cent of the CO_2 emissions in the UK. The process of building causes climate change; uses up our minerals; poisons humans, water and land; uses up fossil fuel stocks and water; creates smog (ground-level ozone that causes asthma and other respiratory conditions); and increases stratospheric ozone depletion, which thins and makes holes in the ozone layer. Construction accounts for around 40 per cent of the total flow of raw materials into the global economy, so there is a lot to think about!

Timber

Timber is a naturally renewable resource that's non-toxic, provided it's from FSC-sourced timbers and without treatments such as pesticides, fungicides and flame retardants. You need to check what has been added to anything made of wood that you buy to guide your decision.

The closer to home you source it, the fewer CO_2 emissions are emitted through its transportation, so buy as locally as you can.

Timber is carbon neutral and easily accessible, whereas steel and concrete construction methods use five times more energy to produce. Some manufacturers have efficient waste processes whereby the excess logs are re-used to create chipboard, paper and energy. At the end of its lifespan, timber biodegrades quickly and can be recycled, making it a generally more sustainable way to build.

Of course, there are other components to a building, particularly if you are converting rather than building from scratch. It might help to consider how sustainable some of the main components of a building are – masonry, roofing, insulation ... I couldn't possibly explain every single sustainable option here, due to the ever-improving technology and information available. But here are some good places to start:

Masonry

Masonry is very durable, to the extent that bricks could be reclaimed and used again even if the building collapses. Unfortunately, only 5 per cent of the 2.5 billion bricks made every year are actually reclaimed; 50 per cent are crushed and used in hard core and fill. The cement used for bricks, particularly Portland cement mortar, is difficult to remove from the brick to enable them to be used again. New bricks rely on clay being quarried, which damages the landscape and creates a high output of CO_2. They also take a lot of energy to produce and are expensive to transport. Concrete blocks are similar, depleting the landscape or marine environment of sand (causing coastal erosion and damage to fish and other marine life) and cement use contributes to global warming. Cement manu-facturing is responsible for 5–7 per cent of the world's carbon dioxide emissions; 40 per cent of that is due to using fossil fuels to heat the kilns and the rest is from de-carbonation of the limestone. Work is being done on these aspects, including using ash/industrial waste in the blocks instead of cement, using recycled aggregate, and using old quarries for water sports. Alternatives include unfired clay blocks, insulated concrete form blocks (mixed with woodchip) and hemp blocks.

Roofing

The best material for roofing is arguably reclaimed slates and tiles, if you can source them and their quality is suitable; this is followed by timber shingles (although these often have import energy and maintenance issues). We used natural slate on our Winchester day nursery building, as specified by the plan-ners, and although they are re-usable, recyclable and very durable, their import energy is high. The Chinese quarry where they were mined will have degraded the landscape, and there is a very high level of waste during production (90 per cent!). They also absorb a lot of heat in summer, requiring us to install air condi-tioners. We have clay tiles on our Wimborne Tops Day Nursery, built in the 1970s. Although they are described as re-usable and durable, we have had a number of breakages and the clay quarry damage to the environment and very high embodied energy costs needs to be borne in mind if ordering new ones. When I built a room into my roof at home, I was able to replace the clay tiles rather than buying new ones – a more sustainable action. The alternative was to buy concrete roof tiles or slates, which are perhaps the most economic form of roof covering, and can be made in various colours, forms and textures. However, they have very high levels of CO_2 and other emissions, and degrade landscapes. Or I could have used fibre cement slates, but they have the same high levels of CO_2, plus the synthetic polymer fibre is derived from oil and responsible for other noxious emissions. The plastic polymer is energy-intensive and, like most plastics, they last for hundreds of years in the environment on disposal. I am so glad I didn't choose those at the time as I wasn't aware of the huge plastic trash problem that we know about now! Recycling tyres into tiles and slates make low-weight, durable roofing, so if these were more consistently available, they would be a good sustainable option. Metal roof coverings are another option as they are recyclable, often made with up to 100 per cent recycled content, are durable, and do not leach into rainwater. However, they do have very high embodied energy if produced with fossil fuel energy and create toxic emissions.

Insulation

There are many different types of sustainable insulation. Cellulose, for example, is made from recycled newspaper, although 20 per cent of that might be borax/boric acid, in order to provide fire resistance and to repel insects and fungi. Wood fibre insulation can sometimes include some non-renewable polyester binder. Hemp and flax are good but may also contain polyester binder, and the fertilisers used to grow it contribute to global warming. Sheep wool can also sometimes be tainted with polyester and, if it's imported, there is an extra embodied energy cost, plus the conditions the sheep were reared in might be unknown. Mineral- and oil-based insulation are not as sustainable.

Flooring

Flooring is also an important choice for your building. If your building doesn't already have wooden floor boards that can be sanded and polished back to their glorious beauty, or perhaps the original tiles, then linoleum is our usual choice because it is durable, non-toxic, renewable and recyclable. However, the linseed used in production usually involves the use of fertiliser, which would have created butane (a hydrocarbon gas) emission and polluted water, so it isn't perfect. Cork is great, although you need to check it hasn't got formaldehyde in it, and sealants can produce toxic chemicals. FSC-sourced timber is perfect. Rubber is great if it really is rubber, but it often contains plastic. Recycled rubber would be a great sustainable option. Ceramic tiles are good, particularly for wet areas, but they carry high embodied energy, and even more so if they're imported. Stone tiles are also good, but quarrying will degrade the landscape and fitting them might include toxic sealants. It's better to avoid polyethylene, poly-propylene and PVC flooring as they're made from non-renewable oil and will not biodegrade for hundreds of years if you want to replace it.

We have tried different options at various nurseries. Sometimes, we've been able to use the existing flooring, which was wonderful, sanding and varnishing it. We've also tried laminate flooring and solid bamboo flooring. While the laminate is cheaper and can still have the look and feel of natural wood, it does wear at the joins eventually. Bamboo flooring is very sustainable in terms of being renewable, it grows incredibly fast and with little water, but it does need importing from the Far East so incurs an embodied energy charge for that. Solid wood or parquet flooring is a treat – it is expensive and high maintenance, but a delight if you find it under your carpets, as we have on a couple of sites. We have sanded it and polished it to provide a beautiful floor – but it does need protecting from water play.

Sustainable materials for rugs and carpets include sisal, seagrass, hemp grass and jute, but you could equally buy second-hand rugs and give them another life. These natural materials are all renewable, biodegradable, naturally insulating, and vary in their durability, stain resistance and mould/mildew resistance.

Window frames

Window frames could be made of FSC hardwood (oak, large sweet chestnut). The factors to be aware of are to ensure that it is FSC, preferably source it locally, and be aware that painting it can add significantly to its environmental impact. You might want to use recycled paint both for window frames and for walls, as we do. Choose windows as large as possible because the metal spaces between the glass panels act as cold bridges and large panes have less perimeter length than lots of smaller panes. Composite materials (combinations) for window frames have been developed innovatively and one of the best combinations is aluminium clad frames with softwood cores, which are expected to have lifetimes of over 40 years. PVC by comparison is around 25 years. Aluminium smelting does take up some energy, though! Steel isn't great because it rusts and takes a lot of energy to make. PVC is made from non-renewable oil and the threat to the environment posed by the manufacture, use and disposal of PVC renders it unacceptable from a sustainability perspective!

The best resources to look out for are anything that uses a recycled content from after the customer has used it. This is much more impressive than recycling pre-consumer, i.e. off the factory floor from during manufacture.

In 2012, Fordingbridge built us a top of the eco range A++ nursery building complete with heat exchanger, automatic LED lighting and ventilation, triple glazing, and a distinctive grass roof. The build cost was high, using steel and wood, and therefore the rent is also high, but the energy use is low. Fordingbridge have since gone on to build the first net-zero energy buildings for Costa Coffee.

In May 2018, we opened an extension to our nursery in Lakeside, Portsmouth designed by TG Escapes, who promised a building that would encourage environmental citizenship, outdoor learning and educational play, and help reconnect students with nature. They said that they do this with biophilic design principles, maximising natural light, providing views of nature and easy access to the outdoors. The building incorporates a timber frame, which has the lowest carbon footprint of any commercially available structural building, red cedar timber cladding (FSC and PEFC certified sustainable), 80 per cent recycled insulation, double glazing, low emissivity glass, pre-insulated flooring with 80 per cent recycled mineral wool, air course heat pump and LED lighting. TG Escapes also offset their activities and CO_2 emissions with ClimateCare, recognising that transporting and the non-sustainable elements of their building do have a negative impact on the environment, despite their best efforts. "Eco Classrooms and Nurseries" built us a new classroom on the Isle of Wight without concrete foundations (metal screws instead) and the children love its funky style as much as we love its eco credentials.[2]

Extras for the building can include features like sun pipes, living sedum roofs, solar water systems, and solar power systems, as well as AA-rated cooling and heating.

A downside to the building is that only 10 years' warranty is provided on the main structure and 20 years on the roof. While 10 years might feel like a lifetime when you are young, it really flies by when you are looking back at 30 years in the nursery sector!

A big issue to be aware of is the phenomenon of greenwashing (also discussed in Chapter 13). This is the practice of using 'eco' or 'enviro' in a product name when it doesn't warrant it. Occasionally, the product is just an ordinary product that has been in production for many years and someone slaps 'eco' in front of the title to gain more market share and keep out the competition, so we need to check there is evidence of any eco claims before settling on a product or supplier.

Worthy evidence to look for are ISO or WRAP standards, the Environmental Product Declaration (EPD), the health and safety sheet for any human toxin content or the pan-European Blue Angel label. The EPD declaration needs to be read and understood; ISO 14025 EPD is *not* a green certificate, although it does give you a list of contents and their environmental impacts – there can be an EPD for nuclear waste just as easily as palm leaves. Like an asbestos survey, it's not just about having done a survey; it's about reading the results and acting safely thereafter. Some labels will be third party national or international standards and some will be self-certificates created by the CEO and marketing department. The only way to work out which is which is to ask the questions and do the research. Beware of the word 'natural'. Arsenic and mercury are natural and no one would claim them to be safe and healthy! 'Non-toxic' is another one – virtually everything is toxic if taken in enough quantities and vice versa. And virtually everything is 'biodegradable' – what we need to distinguish is how long the material takes to biodegrade: 2 days or 2 million years? One constituent may be ecologically friendly, but other parts of the product may be even less ecologically sound than usual: a hidden trade-off. Outright lying is surprisingly more prevalent than I would certainly have expected – I've busted a few!

Heating and lighting

Research shows that a great quality building with good air ventilation and natural light can significantly boost learning progress and children's achievements.

Lighting

Architects can design a building with consideration of its orientation towards the sun, to enjoy the best of the natural light sources. The best buildings can incorporate large windows and doors, even potentially bi-fold doors so that whole walls can be opened up to the garden.

When it gets darker, the most energy-efficient (and therefore sustainable) fittings are high-quality, low-energy light-emitting diode (LED) fittings. There are different shades of LED lights; some are more natural and warm in hue and others are very bright and quite cold. It is worth discussing what you are wanting to light with your supplier to achieve the desired effect, whether for general lighting for children to play under, or displaying their art work. If you have babies lying on the floor and facing the ceiling where the lights are, you might want to consider wall lighting or shading to avoid them looking directly at the lights, which may fascinate them but might not be great for their eyes!

If you want your LED lights to be dimmable (sleep room perhaps), you do need to specify this before the lights are fitted, as a different type of switch and fitting is required.

Passive infrared (PIR) motion sensors ensure lights are only on when needed. Sensors that detect when the light is fading and come on automatically will also help keep the bills down. Otherwise, what usually happens is the first colleagues in the morning will turn all the lights on and the last people at night will turn all the lights off. This is a really inefficient way to light a building, particularly during the middle of the day, or when some rooms are out of use, or perhaps the cleaner is the only person in the building for a couple of hours.

It is well worth changing fluorescent lighting over to LED lighting, although for the long tubes, the whole fitting needs to be changed, which requires an electrician. You do not need to replace every compact fluorescent (CFL) tube fitting with an LED fitting, because LEDs are much brighter. If you still have any halogen light bulbs, you will find that replacing those with LED lights will drop your bills by 90 per cent – these should be replaced immediately as they save their purchase easily within the first few months.

Some of your colleagues may still want to use fairy lights, and light boxes, and maybe standard lamps, and you would continue to run those from the normal plugs. Even for these, you should look for LED bulbs rather than the now old-fashioned incandescent bulbs. LED bulbs last much longer than incandescent bulbs, gradually dimming over time, and are normally replaced when the light output decreases by around 30 per cent.

Figure 10.1 Using a light table and magnifying glass to study plant biology

Heating/cooling

Around 70 per cent of the energy created by an air source heat pump is generated for free. The system doubles as an efficient heating and cooling system to maintain a constant, pleasant temperature through the year. They are a great invention that is more sustainable than most forms of heating/cooling. The biggest difference between a heat pump and ACs is that heat pumps can heat and cool the building, while an AC only cools, so you would also need a boiler (whether electric, gas or oil fired) to heat the building, via radiators or underfloor (wet) heating. A gas boiler is still the cheapest way to heat a building – if you don't also want to cool it – and oil is currently the most expensive. Electric heating can be via storage heaters or electric radiators or through underfloor and wall infrared heating, which is considered a healthier, more pleasant way to heat people (rather than the room). I would strongly advise consulting a heating engineer to calculate how much heating you need for your building so that the system chosen will produce the desired effect, particularly bearing in mind the need for any radiators to be low surface temperature ones to avoid the risk of burning, and that added metal or wood around the radiators will reduce efficiency.

If you are buying your power off your national grid, it is possible to choose the power from a sustainable energy supplier – one that buys their power from wind farms, solar panels, hydro-electricity or tidal booms. All of these are far preferable to purchasing electricity made by burning fossil fuels. I'm sure no one claims nuclear energy is sustainable given the huge problem of disposing of nuclear waste, but at least it doesn't add to global warming gases.

We have our own solar panels on some of our nursery roofs. I had the first set installed on our Wimborne Tops Day Nursery, where we had inherited an oil burning system from the previous owners of the property (a pub) and the heating bills were enormous. I was very pleased when the oil boiler died as I had no excuse for not replacing the system. The finance director was not happy with my decision to install solar panels as the return on them was likely to be 8–10 years, which is a much longer term than accountants like to work with. I was insistent, the system paid for itself in 8 years and, 12 years later, continues to generate as much electricity as the day it was installed – and I'm hopeful it will continue to do so for a while. Here is a case study put forward by our commercial director that you might find interesting on our solar panels' return on investment (ROI):

I've just been working out the money generated by the solar panels at Wimborne for 2018 (for ESOS purposes). It's difficult to get exactly right as we don't have regular readings so I've had to try to estimate readings for the beginning and end of the year and calculate accordingly. I think it's pretty accurate though:

We've generated 3693.5kWh of electricity and we have been paid by SSE £1983.90 for 2018.

On top of that, any of the 3693.5kWh that we've generated we get to use for free, we have absolutely no way of knowing how much of it we have used though. You can't save it up so it has to be used as it's generated. We use very little at weekends, so 28.6% just disappears (apart from anything left on over the weekend, fridges, freezers, etc.). We don't get to use any during the hours of darkness. As you can see it's very difficult to work out how much we've used. The government assume we'll use half, if we go with that then we've also saved about 3693.5/2 x 16p on our electricity bill at Wimborne, that's about another £295.48.

Having the solar panels at Wimborne is worth around £2,280 per year to us and that will increase very slightly every year for the next 15 years (FIT payments are guaranteed for 25 years and index linked).

We've had them for about 10 years so we've already saved about £22,800, minus the install costs of roughly £15,000, £7800 and we've got another £34,200 to come, £42,000 in total.

That's some return on a £15,000 investment.

Something else to consider is having an electric metre that children and colleagues can see – then they can engage in what can be done to reduce electricity use, for example they may see it jumping up when the tumble dryer is on and reflect on using the line instead. There are also systems available that monitor power use throughout the building and can provide a detailed report on where energy is being used in the building and when, but this system does cost many thousands to install and may not be self-financing in the savings generated depending on what is identified. On the other hand, installing just one if you have a group can indicate what savings might be made across the whole group, for example monitoring when immersion heaters are on and off – immersion heaters use a huge amount of energy, so shouldn't be left on overnight or at weekends.

We have solar panels on several further buildings, but they are a significant investment so it can take a while to fund them – although, there are investors who are interested in a return that is measured in impact on sustainability or corporate social environmental responsibility (CSER) rather than just financial who may be keen to invest, such as Triodos Bank and the Bridges Fund. There was a UK government subsidy in place but this has sadly been withdrawn. We are hoping something new and better will replace this incentive soon. There was a limit on the size of array that would attract government subsidy, but this has now gone. You usually need electricity board permission to add to the grid with bigger arrays, and we are therefore likely to apply for bigger systems, aiming to be completely self-sustaining, including the use of electric cars. We have also had permission to install some on leased buildings, not just freehold buildings, which you might want to consider, subject to legal protection of your panels should you move.

Technology and price have drastically improved and I am looking forward to battery technology improving too, and costing less, so that instead of putting the energy we generate over the weekend (when we are closed) into the national grid, it could be stored to run the electric vehicle and the building during opening hours. In some countries you can rent the batteries and share the return with the owners, supported by governments, so that could be something useful for your service.

Wind generation is not something we've tried, although I would love to explore the beautiful tree-type designs in New Mexico that look more like sculptures than generators. Small wind turbines are electric generators that use the wind to produce clean, emissions-free power. You may need planning permission for them. And, as we still don't have cost-effective batteries, if the wind isn't blowing, you won't have any energy, so you would need to stay on the grid for general power. Payback time can be anything from 6 to 30 years, depending on the cost of the turbine, the quality of wind at the installation site, the prevailing electricity rates and financing, so it would still take a good business case to persuade any finance director or bank to take a risk on paying for one.

If you don't want to heat the entire neighbourhood by having your doors open while children free-flow in and out of the building, you might want to install butcher sheets. They are plastic, but they will last a long time! The flaps allow children to go in and out safely while keeping the heat in and the insects and dust out. They work well, and are cheap to install. Some designs can also be taken down quickly and easily for cleaning (put them in a dishwasher) if you don't want to clean them in situ or if you decide you don't want them up for a period.

Infrared heating

I trialled some infrared heating at home while considering whether to install it at the nurseries. I had a 240v system installed, which proved very expensive to run, with few of the known health benefits of infrared today. So if you are considering infrared heat, go for the 24v, such as provided by 'Redheat', which can also be retrofitted attached to LED lights rather than underfloor (saving taking up the flooring), and instead of radiators, which take up space and have to have a low surface temperature in children-inhabited areas. Very high ceilings cause problems for infrared because the panels need to be within 3 metres to be effective. Benefits of infrared heat include: being good for blood circulation, strengthening your immune system, and helping to sweat the toxins out of your body. Infrared heats bodies, not the air, so it is efficient, and feels very different from traditional central heating. The payback time is around 10 years from installation, so it's perhaps only for longer-term thinking operators.

Waste water or grey water

Water is still relatively cheap in the UK (unlike in Saudi Arabia, where it was more expensive than oil the last time I was there). It rains regularly, and the water can be harvested off the roof into water butts and used to water plants (see more about these in Chapter 7), but it can also be used to provide the water for toilets – called grey water. Providing for a grey water system would be a sustainable, water-saving option. However, payback time would be about 40 years unless you install it yourself and don't charge for the labour, and even then it's about 20 years. So in countries where water is scarce and expensive, and internationally this is the case, this is another tool to use in the sustainability challenge.

Painting your nursery

We used to paint our nurseries with the toughest, regular branded paint that we could find, hoping to wash the little handprints off, but having to repaint every three years. Paint was so toxic smelling we tried additives to neutralise the smell, although we have heard since that some of these actually attack nose linings so you just *can't* smell it: a frightening thought!

There are ranges of eco-paints, such as Earthborn, which have the aim of providing an environmental alternative to traditional paints. They consider what the paint is made of, as well as the fumes that arise, and their paints are free from plastic – acrylics, oils and vinyl. They make a full declaration of their ingredients so you can check on those yourself.

There is also an independent accreditation scheme for indoor paints and varnishes: the EU Ecolabel[3] is worth looking out for in the UK – there may be equivalents around the world. EU Ecolabel claims to be unique because it is truly independent of any profit-making organisation and not an accreditation that can be bought.

However, we took quite a different approach by choosing to use re-engineered paint, which is also anti-bacterial! Paint 360[4] collects paint heading to deep landfill or incineration, and then re-manufacturers it, making it the lowest carbon footprint paint available in the UK, while also reducing carbon for its disposal. They add silver ion technology to it to provide the anti-bacterial effect and it comes in a range of colours. It's hardwearing and washable. We love the fact that the core of their workforce is the young and long-term unemployed, that it has a whopping 95 per cent recycled content, that it is a 100 per cent saving on the use of water compared with virgin paint, and that they also make paintbrushes and trays from recycled materials. They are planning to significantly expand and their product competes on quality and price. We've used it since 2016 for all our redecorating and would highly recommend it.

Conclusion

The sustainability of a building is an important component of sustainability for your setting. It can be a significant investment, with a slow return on investment, and it may not be visible to children and parents, but it will have an impact on your sustainability targets, and it is something to publicise as an achievement if and when you put some of these practices in place.

Notes

1. See https://passiv.de/en/index.php.
2. See www.tgescapes.co.uk/ and https://ecoclassroomsandnurseries.co.uk/.
3. See ec.europa.eu/environment/ecolabel/ey-ecolabel-for-consumer.html for more information.
4. Check out www.paint360.co.uk.

Cleaning, sanitising and disinfecting, personal care

Our primary purpose is to keep children safe on behalf of their parents. We all want to protect our children and colleagues from diseases and allergens, but we could damage the environment and even the children's natural immune systems or health while we do it. We therefore need to think carefully about the products we use, and try to stay up to date as science and innovations move us forward in this area.

This chapter looks at why we need to reflect on our policies for keeping our nurseries clean. It considers including sustainability in your purchasing policy, and then the impact of specific types of products such as air fresheners, laundry and cleaning products on the environment. It also looks at products commonly used for personal care, including toothbrushes, hand wash, toothbrushing and insect protection ... and suggests some eco-friendly alternatives

Getting started

If you have no sustainability built into your purchasing policies and procedures already, you might consider taking a more strategic view and consider your overall policy as a first point of call. In our research, we came across the Cleaning, Sanitising and Disinfecting Toolkit for Early Care and Education.[1] This can be accessed online and is a very comprehensive programme, developed by numerous higher education organisations, green solutions and the governmental department of Pesticide Regulation. It provides a thorough list of types of product that we can all use for reflection and action as appropriate, and indeed other countries may already have similar programmes in place. This is, of course, just one aspect of being a sustainable environment for children. You might also consider the carbon footprint of products you are considering purchasing, including their packaging and delivery, and also what happens to the product and its packaging after use. Products that use less or no plastic packaging are more sustainable, and products that are returned to the manufacturers for repurposing or refilling (the circular economy) are ideal. Anything that washes down the drain is of concern, particularly anything with very small bits of plastic in it, as those will bypass the water filtration and enter the sea.

Your purchasing policy can be a standalone document or could be incorporated with your corporate social responsibility documentation (see Appendix II for examples of both).

Air fresheners

Back in the 1970s, we used aerosol air fresheners that contained CFCs, which were later identified as destroying our ozone layer and are now banned. Then we signed up to plug-in air fresheners, which heat up some chemicals and fan them around the buildings. Although they don't use a lot of power (you'd need to run about 30 to match the refrigerator consumption), they are usually made of plastic, and there are concerns about the chemical fragrances/chemicals that they blow out. Physicians with the Natural Resources Defence Council[2] recently discovered distressing levels of phthalates in some major brands of air freshener. Phthalates are hormone-disrupting chemicals that may cause birth defects, infertility and cancer. As a result, some brands were taken off the shelves and another brand volunteered to remove the ingredients in question. Air fresheners may also contain volatile organic compounds (VOCs); look out for acetaldehyde, which is a hazardous air pollutant, benzene and formaldehyde, which are both toxic. Unfortunately, and to my surprise, some of my favourite incense and scented candles contain the same VOCs as the aerosol cans because it's the chemical in the fragrance itself, not the delivery system. Our perfumes and aftershaves have the same problem, so if we really want to keep our world free of this type of pollutant, we need to think carefully about whether the risk is worth it. Pollens and foods that caused our ancestors no problems are giving rise to growing numbers of allergic reactions in today's children. The rise in allergies in the last 30 years has been particularly noticeable. For example 7 per cent of children now have food allergies, compared with 2 per cent of adults in the UK, according to Dr Alexandra Santos of King's College London.[3] She says that the increase in allergies is not simply the effect of society becoming more aware of them and better at diagnosing them, but that allergies and increased sensitivity to foods may well be environmental and related to Western lifestyles, including too much hygiene. The same mechanisms involved in tackling allergies fight parasitic infections, so if the chemicals we use kill all the parasites, the immune system turns against things that should be harmless.

Organic Authority[4] offers six alternatives to toxic air fresheners to sweeten our environments naturally:

1. 'Take out the rubbish.' I'm sure you'd do this anyway, particularly the nappies, which cause many of the foul aromas.

2. 'Open the windows.' Open all the windows, and doors, and let the breeze freshen things up – provided you don't have the heating or air conditioner on!

3. 'Simmer your scent.' For cooler months, fill a pan with simmering water and a couple of cinnamon sticks – this can scent the building for days. But make sure to prevent access to this in a building full of children, and don't let it run dry.

4. 'Make your own natural air freshener.' Creating a customised and all-natural air freshener is easy and inexpensive. You'll need to purchase a small water spray bottle (found in gardening supplies or toiletries) and your preferred scent of organic essential oils (carried by health food stores). Popular essential oils include orange, blue spruce, lemon and lavender, but choose the aroma that appeals to you the most for the current season. Mix a few drops of essential oil into the spray bottle filled with water, and spritz around whenever you need a fragrant boost. The children would love to help choose and spritz.

5. Buy all-natural air fresheners. Skip the plug-in fresheners that waste electricity and choose biodegradable, non-aerosol fresheners. Don't rely on the air freshener's 'natural' label; read the ingredients to make sure all the ingredients are indeed 100 per cent natural. Most organic, all-natural air fresheners are various mixtures of essential oils, so smell before you buy to find your favourite.

6. Use sachets. For places that you can't spray, use small sachets filled with dried organic lavender to spread a sweet, homey scent. Sachets are easy to make yourself if you can manage a needle and thread, or you can purchase them inexpensively as well. Choose pesticide-free lavender blossoms and tuck the sachets into drawers and corners. The children may love to help with this too.

You could also try the following:

■ After cleaning, sprinkle the soft furnishings and carpet with bicarbonate of soda, rubbing into smelly patches, and vacuum up the next morning (once a month).

■ If it is really smelly, use a home-made carpet shampoo of half white vinegar and half water, but wait until it's completely dry before using the bicarbonate of soda.

- Add lemon or lemongrass, lavender, eucalyptus radiata (while *Eucalyptus globulus* is safe for adults, it should not be used near children under the age of 2).[5] or cedar essential oils to your bicarb, as above (best to use a sprinkler rather than straight from the box to avoid clumping).

- Use potpourri bowls and top up the essential oils periodically.

- Use bamboo diffusers in a bottle, with up to one cup of water and eight drops each of three different essential oils, such as wild orange, sandalwood, clove, tea tree, eucalyptus, lemon, pine or peppermint.

We need to risk-assess any items before having them within reach of your children. Watch out with tea tree oil, cinnamon and nutmeg as they can be toxic for babies under six months and is toxic to dogs.

Cigarette smoke

You may share my concerns about colleagues coming into work, or back from breaks, smelling of cigarette smoke. The ideal is to ban smoking on breaks; another option is to at least put a coat on to smoke outside and remove on return, but even then there are many nasty toxins in tobacco smoke, including: nicotine (addictive poison used in pesticides); formaldehyde (preservation of dead flesh); ammonia (toilet cleaner); hydrogen cyanide (rat poison); acetone (used in nail polish remover); and carbon monoxide (car exhaust). So to have a colleague coming into contact with children smelling of cigarettes is unacceptable. Is there a way of neutralising this? The following materials are believed to be capable of absorbing or neutralising tobacco smoke odours, at least temporarily – vinegar, citrus, baking soda, coffee grounds, charcoal – but just because you can't smell it doesn't mean the toxins are not still there.

You might want to consider a HEPA filter (high efficiency particulate air), which would also remove pollen, mould spores, dust and other allergens, particularly if you have asthma sufferers on site. HEPA filters with a carbon filter would remove the toxins and the smells. Biovation produce a spray that neutralises the smoke and the toxins by digesting it, called 'Biofresh', and we have started using that to protect children and colleagues from smokers, but it's quite pungent – smokers just spray once and walk through it, so this is another option. It comes in a large 5 litre container that you decant into a re-usable spray bottle – so it's not perfect, but it is an option.

Clean air ioniser/purifier/ozone generator

If you are near a busy road, or perhaps near fields of rapeseed, etc., and you have children who suffer from hay fever or allergies, you could consider an air purifier. Certainly, I know of nurseries who have these in the UK thanks to a Dyson[6] who has started distributing some cost-effective air-purifying fans considerably more economically than the commercial ones available. It is definitely worth knowing the difference between an air purifier and an ioniser. Air purifiers suck air into the device through a filter that traps airborne contaminants and then pushes clear air into the room. An ioniser, on the other hand, attracts airborne particles to an electrode and removes them through a process similar to static electricity. The ions collect on walls and ceilings, and you have to vacuum around an ioniser frequently to pick up the dust. Ionisers can sometimes produce excess ozone as well. Ground-level ozone is harmful to the respiratory system, can reduce lung function, exacerbate asthma and make lungs more susceptible to infection. Ozone generators are also used sometimes to return air to basic elements, carbon dioxide and hydrogen, which have no odour, but beware because ozone is dangerous and ozone generators should only be used in unoccupied spaces. Large retailers use air filter facilities management partners to supply air filter products that also contribute to energy conservation and waste reduction, for example CFP works with M&S and supplies, fits and removes filter banks and housings.

Plants that purify air naturally are covered in Chapter 7.

Adult perfumes and deodorants

I recently had a member of office staff threaten to quit due to other members of staff using strong perfumes and deodorants. This is quite a touchy subject.

It's bad enough when an adult suffers from body odour and that has to be raised, but this did lead me to do some research and what I found was concerning. Many perfumes and deodorants, which are often used on bare skin, contain a number of nasty chemicals. Some to avoid include **triclosan**, which has been banned in antiseptic products for hand-washing yet is still allowed to be applied to our under arms for hours at a time and in some other products. A long list is available online. **Parabens** are another nasty, added to products as a preservative, but may interfere with the regulation and production of hormones including oestrogen, leading to an increased risk of cancer cell growth in the surrounding area, for example breasts. And **propylene glycol**, found in most deodorants to give a smoother application, could be linked to damage of the heart, liver and central nervous system. Why not pick products that use coconut oil for the same effect?

TEA and DEA (acidity controllers) have been linked to an increased risk of liver and kidney tumours and **phthalates** have been linked to hormone production, risk of asthma, adverse impact on foetal development and even a lower IQ. But can you require your staff to use only natural deodorants and perfumes? Probably not, and you probably couldn't identify what they are wearing by smell either, could you? Phthalates are also found in nail polish to reduce cracking, in eyelash glue and as a solvent and fixative in fragrance. Should we not all have been made aware of the risks we are taking with our own health as well as the health of the children we are cuddling, or do we accept that just about everything carries a health risk these days?

Bleach

Bleach is a known carcinogen that can cause burns, respiratory problems and gastrointestinal issues. If it is mixed with anything that contains ammonia, it produces an extremely toxic gas. Rightly so, most early years establishments do not use it, other than maybe small amounts in Milton for sterilising. Studies have shown that volatile organic compounds (VOCs) skyrocket when you clean with bleach.

Alternatives to using bleach include:

- Oxygen bleach disinfects and cleans just as well as chlorine bleach.
- A thick paste made of a half cup of vinegar and a quarter cup of baking soda will clean tiles.
- A spray of equal parts white vinegar, baking soda and water is an excellent multipurpose cleaner – e.g. for spraying tables.
- Sprinkle a cup of borax and a quarter cup of vinegar into your toilet bowl, let it sit overnight, scrub and flush in the morning.
- Unclog a drain by pouring a handful of baking soda and a half cup of vinegar, cover for 15 minutes and then flush with boiling water.

Insect killers, fungicides and herbicides

Borax is a natural mineral, also known as sodium borate, with the sustainability issues that come with being mined. If you somehow consumed a large quantity, it would cause nausea, vomiting and diarrhoea, and the dust can cause respiratory irritation. It is commonly used in insect killer, fungicides and herbicides, as well as for water softening and food preservation (banned in some countries). Borax is linked to hormone disruption, so it's not something you'd want to use much, if at all, and definitely to keep away from children.

The chemicals in fungicides and herbicides are the subject of legal challenges. Evidence has been brought against large chemical companies such as Procter & Gamble and Monsanto accusing them of making products that kill bees and cause cancer, and some have been banned in some countries. So there are strong arguments for being as organic as possible in our nurseries and nursery gardens. There are alternatives such as using a weed spray made from 4 cups of vinegar and 1/4 cup of salt, or just pouring boiling water onto the organism you wish to kill. Coffee grounds repel common garden pests like slugs, snails, fleas, and mosquitos. Children are unlikely to try and eat these products and they aren't poisonous if they do, but obviously you wouldn't be able to use boiling water while children are present.

Use a steam cleaner

Steam cleaners heat water to a high enough temperature to produce a high-pressure steam, which in turn gets rid of germs, dirt and grease, with no need for any chemicals. With appropriate attachments, it will clean glass (a squeegee), tile grout (scrubbing brush), windows (angled nozzle), and dust (various absorbent machine-washable cloths). They use power, of course, and quite a lot of it, so ideally they should be powered by a renewable energy source.

When you buy one, check out comparison sites, like IndyBest[7] or *Which?* magazine,[8] where you can compare prices, heat-up time, how long it lasts on a full tank, how you clean the pads (washing machine?) and what surfaces it can be used on – some are only good for hard floors, others will do ceramic, lino, stone, wood, parquet, marble and carpet. If you are in a hard water setting, you will need an effective limescale filter for your steam cleaner. As with any machine in a childcare setting, you will need a risk assessment and would probably choose to use a steam cleaner after the children have gone home.

Washing-up liquids, floor, surface and toilet cleaning products

We considered whether to change our washing-up liquid to a more eco-friendly brand. We looked up the *Which?* magazine's analysis of washing-up liquids, which considers the performance of each product and a report on eco-friendly washing-up liquids. Based on a *Which?* member survey in February 2019, consumers expect the following from an eco-friendly washing-up liquid, in this order:

- biodegradable ingredients

- can be recycled

- uses recycled materials

- not tested on animals

- suitable for septic tanks

- ethical supply chain

- meets Paris Agreement.

However, under EU law, washing-up liquids have to meet specified standards for biodegradation – the extent to which the substance breaks down into carbon dioxide, water and minerals, and salts and can be absorbed back into the environment. This means all washing-up liquids sold in the UK can be considered eco-friendly. The main difference that *Which?* found between 'eco' branded and standard washing-up liquids is in their ingredients. The eco brands were all free from crude oil as an ingredient. Ecover was the only brand to meet every eco criteria that *Which?* asked about, using a 100 per cent recycled bottle and a refill scheme. Tesco's own brand had its range certified by the independent EU Eco Label, which says that 'its factory recycles all materials including plastic waste, metal waste, cardboard and all liquids. Everything is processed to be used again.'

However, we found another company, Biovation, an advanced and innovative technology, based on natural bacterial cultures that are specially selected to quickly decompose organic matter. It basically eats up the bad bacteria and replaces it with good bacteria. *Which?* hadn't tested it as it's a commercial brand rather than a product found in supermarkets. It comes in bottles made from ethanol sugarcane, which is more sustainable than plastics made from oil, and can be recycled within the same chain of recycling of traditional polyethylene. The washing-up liquids come in super concentrated form that we water down, so fewer bottles to recycle, plus it works best with warm or cool water, saving energy usage. The same range can be used for floor cleaning, carpet and fabric cleaning, surface cleaning, and has significantly reduced the quantity of plastic containers entering our premises. Something to bear in mind with all surface cleaning products is how many seconds or minutes it requires to be left on the surface before wiping it off. This time period is likely to be longer in a kitchen, where nasty bugs found on raw meat and other products need to be allowed for, but, as ever, read the instructions before use.

Biovation also works out cheaper, and when we shared our research with our main supplier (they say they are the biggest educational supplier in the world), they agreed to start distributing this product range along with more traditional products. It is much easier for our accounts department to have as many products as possible coming from main, preferred suppliers as it reduces the number of invoices, so is cheaper, plus we are more likely to get a discount through bulk ordering. It is better operationally to be dealing with fewer companies, as there is less checking to do regarding deliveries, CSER, and quality. This shows that working with your supplier, explaining how important sustainability is to you, and giving time for adaption can be a win situation for us in the sector, a win for our suppliers, and a win for the sustainability of the planet.

Sponges, brushes and wipes for cleaning up

There are alternatives that are more sustainable, but they aren't appearing in our standard supplier catalogue – talks are in progress, so again we have started working with local artisans. For example, Stitchery Dorset, who you can find on Etsy, do all-purpose 'Crim cleaning cloths' made from natural scrim – 60 per cent linen and 40 per cent cotton – an eco-friendly linen mix which makes it very absorbent, lint-free, and able to dry out quickly. We found this great for most cleaning tasks. They have also colour-coded them for us with a strip sewn down the sides to help prevent cross-contamination (green for kitchen, blue for bathroom, red for bodily fluids, yellow for playrooms), which is a more professional solution than you might use at home, perhaps cutting up old towels and flat nappies into hand-cloth sizes, and certainly much better than using plastic-based single-use wipes or J-cloth-type cloths that contain plastic and are only washed a few times.

Use brushes that will be compostable in the garden afterwards, typically made of wood, bamboo or coconut husks. Replacement heads will help them to last longer. Use coconut husk-based pads instead of plastic pads; Brillo pads, made of steel wool and soap are actually a sustainable choice. The coconut waste in countries such as the Philippines and Indonesia litters many coconut-growing areas when it could be utilised. For more information on green cleaning products, there are a wealth of websites to visit, such as Mommy is Green,[9] Organic Mania[10] and Eco Efficiency,[11] to name but a few.

Laundry

Eco eggs or soap nuts are an option for washing clothes. These are both cheaper than powder or liquid detergents and do not cause eczema. Eco eggs are plastic egg shapes that you put black ceramic balls and white mineral pellets into. You top up the white mineral pellets every 720 washes. Eco eggs are stored in a very small area and are very easy to use (just don't let staff put them into the dryer as the white mineral pellets get used up much quicker if they do). They avoid all the heavy boxes and plastic bottles, which then need to go into the waste, they work out much cheaper per load than powder or liquid detergent, and they are certified as not causing eczema.

However, there is evidence that eco eggs and soap nuts are not as good at getting rid of bacteria as commercial detergents, so if laundry has a lot of food or excrement on it you need to clean the washing machine itself periodically. And you might want to use their stain removal for hard-to-shift stains too.

Commercial softeners or fabric conditioners coat fabrics, so cannot be used for laundering nappies as it stops them from absorbing properly, which will cause leaks. Also, be very careful to rinse out nappies and children's clothes, as detergent remaining in them can cause unpleasant smells and irritate the skin. Wool dryer balls help to soften fabrics when used in a dryer if you are finding towels and garments are coming out a bit hard and prickly. One-use plastic sheets to pop into your tumbler drier are a sustainability disaster; like wet wipes, they are likely to end up in general waste/landfill or blocking drains.

Drying clothes in the sun is the most sustainable way to dry clothes. The sun will help to kill the dangerous bacteria and also bleach stains out naturally. Rain is good for clothes washed in detergents, too, helping to rinse out any remnants.

However, if time is important, you might consider the Scandinavian dryer cupboards. If you are using a tumble dryer, do not use it hot on bamboo nappies. A great discovery are the dryer balls – little prickly balls that reduce drying time by around 20 per cent. Dryer balls accelerate separation and allow warm air to flow between garments faster and easier; they are a 'no-brainer' for saving energy if using a tumble dryer.

A lot of our clothes are made of acrylic, nylon and polyester, including our nursery uniform fleeces and sports shirts. Every time we wash these synthetic fabrics, millions of microfibres are released into the water. Microfibres are too small to be filtered out by waste treatment plants, just like microbeads in makeup and microplastics such as glitter. One research paper[12] showed that microfibres are responsible for 85 per cent of shoreline pollution across the world.

The Guppyfriend wash bag[13] or a washing machine lint filter are two ways to reduce the microfibres from escaping down the drain apparently. Guppyfriend was developed in the campaign STOP! MICRO WASTE,[14] a German non-profit organisation funded by a group of surfers and nature lovers to find solutions to the micro-waste problem. Patagonia are now retailing the Guppyfriend bags, as are other online retailers, but they aren't cheap. They also only take 2.5 kg and you must only fill it half way. Then you load your non-polyester/nylon clothes around it and wash as usual – but not with powder, as that increases abrasion and damages the fibres. You then have to empty the microfibres into your waste bin (don't rinse down the sink), as it is better there than in the sea. This is yet another extra job for nursery staff to do, but clearing a washing machine filter like we already do for dryers is a small price to pay for reducing plastic pollution in the ocean. The additional benefit is that clothes will last longer without having the plastic fibres washed out of them. If your uniform includes fleeces, like ours does, the responsible thing to do would be to issue a Guppyfriend bag at the same time. Unfortunately, the expense is a huge barrier – as much as another fleece.

Baking soda

Baking soda is a product that most environmentally aware people go through in significant quantities as it can replace countless laboratory-made substances. We use it for cleaning nurseries, deodorising furniture, unclogging drains, cleaning pots and pans, freshening mattresses and carpets, cleaning the oven, fridge and freezer, counters, tiles and floors, grout, toilets, linens and getting the onion smell off your hands. We could also use it for washing hair, making deodorant and killing mould. Amazing stuff. It's even edible, used as a raising agent in baked goods. Treehugger has a long list of articles suggesting household uses for baking soda.[15]

While we sing the praises of baking soda, have we really considered how renewable it is? It comes in a recyclable cardboard box, so that's a good start. Baking soda (also called bicarbonate of soda or sodium bicarbonate) is made by mining soda ash from minerals called trona and nahcolite. The soda ash is dissolved into a solution through which carbon dioxide is bubbled, and sodium bicarbonate comes out, forming baking soda. So ... baking soda comes from a natural source, but a non-renewable one. There is apparently no risk of running out for thousands of years because there are huge quantities worldwide, but it is mined and therefore invasive and destructive. The mines use energy and emit toxic volatile organic compounds (VOCs) and methane. Plus, if the mines or processing plants are powered by non-sustainable means, such as fossil fuels, they contribute further to greenhouse gases (GHGs). In the US, mines endanger the sage grouse's habitat, and in Eastern Africa, the soda ash processing plants have disturbed flamingo populations. It is not a perfect option, but better than using more toxic chemicals.

Toothpaste

There are two elements of toothpaste that we need to consider with regard to sustainability: the toothpaste itself, and the container that it comes in.

The risks from swallowing fluoride include permanent tooth discolouration, stomach ailments, acute toxicity (allergic reaction), skin rashes, impairment in glucose metabolism, brittle bones and behavioural change! The difference between adult and children's toothpaste is that there is slightly less fluoride in children's toothpaste and they are also more of a gel than a paste to be less abrasive on the sensitive enamel of babies' teeth … and of course, they tend to come in a range of flavours. Studies show that we ingest about 33 per cent of the toothpaste that we put on the brush. While most of us have been taught that fluoride protects teeth, research is beginning to surface that contradicts this. The vast majority of Western Europe (98 per cent!) has rejected fluoridation in the water supply. What else is lurking in children's toothpaste?

There is a major problem with tooth decay in children in the UK. Children consume a lot of sugary foods and drinks (although not at the nursery, of course), so we have a battle on our hands. Without question, we must teach children to brush their teeth well, and we do this daily in our nurseries. Our local dentists recommend that we use a children's fluoride toothpaste, but only a very small amount: a smear on the brush. Just enough to flavour the brush really! As children's toothpaste is quite low in fluoride, and as they use such little amounts and we haven't found an alternative when we experimented offering staff children free samples, we haven't changed our supplier – yet!

The other issue is the plastic packaging that toothpaste generally comes in. Our children's toothpaste comes in plastic tubes, with caps of a different plastic which are difficult to recycle. It is unusual for councils to collect them as part of their recycling collection schemes, or for commercial waste companies to do so either. We always separate the cap when we throw it in the general waste bin. A good option is to work with TerraCycle,[16] who are working towards zero waste. You can send them any brand of toothpaste tubes, caps, toothbrushes and toothpaste tube outer packaging. They will mechanically and hand separate them into fibres, like wood, coated paper, plastics and other materials, and then hydro-pulp them to separate coatings such as wax and plastic. Then they recycle them into new paper products or compost them. Mission accomplished, perhaps. However, this is dealing with the waste rather than preventing it; a good step, and not a free step, as you have to pay for the box.

Another option is to make a homemade toothpaste using baking soda and put it in a glass jar, but I doubt the dentists will approve?

Toothbrushes

Dentists recommend that we replace toothbrushes every three to four months, depending on how often they are used and wear and tear, so we were getting through thousands of little plastic toothbrushes every year and then throwing them into the general waste. While doing beach cleans with the children we have periodically found toothbrushes there, too, so trying to change our toothbrushes is one of the earlier changes we considered.

We sourced bamboo toothbrushes, which are fully compostable and are the gold standard of zero-waste toothbrushing. There are many brands available, so choosing between them comes down to which ones are offered in minimal, recyclable, and compostable packaging, and which are made closest to where you live. They are more expensive than plastic toothbrushes, and be aware that some bamboo toothbrushes have bristles made of boar hair, which is not acceptable to either vegans or Muslims. Some have 10 per cent nylon bristles, or all nylon bristles, which aren't compostable. Our current choice have 10 per cent nylon bristles, which we have been told are compostable – we are still waiting to see if they will compost in our home-style composters, though.

We found the most economic way to buy toothbrushes was to order them in bulk from China through a local eco-supplier who checks on their production systems, so unfortunately fossil fuels must have been used to deliver them across the world. But bamboo doesn't grow locally, so there is not a more ecological

Figure 11.1 Brushing teeth with a bamboo toothbrush at Tops Day Nurseries

Figure 11.2 Learning about toothbrushing at Tops Day Nurseries

option known to us currently. This is another example of making a better decision but not a perfect decision, and there may be better decisions to make in the future.

Hand wash

We trialled using blocks of soap rather than bottles of liquid hand wash and had complaints from parents, who thought that the blocks were not as hygienic, especially if dropped on the floor or covered in paint from the last child. Research shows that washing hands with a block of soap is just as efficient as liquid soap from a pump (the pump having been used by dirty hands) but they looked fairly dirty so we had to continuously clean them. We had complaints from staff who found them on the floor and thought they were a slip hazard, and the children seemed to enjoy dropping them down the toilet. The answer to this is to put the blocks of soap into little nets and attach those to the taps, or have 'soap on a rope' and tie them onto the taps.

We looked at what the standard blocks were made of and found them to be full of fairly nasty chemicals, but when we looked at our liquid soaps we found they were just as bad. Triclosan and Triclocarban are two ingredients commonly found in some commercial antibacterial bar and liquid soaps, but both are harmful and have been banned by the Food and Drug Administration in the US as a result. Some products in the UK still have these ingredients as they have not (yet) been banned by the EU, and they can also be masked under another chemical name or replaced with worse chemicals. The antibacterial soap was worst of all; in fact, it was so much worse that we decided to stop ordering antibacterial soap for adults also. Initially, the nursery managers were horrified at the suggestion, until we produced the research that substantiated this change. The antibacterial chemicals stop good bacteria as well as bad, and could have nasty side effects on the immune system and digestion if they gets into stomachs. Anything on our hands is likely to get into people's stomachs, that's why we wash our hands, and children put their hands in their mouths often. As the main time for washing hands is immediately prior to eating, there is a very high likelihood of ingesting chemicals in a hand wash, so far better to use natural products in hand wash, basically edible products. It seems that by temporarily killing nearly all the bacteria on our hands, we could be paving the way to allow bad bacteria to take hold.

We have looked into making our own soaps at nursery, and given it a try as a play activity rather than as the main source of producing soap. There are many recipes and videos freely available on the internet.

You may be lucky enough to have a local artisan who can help you, like we do, with 'Love to b Skincare'. They have made us some lovely, super mild children's soaps with a 'tutti frutti' smell and look, on a rope so we can tie them to taps or hooks, safe enough to eat, but effective enough to wash little hands and not kill the good bacteria. It's actually made with olive oil, coconut oil, shea butter, pink clay, plus turmeric, indigo, spirulina and wheatgrass. It smells and feels lovely, making handwashing a safe and a sensory experience too, which encourages children to wash their hands thoroughly. (A handwashing song helps along as well!) The soaps also came beautifully packaged in cardboard and paper, no single-use plastic anywhere.

> Should you need the evidence for your colleagues or parents, look at www.tealwash. com/11958-antibac-gel-vs-soap-and-water-which-was-the-winner/ from Drs Chris and Xand Van Tulleken's BBC TV programme. Or www.care2.com/greenliving/ which-is-better-liquid-soap-or-bar-soap.html; www.telegraph.co.uk/news/2017/06/25/ antibacterial-soaps-may-do-harm-good-scientists-warn/; www.theguardian.com/lifeand style/2016/sep/12/should-i-stop-using-antibacterial-handwash-and-gels.

There is certainly an art in making great soap, but it is also fun making soap by melting down glycerine bars, adding a little coconut oil, perhaps mixing them with a drop of colour or essential oil, and then putting them into a playful mould, perhaps with a tiny shell or plastic dinosaur inside. Cold-pressed soaps and those containing lye do look rather more complicated, though. Glycerine (glycerol) soap is gentle and doesn't contain alcohol or other chemical-based ingredients that could irritate skin; it's vegan-friendly too. Glycerine is usually made from soy or palm, but could be made from animal fat, so you need to check the source if you are vegan and if you want to make the most sustainable choice. Both soy and palm are implicated in deforestation (palm in Indonesia and soy in South America). Both are also used for feeding livestock, so we need to check that these ingredients are from sustainable plantations, if possible.

Paper towels, tissue paper and toilet paper

I think it's important to consider what packaging they are delivered in as well as what they are made of. Paper that arrives covered in plastic is a waste of plastic, with very little advantage unless storage or delivery is likely to be in the rain. Many companies are now delivering paper products without covering them in plastic, so it's worth raising the issue with your suppliers. But you might still be obliged to continue with your plastic-wrapped paper because it is usually so much cheaper than non-plastic-wrapped paper, stupid though that is. I buy a brand for home that comes in cardboard boxes and paper wrapper that I can't afford to buy for the day nurseries due to the quantity we get through and therefore cost. Plus, it's named 'who gives a crap', which is a word I don't feel comfortable using with small children about!

You need to be aware that anything made of recycled paper, which could include paper that has been printed on such as till receipts, will include some plastic, as that's apparently unavoidable. Beyond that, follow the same logic as for the wood it is largely made from, which is covered in Chapter 13.

Sunscreen

Although not a cleaning product, I add sunscreen here as it's another item that we need to consider in the sustainability frame that can be a protection to our children. Sunscreen, or sunblock, absorbs or reflects some of the sun's ultraviolet radiation and therefore gives us some protection against sunburn. It has become the norm in the UK to apply sunblock during the summer months before children arrive at nursery, and depending on the intensity of the sun, to reapply during the day. Unfortunately, there has also been an increased number of cases of rickets in the south of England, which is caused by a lack of vitamin D. Lack of vitamin D has also been implicated as another possible reason for the increase in children with allergies. Vitamin D can be found in some foods but is also produced naturally by the sun and our skin. Some sunshine is clearly good for us, as well as being very bad if it burns us.

I would like to alert you to the concerns that have led to Hawaii banning sunscreen from its beaches due to environmental damage, mainly caused by the ingredients oxybenzone and octinoxate. All our oceans join each other, so I think there is an argument for banning these worldwide. One also has to consider whether it is better for our children to have this potentially toxic cream on their skin, or to limit times in the sun, play in the shade, and wear protective clothing and hats. There is another option: there are some natural sunblocks being produced and marketed in tins rather than plastic, such as the Eco Vibe products. Their all-natural sunscreen is made of shea butter, coconut oil, zinc oxide and beeswax. No good for most vegans, but it is an alternative worth considering, and has an SPF25 rating. Zinc will be available with continued sustainable practices for centuries to come, according to the Zinc Association.

For several years, we were advised by our health and safety reps to wear single-use plastic gloves for putting cream onto the children. Unless the child or the adult doing the creaming have skin lesions or infections that mean their skin shouldn't be in contact, gloves are not required for applying sun block.

Insect protection

Rather than smothering children in toxic DEET, there are other options in countries that don't suffer from malaria, West Nile virus, Lyme disease, or similar life-threatening diseases. If you decide to use DEET, though, it's less damaging to your nervous system if applied onto clothing rather than directly onto skin. The American Academy of Paediatrics recommends using repellents with no more than a 30 per cent concentration of DEET for children over 2 months, and not at all for children under 2 months. A 2002 study of mosquito repellents found that the soy-based Bit Blocker for Kids was the most effective natural alternative to DEET, offering more than 90 minutes of protection, which is better than some low-concentration DEET products. Oil of lemon eucalyptus (PMD) is a natural oil recommended by some, repelling mosquitos and maybe ticks. Oil of lemon eucalyptus may be poisonous if ingested, and according to the CDC should not be used on children under 3 years old. Citronella, peppermint oil and other plant-based oils have unfortunately been found not be particularly effective, and Avon's Skin-So-Soft Bath Oil only kept mosquitos away for half an hour or less.

The best approach is to avoid chemicals altogether and instead dress children in lightweight clothing that covers their skin, such as long trousers perhaps with elastic around the ankles and long sleeves. The use of mosquito netting over areas being used for outdoor sleeping is also highly effective. We should also avoid having any stagnant pools, buckets or containers of water or rubbish bins near where children play, or leaving food uncovered in gardens where flowers are in bloom. Bright colours, flowery prints, some scented soaps and perfumes seem to attract insects, but fans and sea breezes give mosquitoes trouble manoeuvring, so positioning yourself and the children in a draft is a good idea. Do not bother with bug zappers as they usually kill beneficial insects that eat pests or feed birds. One study showed that a mere 0.13 per cent of bugs zapped were biting mosquitoes. Ultrasonic devices also don't work effectively.

If you feel you need to use a repellent, don't use a sunscreen combined with a repellent. It is better to apply sunscreen first, then a separate repellent. It's better not to allow the children to handle repellents because of the risk that they might put their hands in their mouths. Avoid all types of aerosol sprays because they increase the amount of repellent inhaled, and that's incredibly bad for health. There is also a risk that insect repellents will be bad for bees, and bees are crucial to plant sustainability, so this is another factor to bear in mind.

Conclusion

We have looked at a number of types of protection that we use to keep environments and the children clean, smelling sweet, and healthy. Science and innovation is moving on in this area, as manufacturers become more aware of the risks and benefits to human health, so we can expect to learn more and to adapt and improve our policies and procedures as they publish their reports and offer new products.

Notes

1. University of California, Center for Environmental Research and Children's Health, and Informed Green Solutions. (2013). *Green Cleaning, Sanitizing and Disinfecting: A Toolkit for Early Care and Education* [online]. Available from: www.epa.gov.
2. Cohen, A., Janssen, S. and Solomon, G. (2007). *Clearing the Air: Hidden Hazards of Air Fresheners*. Natural Defense Council.
3. See www.foodbeast.com/news/food-allergies/.
4. Urban, S. (2012). *6 Natural Alternatives to Chemical Air Fresheners* [online]. Organic Authority. Available from: www.organicauthority.com.
5. www.healthline.com.
6. www.dyson.co.uk.
7. Part of the *Independent* newspaper, available at www.independent.co.uk/extras/indybest.
8. Available at www.which.co.uk/.
9. www.mommyisgreen.net.
10. organicmania.com.
11. www.eco-officiency.com.

12. See www.theguardian.com/environment/2016/jun/20/microfibers-plastic-pollution-oceans-patagonia-synthetic-clothes-microbeads.
13. Available from http://guppyfriend.com/en/.
14. Read more at www.stopmicrowaste.com/.
15. For example, Badore, M. (2014). *13 baking soda uses to clean almost everything* [online]. Treehugger. Available from: www.treehugger.com.
16. See www.terracycle.co.uk for more information.

12 Sustainable food

Providing sustainable food in our day nurseries is an important part of our service. We have to consider the health of the child eating it, but also the health of the planet. We can contribute to society, the economy and the environment by making sustainable decisions.

Ideally, food should be grown in the local community, with some grown in the nursery. Growing the food should not use any toxic or non-sustainable chemicals, and not too much water or energy. Plant-based food is far more sustainable than animal-based because we also have to grow plants to feed the animals.

However, in practice, we're rarely going to reach such high ideals. If we break the food service down into parts, we can consider each area to see if there is a way of making more sustainable choices.

The different areas to consider are planning, buying, storage, cooking, and waste. Waste is covered in more detail in Chapter 15.

Planning

Mealtimes are an educational and social experience, and the more we can involve the children in choices and preparation of food, the more opportunities we are providing for them. This isn't always possible in daily routine, which is why our nurseries also run cooking schools, where child-friendly recipes are followed that the children can complete and take home afterwards. Touching, smelling and tasting the food is an opportunity to develop senses, maths and science, form opinions, make decisions, as well as to talk and socialise.

Advice to support planning of menus in the UK is available from the Soil Association[1] and from the Food for Life programme,[2] but they are heavily meat- and dairy-based. The more sustainable, and also healthier, option is vegetable- and fruit-based, which is why, although we do use their advice ... we don't use all of it! The numbers of vegan and vegetarian families are increasing every-where, and that includes in all our nurseries. We also have increasing numbers of families wanting to just eat less meat and are happy that we reduce meat content in meals and have meat at fewer meals. I think the UK has much to learn from food pyramids being created in other countries, and also the whole-food vegan food pyramid (Figure 12.1).

So having made sustainable choices for your children, publicise where your food is bought from and why, so you can explain to stakeholders (parents, colleagues, local communities) why this was the most sustainable choice you could make for your setting. But be prepared to keep checking as you learn more about sustainability and the farmers adapt as well.

Organise trips to local food producers and shops so the children can see where their food comes from. You might be able to encourage parents to come along too,

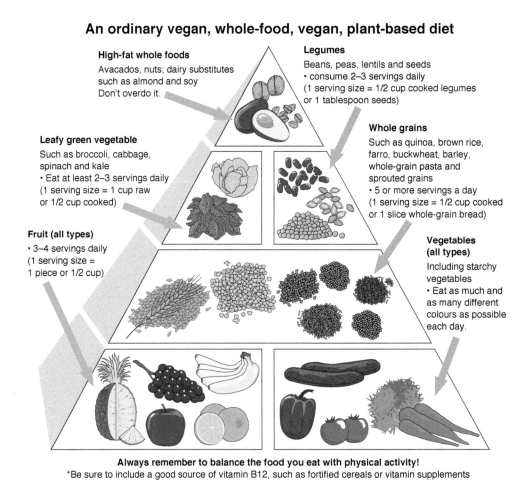

An ordinary vegan, whole-food, vegan, plant-based diet

High-fat whole foods
Avacados, nuts; dairy substitutes such as almond and soy
Don't overdo it.

Legumes
Beans, peas, lentils and seeds
• consume 2–3 servings daily
(1 serving size = 1/2 cup cooked legumes or 1 tablespoon seeds)

Leafy green vegetable
Such as broccoli, cabbage, spinach and kale
• Eat at least 2–3 servings daily
(1 serving size = 1 cup raw or 1/2 cup cooked)

Whole grains
Such as quinoa, brown rice, farro, buckwheat, barley, whole-grain pasta and sprouted grains
• 5 or more servings a day
(1 serving size = 1/2 cup cooked or 1 slice whole-grain bread)

Fruit (all types)
• 3–4 servings daily
(1 serving size = 1 piece or 1/2 cup)

Vegetables (all types)
Including starchy vegetables
• Eat as much and as many different colours as possible each day.

Always remember to balance the food you eat with physical activity!
*Be sure to include a good source of vitamin B12, such as fortified cereals or vitamin supplements

Figure 12.1 The Vegan Food Triangle

Buying sustainable food

Sustainable versus organic

Everyone needs to be aware that *sustainable* and *organic* do not mean the same thing at all. I came across a useful article on *The Balance: Small Businesses*[3] that describes the difference between the two terms well:

> Sustainable is not a certified label, most people consider sustainability a philosophy that describes planet protective actions that can be continued indefinitely, without causing damage to the environment. However, sustainability is observable and measurable via economic profit, social benefits for the community and environmental conservation.

Sustainable is small

Less is almost always more sustainable than more.

> A sustainable farmer may own less land and grow diverse crops to help enhance the soil and conserve land resources. A sustainable farmer might also experiment with vertical planting or allow animals to graze on cropland to save space.

I think that asking the size of the farm you buy from is not particularly practical, but bear in mind that an organic farmer may use more land than necessary and waste resources because being sustainable isn't part of the remit for being organic.

Sustainable is water-efficient

Organic policy doesn't require that farmers or processors conserve water resources. Sustainable farming and processing methods do try to conserve water.

Sustainable farming methods may include using reclaimed water for some crops, planting drought-tolerant crop species or using reduced-volume irrigation systems. Organic policy just says that reclaimed water can be used to water crops. Again, you might not have the time or inclination to ask such questions – but maybe your food supplier does, so we ask ours to source sustainable farmers if possible.

Sustainable is energy-efficient

Farms need energy, for transporting and for their machinery. Electric vehicles are approximately four times more efficient than diesel or petrol, and if that electricity is generated using renewable energy sources such as wind, solar or water-based power, you have more sustainable food.

Sustainable is low-emission

Ideally we want our food produced and made using as little fossil fuel as possible. The best way to do this is to source locally grown food, grown by farmers who use renewable energy, and then transport it to you using a bicycle, or an electric or hydrogen vehicle!

Sustainable is more humane

Organic certification policy includes few rules about animals' freedom to roam and to root, peck and graze naturally. Organic livestock can spend a lot of time locked inside with little thought given to their overall well-being.

A more sustainable farm provides lots of natural outdoor space as well as comfortable indoor space in times of inclement weather.

Treating animals well is not part of organic certification, but it is relevant to farmers wishing to provide a sustainable environment – although the most sustainable farming does not include the use of animals at all.

Sustainable is eco-friendly packaging

Organic food is not concerned with the packaging, so you might have a farmer grow organic cherries, then put them in plastic tubs, cover them with plastic shrink wrap, then wrap everything in a bigger plastic box. That's a lot of single-use plastic, which we want to avoid.

We can also buy products like milk and oil in glass, which is more sustainable than single-use plastic.

Sustainable packaging uses the least amount of resources necessary. Ideally, sustainable packaging should be minimal, 100 per cent recyclable and printed with vegetable inks as well. You are likely doing your own labels for foods to keep once opened, so do look for paper labels, although we are finding this hard as they sometimes go black and unreadable!

Sustainable is ethical

Organic certification doesn't mean that a farmer or company acts ethically. For example, farming decisions based on sustainability should extend to other issues, such as a paperless office, incentives for avoiding diesel and petrol vehicles, protecting the local community, and fair working conditions for workers.

or they might be producers themselves, of course. There was a joke on national TV many years ago on 1 April (April Fools' Day) where the press showed spaghetti trees, with spaghetti hanging from the branches. Our children do not know where their food comes from unless we show them first-hand, or with photographs, books and computer programs. Undoubtedly, the best learning experience is to see it, touch it and smell it where it is growing, and then to be involved in cooking it, and of course eating it.

Local producers or greengrocers/retailers are usually delighted to prepare and supply a regular box of food for the nursery and maybe even for parents – ideally organic, and definitely seasonal local fruits and vegetables. There is a feel-good factor about supporting a local shop.

There is also the possibility of using national food distributors, but many nurseries are barely big enough to benefit from these schemes, so the spend ends up increasing, not decreasing. We looked for national distributors that used local farmers and had mixed success with these; one awful one kept distributing food that wasn't fresh enough to serve, or served alternatives that weren't suitable; but another one understood that while we want to support local farmers, sometimes the benefits of consolidated invoicing, and being able to control purchasing quantities compared with numbers of children/budgets could be easier through a national distributor who would also source locally from the farms.

Some of the national distributors not only embrace their own corporate, social and environmental responsibilities; they can actually help ours. For example, CREED has a very strong sustainability vision: 'To drive down our carbon footprint (CO_2 emissions – tonnes) by 7.5% each year for the next 3 years ahead of the UK Government's 2050 commitment.' And to do that they are focusing on responsible water management, using a fleet of vehicles with very low carbon emissions, recycling cardboard and plastic, and also committed to sourcing products that are 'sourced and manufactured in an ethical and environmentally responsible way'. All their suppliers have to be accredited and meet a strict set of standards. They are also a zero to landfill business on both their sites.

The problem with supermarkets is that they can put local growers and retailers out of business. Although they offer jobs in the supermarket, they take more jobs out of the local economy than they provide; little shops shut and high streets die. The profit that would have been recycled locally is then taken away to national profit centres. They are notorious for underpaying the growers. On the other hand, they provide relatively cheap, reliable food and deliver in containers they take away again. There is another problem in the UK, in that supermarkets aren't really meant to supply food to food businesses. While day nurseries are not food businesses, they are selling food for children to the parents, so it's a bit of a grey area.

Some local supermarkets, though, run a fantastic past 'best by' service, where the nursery manager can collect food once or twice a week to either use in the nursery or distribute to families who are going hungry. This doesn't help with planning nursery meals, but it certainly supports those finding it hard to make ends meet, and for that we are very appreciative.

There are logos to look out for to identify good organic food, such as USDA Organic and Soil Association Organic Standard. There are no such labels to identify sustainable food, because sustainability is a process rather than a yes or no status. We are all at different stages along the journey, making it much more difficult to implement a 'sustainable' logo system.

Other accreditation or assurances to look for include RSPCA Assured, Assured Food Standards and Lion Quality. The RSPCA monitors on-farm health and welfare, including stunning and slaughter processes, and is the best standard to look for.

The Red Tractor Food Assured Standard has some of the most comprehensive farm and food standards in the world, covering more types of food and drink than any other.

Hens eggs must, by law, carry a stamp with a number indicating whether they have been produced in an organic, free-range, barn or cage system, but the Lion mark just means the eggs or meat meet food safety criteria and that eggs were laid in Britain.

True sustainability extends beyond basic farming goals into management and individual goals and lifestyle choices. Organic policy doesn't cover much in terms of full company or full farm sustainability, but a truly sustainable business attempts to be eco-friendly in many ways, not simply with how food is grown.

This same website is also very useful in helping consumers avoid being scammed by companies selling what they call organic food when it isn't, in order to bulk up prices: what a minefield!

Buying fish

If buying fish, look for the MSC logo. If we carry on fishing the way we are, even with lines rather than nets, we will simply have no fish left and millions will starve. Those who are in a position to make further choices should either not eat fish, reduce the amount of fish they eat, or choose certified sustainable fish. Do be aware that almost 100 per cent of shell fish contains plastic, and farmed salmon is arguably the most toxic protein on the planet. I don't eat fish at all anymore myself, but we do have it once a week in the nurseries currently – until I can per-suade colleagues and parents not to! The Marine Conservation Society also has a lot of information on what fish is sustainable and what isn't.

Palm oil

If you are buying whole foods, you won't have a problem with palm oil, but be aware that around 50 per cent of products in the supermarket have palm oil in them, which is neither healthy nor sustainable. Often, the palm oil is hidden in products you may not expect, such as non-dairy spread, vegan cheese, bread, pizza, crisps and ice cream. It is possible to buy sustainable palm oil that hasn't involved destroying the habitats of orang-utans or the rain forests. The other problem with refusing all palm oil is that the alternatives are potentially even less sustainable, so it's not quite as straightforward to make this choice.

Buying milk, and sustainability of its delivery

The UK government pays day nurseries and schools providing care and education for under-5s to supply one free 189 ml serving of milk per day. The cost is as invoiced, so there is no penalty or advantage for using the more expensive milk delivered from a dairy rather than buying and collecting it from a supermarket; most day nurseries and schools in the UK have their milk delivered for convenience. They can choose whether it comes in glass, plastic or cartons as well as the size of the cartons.

Tops Day Nurseries accommodates approximately 3000 children per day and purchases around 250,000 2-litre glass bottles of milk per year. I would stop it now if I could without losing customers! Many children are suffering from obesity and replacing cows' milk with oat milk and more vegetables is an obvious way to reduce the mistreatment of so many cows while giving our children a healthier diet. Cows' milk is meant for growing large, grass-eating cows with extra stomachs, not humans. Unless fully organic, it'll also likely contain many hormones and chemicals that the cow has been given and has come through its milk.

There are approximately 700,000 births per year, and children are at nursery for four years. If every child is given 0.19 litres of milk a day, that equates to about 1 billion litres of milk per year … at preschool alone. They get another 24 million litres of cows' milk in reception (remember, reception is term-time only!).

Cows produce about 50 litres of milk per day, double what they produced 40 years ago (due to selective breeding and management) and 6–10 times what a cow would naturally produce to feed her calf. They are artificially impregnated every year to keep the milk flowing, and the calf has to be removed shortly after birth and fed artificial milk so humans can have the cow's milk. We won't discuss what happens to the poor male calves here. It's brutal, but it's a way of life for dairy farmers. Dairy cows also produce large quantities of methane

(92–98 per cent orally, not out of their rear end), which is twice as much as beef cows. Methane is a powerful greenhouse gas, which is currently doing more damage to our climate than all our diesel and petrol cars put together. You could run a small fridge off every dairy cow! Some schools elect to have 1/3 pint cartons, supplied with plastic straws. More responsible teachers open the cartons and wash them out ready for recycling as part of their education in caring for the environment. A more responsible choice still would be to stop the plastic straws!

Consider for a moment the amount of plastic this creates, even without straws. If one 2 litre plastic bottle weighs approximately 42g (I checked), and preschool and reception get through 62,000,000 of them, that's 2604 tonnes. At a waste disposal cost of £345 per tonne, that is £898,380 in milk bottle packaging alone, per year.

Plastic milk bottles are generally made from high-density polyethylene (HDPE) plastic. Very little recycled HDPE plastic is included in new milk bottles (about 10 per cent, although the target by 2015 was 30 per cent) because the recycled material currently has a green hue to it, which consumers don't like. Along with the plastic are the labels, adhesive, ink, seals, closure liners, lids, barrier coatings and layers. In the UK, only about 30 per cent of milk bottles are recycled; the rest go in general waste and landfill, and even the 'recycled' ones have actually been exported to China until very recently; now some go to Malaysia and are dumped. Some are discarded by people, ending up on roads, pavements and washing into rivers and the sea (covered in Chapter 4).

A more sustainable solution is to have our milk delivered in glass bottles with foil lids. Glass is made using a combination of sand, soda ash, and limestone. These materials are not renewable, but they are plentiful, and once they are used to make a glass bottle, the bottle can be re-used several times. If it does not re-enter the recycling system, it can be melted down and remanufactured into any number of glass products without a decrease in quality. When a bottle is returned, far less energy is required to sterilise and refill a glass bottle than that needed to make new dairy packaging.

However, glass is heavier and therefore more expensive to transport – particularly if diesel vehicles are used rather than electric vehicles. If renewable energy electric vehicles are used, which are much more sustainable to run, the additional weight becomes insignificant.

Paper milk cartons can also be used. These are very light, but they need to be made using virgin materials. They often have plastic linings, and large amounts of water, fuel and chemical bleaches are involved in the manufacturing process. Often, the cartons are thrown into general waste landfills after use, particularly if they contain a combination of paper and plastic.

By returning glass bottles, we are *reducing* the amount of new bottles that need to be made, allowing them to be *re-used* many times. Then once they are *recycled*, they can be remanufactured without any decrease in quality. I think the choice is clear: glass milk bottles are the best choice for the environment provided they can be transported efficiently to where they are to be used (i.e. no fossil fuels).

Many dairies have been using plastic for some time, so a move to glass is not something that can be done overnight, particularly if not everyone wants to do it immediately. However, some dairies are still supplying milk in glass bottles and consumer demand has already increased. The bottles are returned to the dairies and cleaned and re-used. The bottles of milk are currently more expensive than milk supplied in plastic – but it wouldn't be, if the government were to intervene and charge companies using virgin plastic an environmental damage tax. I also think there is a strong argument to start phasing out the subsidy of milk for under-5s and put the funding saved into their education or into plant-based food.

So here are a few tips for sustainably minded childcare professionals regarding buying:

- Buy less stuff, create less waste.

- Buy less fish and meat, and dairy products. Buy more local fruit and vegetables and look for organic, sustainable and local labelling.

- Complain about excessive delivery packaging; take photographs, as they often deny it. Try giving it back – particularly if it's plastic or polystyrene!

- Watch out for hidden high deforestation risk products like soy and palm oil.

Storage

Storage is generally an issue because if food is not stored appropriately it may be wasted, and the wastage and massive over-ordering is a problem.

However, most nurseries order weekly and expect to use most of the food ordered within the week. Some nurseries are still ordering food such as pasta, rice, baked beans and jelly as sensory play items, but there many alternatives (see Chapter 13). If nurseries do not use their food within the 'best by' date, they can of course use it for play rather than throwing it away, as long as it isn't 'off' (just smell it).

Another place to use food that is on the way out is to allow the children to play with it in home corners or play kitchens. As children are actually practising food preparation and possibly tasting and serving it, this can be a wonderful opportunity to extend their play and to discuss where the food comes from, the food itself and waste.

Cooking and serving food

Linking food to gardening activities or visits is ideal, but otherwise we can talk with the children about where their food has come from and show them photographs and videos.

Some of our most active Facebook communications are when we share our recipes, so we make sure we share the sustainable ones!

Most nurseries share the daily menus with parents, particularly those like ours, where parents have a choice of whether to provide a pack lunch or pay for a cooked meal. Daily menus are a great opportunity to show off sustainability. Including words like *free range*, *organic*, *homemade*, *seasonal fruit and vegetables* or *locally farmed* show that you care about where the food is from and what is in it. We do sometimes struggle with this aspect: we produce our menus centrally, but they sometimes need to be adapted due to the nursery's location and the needs of the children. They're usually then displayed on blackboards in the nursery entrance. In some nurseries, parents have the opportunity to bring a tub in and take a meal home, too, but it very much depends on the chefs' capacity at each site.

Our nurseries have looked at the Food for Life programme[4] to help us provide good, healthy, tasty and sustainable meals for our children. The programme also seeks to reconnect people with where their food comes from, teaching how it's grown and cooked, and championing the importance of well-sourced ingredients. Food for Life early years settings can access digital resources from Jamie Oliver's Kitchen Garden Project, which includes recipes. Unfortunately, the awards packages start at £360 including VAT (which UK nurseries do not get back but schools do).

Food for Life co-founder Jeanette Orrey says on their website that they have 'a clear vision that every child has a right to good, wholesome school food and that food poverty will one day be a thing of the past'. They have an Early Years Award endorsement for nurseries and children's centres that serve good-quality, nutritious food and support the babies and children in their care to develop good eating habits for life.

Another advantage of using a national firm to provide your food is that they may have software to help plan and balance menus, plus support from nutritionists and chefs for your cooks, included as part of the service.

We have the opportunity at nursery to avoid over-feeding children, and also to enable them to make healthy choices about what food they choose and how much they have on their plates. To help colleagues and cooks put the appropriate amount of food on children's plates, you can use 'spoodles', but in general start with a small amount and allow seconds rather than overload a child's plate.

Waste

According to WRAP (2010):

> It is estimated that 20% of the UK's greenhouse gas emissions are associated with food production, distribution and storage. If we stopped wasting food that could have been eaten we could prevent at least 200 million tonnes of carbon dioxide equivalent emissions each year.[5]

In other words, our wastage of food is contributing to global warming and we need to stop ordering food that we don't eat. In fact, the UK orders 150 per cent of the food we need now: little wonder there is an obesity problem and a waste problem.

We have a cultural issue here, too; we like to show love by the giving of food. We celebrate birthdays and successes with food and drink, and we also commiserate with each other with food and drink. Who doesn't have a parent, relative or friend that is a 'feeder', who enjoys nothing more than seeing loved ones clear their plates of goodies?

I think baby rooms might also be excused some food for play purposes. Babies need the extra opportunities to practise their hand/eye coordination and develop their senses while they try and get the food from plate or tray into their mouths: I wouldn't call this waste at all!

Please see Chapter 15 for more detail on what to do about food waste.

Conclusion

We have looked at the stages of providing meals to children in day nurseries, from suppliers and purchasing through to an alternative food pyramid, and how to make sustainable choices throughout, including recognition of accreditations and certifications to help assure you of your choices.

Notes

1. Soil Association. (2011). Current National Guidance [online]. *Good Food for Under 5s.* Available from: www.soilassociation.org/certification/catering/sectors/early-years/good-food-for-under-5s.
2. Food for Life programme, in partnership with the Soil Association. Information can be found on their website: www.foodforlife.org.uk/.
3. Chait, J. (2018). The Difference Between Organic and Sustainable Food [online]. *The Balance: Small Businesses.* Available from: www.thebalancesmb.com/difference-organic-sustainable-food-2538316.
4. See www.foodforlife.org.uk/.
5. WRAP. (2010). *Estimates of Food and Packaging Waste in the UK Grocery, Retail and Hospitality Supply Chains* [online]. Available from: www.wrap.org.uk.

13 Sustainable resourcing

Those working with young children are perfectly placed to be recyclers for local companies, as our children can be so creative and learn so much with almost anything that engages their senses. This chapter looks at how sustainable various resources are, including free, cheap and second-hand resources; wooden, resources; and resources to invest in. The chapter also looks at some aspects of resourcing that will help you make better sustainability decisions, such as packaging, delivery, greenwash (including biodegradability and composting descriptors), vegan resourcing, core lists and carbon offsetting.

Free resources

We can scavenge free food and resources from the woods, the hedgerows, the beach, tips, dumps, or even shops waging a war on waste. In days gone by, perhaps there was some shame in this kind of resourcing, but not now; this is now best practice, providing open-ended resources for children to really learn with.

Fruit-picking in areas of heavy traffic is not a good idea, not only due to the toxins pumped into the plants but because children will be suffering the air pollution while they pick.

Only scavenge food that you are 100 per cent sure is safe. I'm told the sense of smell is the safest way to identify safe food, as once you know the smell you will recognise it again.

Finding fascinating items for the children to explore is a hobby all on its own if you have the time. The list is too vast to contemplate trying to make into a complete one, but our job is to make sure that there are no hazards in the items we pick up. The very last thing we want to do is cause injury to a child through our negligence. Sometimes, items from building sites may carry a risk of toxic substances, such as asbestos or dangerous preservatives, so unless you know the provenance, you have to avoid these.

Ideally, we take the children with us. What a brilliant learning experience that can be – looking carefully, spotting some leaves, twigs, stones, shells, fallen petals or pine cones and bringing them back to work with or perhaps identify. This is sustainable resourcing, and the more we do of this, the better for the children, and also the less we have to spend on buying things. Although it can be time-intensive and we need to be alert to risks and hazards around us as well as from the items, the benefits are surely worth the effort.

Of course, your *children's parents and extended family* can be a tremendous resource for finding items. They are often delighted to be involved and we can recycle their unwanted bits and pieces: wool and material, pots and pans, buttons and tablecloths! Our nurseries tend to put up a list of what they need, and sometimes the neighbours give us more than we can handle, so a bit of diplomacy is required. Everyone wins – except perhaps the toy manufacturers and shops, although we do still need them for really good quality, craft goods – see below.

We use a lot of wooden pallets, which we often get for free because local hospitals have a lot of goods delivered on them and they are just left out by their skips. Occasionally, people have to pay for them depending on the local supply and demand. Pallets are made from leftover wood from trees often used for furniture and cabinets so can be very good quality. These days they also come from sustainable forests, which contributes to carbon-reducing due to forest regeneration. However, there a few old pallets around which are very dangerous, because methyl bromide was used to fumigate them back in 2005. Fortunately, every pallet has a label stamped on it somewhere. If your pallet does not have a label, don't use it. Pallets should be marked HT (heat treatment), and DB just means that the wood was debarked.

We use pallets to make play houses, low climbing frames, fencing, partitions, plant hanging frames and mud kitchens. The children use them to create whatever their imagination can come up with – boats, planes, fire engines, spacecraft, tanks, submarines, anything.

Some risks are acceptable, such as items which could cause splinters or items with sharp corners or edges that could be sanded down. I'm not suggesting you sand and smooth absolutely every item, though, even if that were possible, because who hasn't had a splinter and learned from it? There are some useful first aid tips for removing splinters painlessly – but beyond the scope of this book.

Adults can find bigger items such as tyres (which make great planters or tables, and can be climbed on with very little work), logs, tree stumps, planks, cable reels, and large containers – usually for free – to bring back to the nursery. Tyres do need a very good clean, and ideally a coating of something like Rust-Oleum Ultra Cover, which you can pick in different colours, and then add a clear coat of the same brand to prevent the microplastic and road oil lifting off onto little hands. You can fix them together to make tyre climbers, or add a plank for balancing, or again just use your imagination, plus there is a Pinterest site that you could check out for ideas.

This type of purchasing/acquiring needs to be done by key workers and their managers who know the individual interests of the children that they are aiming to fascinate. The nursery managers therefore need their own acquiring and buying power and they need to be able to pass it on to their passionate and responsible colleagues too. They might well do this when they are out shopping for themselves, although it would be wrong for owners to expect or assume that.

Other resources may be delivered free of charge to your door, such as crates or boxes that contained other products. Some resources will be your own cooking waste, such as melon and butternut squash pips, avocado stones, pineapple tops, even onion skin – which can be used to dye things – and many make great activities, which we cover later. Even loading the wormery with food scraps is a fascinating activity for some toddlers. You might be able to collect free stuff using a local free recycling website or Facebook page; even small electric irons, kettles and microwaves can be used – just cut the plugs off!

Cheap resources

From free we might move to cheap. I'm proud to shop in a thrift or charity shop, a tip, a car boot sale, a nearly new sale, or a shop that specifically sells scrap from businesses at rock-bottom prices. Some hardware and builders' merchants, kitchen suppliers, and discount stores sell normal domestic items such as cutlery, crockery, pots and pans, sieves, colanders, whisks, spoons, ladles – made of metals, glass, pottery and wood, in all different sizes – which are amazing resources at much better prices than from a toy or equipment catalogue.

Charity shops can be a goldmine for second-hand furniture. Some useful items to look out for include: dining tables that you could lower by sawing some chunks off the legs; rocking chairs that you can take to bits to use the curved pieces of wood; chests of drawers and dressers; and crates and suitcases you can upcycle to display in or on. We buy old trunks and electric cable reels for around £5 currently and they make tremendously versatile pieces of equipment. You might pick up scarves, quilts, sheets, tablecloths, hessian sacks, bags, baskets, tins, boxes, cases – anything to make dens and wigwams with, or display other items on or in or under. Or you might discover small items such as buttons, marbles and pebbles, cotton reels, cardboard, paper, coconut shells, sea shells, wooden bowls, bamboo, plants, slices of wood, wooden cup holders, wooden kitchen roll holders, and larger items such as crates, large tubes, cable reels, old radios, or even tree stumps. You might find dolls and dolls' clothes – handmade, crochet, knitted, multicultural, all different sizes, colours and shapes.

Do not buy very old mirrors because, apart from the glass potentially breaking into sharp shards, they used to be made with mercury in the back, which is highly toxic. There are also old pendulum clocks with mercury in the case or pendulum and old lamps with mercury in the base. Mercury normally falls as liquid silver/grey droplets. Vacuuming it up can heat it and turn it to vapour, which can harm the nervous, digestive and immune systems, lungs and kidneys. Babies in the womb are very vulnerable if mum breathes mercury vapour or eats mercury (shell fish and some fish). Its nickname is quicksilver – it's very difficult to pick up, so if you spot it, get the children and yourselves well away and call a professional to come and remove it safely. Old paint can have lead in it, so also avoid very old toys including little soldiers.

Also, very old Lego and other small plastic toys, very old building blocks, figures, dolls and puzzles have been found by Dr Andrew Turner of the University of Plymouth[1] to have toxic amounts of barium, lead, bromine, cadmium, chromium and selenium in them. There is no Toy Safety Directive regulation covering the recycling or resale of older toys, so be wary of antiques.

If you provide some of the items above for group or individual play, display them attractively to interest your children, and perhaps combine with more traditional toys such as cars, animals, insects, dolls and, of course, a relevant book. You will have set up your environment for hours of education and activity with sustainable resources, very cost-effectively.

Figure 13.1 A good shopping trip for resources from a local charity shop

Resources to invest in

Fortunately for our equipment suppliers, there are times when we need to consider investing in some really good-quality, perhaps solid wood resources. Having saved money with our sustainable items, we can refocus our funds on the long-lasting equipment.

When we reflect on this, there are several different aspects to consider:

- Do you really need it? Order just enough for your needs in order to avoid waste of the product, as well as money.

- Could we borrow or rent it instead?

- Who made it? (We have a moral and legal obligation in the UK to ensure we do not purchase from anyone using slave labour.)

- Is the packaging that the products are delivered or purchased in sustainable?

- Is the delivery method for the products sustainable? Do you really need it next day, every day, or would once a week be better for the environment?

- Where is it coming from – is it a long way?

- What is it made of?

- Will it withstand the use of lots of little hands for a long time?

- What will you do with any waste packaging?

- What will you do with any waste product?

- What happens at the end of its life?

Sometimes, it's tricky to find the answers to these questions, and you may have to make some decisions without being fully satisfied – just to be pragmatic about running your nursery. But I believe that having a checklist will help you make the best decisions that you can from a sustainability point of view.

Arguably *eco* and *green* are subsets of *sustainability*, as sustainability is a very inclusive term; it considers all aspects of philosophy, production and consumption. People using the terms *eco* and *green* may be focusing on specific attributes of their product – perhaps it is home-compostable, which means they can label it as eco or green and potentially attract a premium. Companies, rather than products, are certified as sustainable. This will underpin their entire philosophy and denote that they have embarked on the sustainability journey. They may self-certify or use external companies such as Green Globe,[2] who certify hotels and resorts and similar. Green Globe define sustainable companies as those that are

Figure 13.2 Investing in top-quality wooden resources, e.g. from Community Playthings

focused on saving the planet from waste, as well as potentially saving money. It is likely that Green Globe accredited hotels benefit from higher bookings from consumers interested in the most eco-friendly options.

You can buy certification for your company through completion of an online course. Not many products carry a sustainable logo or label, but there are a few that we can look out for: for wood, wood products, paper and cardboard, look for the Forest Stewardship Council (FSC) or Endorsement of Forest Certification (PEFC) logos and labels. These are globally trusted trademarks that help us identify resources and goods from forests that are managed sustainably.

When I was talking to a supplier recently, he pointed out that some woods are more sustainable than others, and advised me to study this further. For example:

- Bamboo is amazingly light and strong, it grows incredibly fast and can be harvested in three to five years, compared with 10–20 years for most softwoods and even longer for hardwoods. Check the International Network for Bamboo and Rattan website to check it's not been harvested unwisely, as giant pandas and West African mountain gorillas like bamboo! However, making fabric from bamboo is chemical-intensive, so it is less sustainable the more it is changed.

- Eucalyptus wood is an extremely sustainable material. Some plantations can produce up to 30 times more volume per year than other wood-bearing trees. The wood is versatile, hard and strong. It can be shaped well and absorbs stains evenly, so it's great for children's furniture and toys.

- Beech, oak, pine and fir are sustainable because they're replaceable, fast-growing species. Sycamore can be sustainable too.

Top-end, ethical suppliers like Community Playthings[3] specifically care about the environment and make sure that they use sustainable wood. They make sure more trees are planted than are cut down and they try to source wood local to where it is going to be supplied, so European birch to the European market. They use woods such as Radiata pine (abundant and fast-growing) made into Accoya® to make their Outlast products.

You should never buy new teak or mahogany because they are two of the world's most endangered wood species. A full list is available on the rainforestrelief[4] website but includes balsa (that very soft wood we used to use for children's woodwork), ebony (used to be used for piano keys), iroko and rosewood. Both Friends of the Earth[5] and the United National Environment[6] websites have up-to-date details on which woods are endangered or threatened.

MDF (medium density fibreboard) has some sustainable features about it, but is usually glued with formaldehyde, which is nasty, toxic and not sustainable, so you need to check what it's made with.

This supplier also pointed out that although wood is a lovely, sustainable material, it is expensive and not mouldable, so some resources just have to be made of plastic. He argued that plastic is also very durable and can come in a vast array of colours, so as long as something is to be kept for a long time, plastic can be an appropriate material for some products (TVs, computers, moulded plastic pegs for developing a pincer grip, for example).

Where are your products coming from?

A long sea voyage is not only a drain on fossil fuels (ships aren't running on solar power yet), but tankers make a horrific noise when driving through the oceans, which can damage the reproductive ability of cetaceans, along with destroying their underwater peace. I learned a lot from listening to Pavan Sukhaev[7] on a TED Global Talk from 2011. He talked about putting a value on nature, something humans have not done to date but which has caused the world serious harm through not paying attention to it. The economics of ecosystems and biodiversity is something the world does not currently value or take into account, although big thinkers like Pavan have been pointing this out for years. What are the true costs of our purchasing?

Air transport is even more of a drain on fossil fuels, even with ever lighter cargo planes. And transport by road also has a carbon cost. Both cause air pollution, so a preference has got to be to buy as local as possible.

Supplier sustainability improvements

One supplier I talked to invited me to visit his warehouse and distribution centre, proud to say that his state-of-the-art packaging machine had cut their CO_2 emissions by 46 per cent. Findel is advertising not only a 45 per cent reduction in cardboard, 200,000 fewer vehicle miles per year, and their latest investment in an energy management system (EMS) to deliver accurate heating control for different zones at different times in order to reduce energy use, energy bills and CO_2 emissions. These are significant improvements and worthy of our support and acknowledgement. Perhaps these are just some elements in assessment of a particular supplier and their products. I think with all these types of statements, one ought to ask for independent evidence, if possible, or companies might be tempted to go the greenwash route. But I think it is significant that companies in our supply chain appear to be making an effort and publicising this in order to attract our business because they know this may influence the buying decisions of other day nurseries also wishing to be more sustainable.

An alternative to plastics such as nylon or polyester in fabrics is viscose, but is it a sustainable fabric?

Viscose is made from renewable plants, frequently described as being environmentally friendly and sustainable. Viscose is the oldest manufactured fibre, first produced in 1883 as a cheap alternative to silk.

To create viscose, and make it stand up to regular wearing and washing, the wood pulp must be treated with chemicals such as caustic soda, ammonia, acetone, and sulphuric acid – all fairly nasty chemicals which are not sustainable. However, viscose is increasingly being manufactured using the Lyocell process, which uses N-Methlymorpholine N-oxide as the solvent. This method produces little waste product, making it far more eco-friendly.

When I was recently approached by a distributor in China who was offering baby wipes and clothes made with cotton and viscose (no plastic), I asked how the viscose is made, having a little knowledge of the above. We still make our own baby wipes with paper towels, or use re-useable ones and wash them.

Packaging

The Soil Association has recently announced some work on packaging in recognition of the plastic pollution problem. It's useful to know what they are working towards, as consumers like ourselves can contribute to this agenda:

- reducing the total amount of packaging used in the first place

- banning or phasing out the most harmful types of packaging to people and the planet

- supporting innovation and investment in truly sustainable, biodegradable and compostable packaging – especially non-oil-derived, non-GM, renewable alternatives to plastic

- working towards a world that is free from plastic pollution – a rapid phase-out of single-use plastics: all plastic to be re-usable, recyclable or compostable by 2025 – or earlier

- focusing on changing the system – helping organic businesses minimise their packaging footprint; helping citizens and consumers find products with less or no packaging, plastic-free options, and the most sustainably packaged organic produce.[8]

Wastepack is a compliance organisation that checks that companies fully comply with the Producer Responsibility Obligations (Packaging Waste) Regulations and produce a certification. Only very large companies handling over 50 tonnes of packaging a year and turnover of over £2 million are obligated to comply with waste legislation.

Should we buy products that are biodegradable or compostable?

A good understanding of definitions helps us make informed choices about the products we buy and how to dispose of them.

Merriam-Webster defines biodegradable as 'capable of being broken down especially into innocuous products by the action of living things (such as microorganisms)'.[9] I think that's what most of us believe: if it's labelled biodegradable, we can throw it into the bushes and it won't cause any problems or mess.

Some people think that leaving litter behind is acceptable, even with non-biodegradable products – just look around the fields after a festival or the beaches after an air show or the commons after a bank holiday weekend. So calling things biodegradable when they actually only biodegrade in a commercial machine has almost given people permission to litter without consideration or guilt.

According to Science Learn,[10] a **biodegradable** product:

> breaks down into smaller compounds with the help of biological organisms, such as fungi and bacteria. In aerobic [with oxygen] conditions, biodegradable products will break down to produce carbon dioxide, water and biomass. In anaerobic conditions, they produce carbon dioxide, methane, water and biomass.

There is no time limit to this, so products that take 400 years to break down in sea water – and may break into tiny bits of microplastic which can be eaten by fish and passed up the food chain before they biodegrade – could be described as biodegradable by some. No one appears to be regulating this! So if your balloons or other plastic or bio-plastic products are labelled biodegradable, do not think they can't still kill or maim turtles, whales, seals, etc., because they can, and could do this, if you let them escape into the sea. The description on the product normally gives us no idea of how long it will take to biodegrade, but even if it is four weeks, it is too long if it escapes into the water.

Sadly, some companies describe products as being biodegradable when they biodegrade into substances even more toxic than the original – surely not what the public understands as biodegradable:

> A **compostable** product also breaks down into smaller compounds with the help of biological organisms, but it does so in specific conditions to a defined outcome. In general, a compostable product breaks down in a specific timeframe in a controlled moist, warm, aerobic environment to produce compost that is non-toxic and can enhance soil and support plant life.[11]

So if something is certified compostable, it must decompose in a certain time (say 12 weeks), with certain environmental conditions (50 degrees) and produce a defined quality of compost that is no more than 10 per cent of its original dry weight (no toxic effect on plants or earthworms). But watch out, unless it says otherwise, this is when it is put into an industrial composting facility – and how much, if any, of your waste goes to one of those?

I suggest what you are really looking to buy are products that are **home compostable**, or make sure nothing escapes into the environment and put all your waste that you cannot deal with yourself into your normal bins for your waste management company to sort out. There is more about practical waste management in the next chapter.

We found a very helpful children's clothes catalogue. The producers had marked items that are fully home compostable with little blue dots.

How sustainable are natural products such as leather, fur, wool and feathers?

Obviously, animal products are natural and will degrade and rot in time. However, don't kid yourself that all of these are by-products of meat-eating because, in the vast majority of cases, animals are farmed purely for their outsides. There are some incredibly cruel processes in place, such as plucking and skinning animals alive. Toxic chemicals are used to cure leather, and it's very difficult to check on the origin of such goods, particularly those coming through the Far East. So if you are against cruelty to animals, the better decision has got to be the vegan one.

Vegan decisions, both in what you eat and what you buy, are growing significantly year on year as alternatives improve and knowledge is shared. The cost in resources of animal husbandry (feed, water, vet bills, shelter, fencing, etc.) far outweigh the cost of growing alternatives, such as bamboo for fabric, flooring, etc., and Pinatex. Pinatex is an environmentally friendly textile created from the fibres of leftover pineapple leaves, which are extracted through a process known as decortication. Even when you account for the water used in processes, the sustainable choice is a vegan choice – although not all vegan choices are totally sustainable. Some companies now mark their products as being vegan, having put their whole supply chain through an authentic, international vegan standard that was created by the Vegan Society.[12] The process is not cheap, and if just one step in the chain does not comply, distributers and retailers may not use the trademark.

Greenwash

This describes products which are described as *eco* or *green*, *biodegradable*, or *compostable*, when the product is not really what you think it is. The reason for companies describing their products as eco can be because it's a selling technique.

Manufacturers sometimes call products eco if they are an improvement on theirs or someone else's previous model. For example, products that are 10 per cent plastic when they were 100 per cent plastic could be described as an eco-alternative. Buyers don't realise that a proportion of that product will still not biodegrade, nor compost, and will continue to litter the world until someone else picks it up and processes it correctly.

Some products do not have all their ingredients detailed on the packet, such as baby wipes. On a baby wipe packet, you generally find the ingredients of the lubricant, not the wipe itself. There are manufacturers saying that their product is pure because the liquid is indeed nearly 100 per cent water, but then it jams up your plumbing if you flush it down the toilet, because the fabric is *not* compostable and will clog up your plumbing and the sewage works and pipes in between. There are no warnings on the packaging, so you may think you are buying an eco or even sustainable, product but you aren't. I have challenged this with the advertising authorities and received a polite letter in response, but there has been no action on the packaging to date. BBC's 'War on Plastic'[13] recently highlighted exactly this issue.

Reading the information on manufacturers' websites can also be misleading. They may certify their products are compostable, or conforming to EU standard, but if you investigate, you may find that the company self-certified, or the standard has expired. These self-certified standards are not helpful, but of course help them sell more – it should be illegal.

According to the United Nations Sustainable Development Solutions Network 2019 World Happiness Report,[14] the three happiest countries in the world are Finland, Denmark and Norway. These countries observe a more frugal way of life, where repairing and re-using products is praised and respected, rather than the throw-away culture still prevalent in much of the USA, UK, New Zealand, Australia and China. However, shops do exist now that sell primarily second-hand items; where customers bring their own bags and containers; local farm shops and markets are making a comeback; items are upcycled and repurposed; and repair cafes are being set up in many cities, towns and villages. This model is gradually being adopted worldwide as societies start to show signs that people recognise that there is 'no away'[15] in our throw-away culture. Now is a good time to celebrate being frugal to our communities and families.

Organic products are covered more in Chapter 12, but some catalogues are now beginning to promote their products, such as clothing and soft furnishings, as being organic. Companies such as Rapanui,[16] on the Isle of Wight, only use certified organic cotton for which every step of the supply chain is checked. They also commit to the whole circular economy – you send their clothes back to them at the end of your use. Kite Clothing[17] in Poole, Dorset offers a catalogue of clothes and fabrics which are predominantly organic, and where individual items in their catalogues are marked up with a blue dot so you can instantly tell whether each item is totally organic or not.

Organic does not necessarily mean sustainable. Cotton production uses enormous amounts of water, but with attention to the types of dye used and what happens with the used water, and avoiding toxic herbicides on the plants, it can be more sustainable. There is currently no standard little dot nor trademark to help us identify how far along the sustainability journey companies are – yet.

Core lists

If you are a sole proprietor and you've made a decision to purchase sustainably, it is just up to you to do the work and make the best decisions that you can with the information you can find and in the time that you have.

If you are a committee-run group, or run a group of services, you have more of a challenge; despite your new purpose and good intentions, others may not have bought into the same ethos. What is to stop them continuing as they were and buying cheapest, or most convenient, or wrapped in plastic? We not only need an agreed purchasing policy but a way of encouraging and incentivising, or picking up those not following the policy.

There are various ways to do this. One group of nurseries I know were having the managers instigate the orders (online), which were then individually approved by the daughter of the owner at their head office in line with the ethos of her parents. Orders were then combined so the owners were bulk-buying the same items for each nursery.

A useful tip is to have a core list of products from one or two suppliers that you have pre-researched and approved, and a budget allocated to each purchaser. If you limit the number of suppliers you work with, you can check their credentials and research their procedures for checking the sources of their products more diligently than trying to work with multiple suppliers. But we all need to keep asking the sustainable questions so that they know that is influencing our purchasing decisions.

A core list can further help indicate to your team which products you approve of and which you don't. You could also put a post-order approval process or a pre-ordering system with this to give you, or your trusted top operational staff, the opportunity to block any items that you wouldn't approve of from a sustainability, budget or individual limit angle.

It is good practice to also analyse purchases at month end and query purchases that are not in line with your ethos. It is generally too late to return them by this point, but you can reflect on the different sites for good and poor practice, so it's a learning experience ready for the next month. The combination of information, on-boarding your colleagues with purchasing power, and then monitoring purchases is a challenging one, requiring skilled delegation if you are to achieve the most sustainable purchasing procedure possible.

Carbon offset

If you do feel bad about buying unsustainably, perhaps travelling on holiday or doing a lot of driving, there is now a way to carbon-offset any purchase by buying on the green carbon market. This is generally something big manufacturers use, but you will find when you buy holidays or flights that you are sometimes given the opportunity to donate to a fund that replaces the carbon you have caused to be emitted,[18] by planting trees, for example. Thus, your business can become carbon neutral – definitely something that would generate goodwill amongst those who understand what a great achievement this is!

Energy

Finally, we all need to buy energy to light, heat, cool, and run our buildings and systems. These days it is easy in most countries (not all) to buy renewable energy. You can generate your own energy (solar panels, windmills) or you can buy from suppliers who only purchase and therefore re-sell renewable energy. Some even offer carbon-neutral gas as well – by offsetting the gas purchase against carbon credits. The biggest supplier in the world is Orsted,[19] who mostly use offshore wind, but there are many brokers such as Bespoke Energy[20] and suppliers such as Good Energy[21] and Octpus Energy[22] who offer a similar service. The energy all goes into the same grid, but overall we are looking for our countries to phase out fossil fuel energy as quickly as possible to reduce climate change.

Storing the energy is another issue, and one where technology is advancing quickly, but there are problems with lithium (a small percentage of the labour is slave labour), and there is a global shortage currently. It's a finite resource, so this is an area to consider. Early adopters are already installing batteries to store their home- or business-generated energy so that they can use this energy at times when it isn't being generated, such as at night for solar energy.

Also people are beginning to be smarter about when they use energy, for example is it cheaper to run your washing machine during the day when your solar power is on? Or in the middle of the night when your grid electricity is cheaper to use? As electricity usage increases, power companies are expected to charge more for premium-time electricity, so look ahead to timer-operated equipment and perhaps a new generation of batteries.

Preschoolers can also engage in energy use if you install a visual electricity usage gauge. They are not expensive and are easy to install, and you will be able to show staff and children what happens when the tumble dryer or fan goes on and off.

Water

It's often said that a drop of water is worth more than a sack of gold to a thirsty man. The world is very, very short of drinking water – less than 1 per cent of the world's water is drinking water. Many countries/large businesses are draining deep water aquifers rather than using rain water, and that is having devastating effects, with lakes, rivers and canals drying out. Many crops (e.g. cotton and wheat) and animals also use a lot of water, so demand is increasing even though supply is not. Even the great Panama Canal is having to consider restrictions on boat sizes due to the drop in water level. Despite the rainfall in the UK, London is in the top 10 cities in the world where demand exceeds the supply of water. Water in the UK is cheap, so it's not really financially viable to replace existing plumbing and install grey water/recycled rain water for toilets, etc., although this is feasible in new-builds. However, we can recycle rain water for watering the plants by simply installing water butts – with fastened down lids so no child can get into them. You can add to the learning experience of a water butt by adding a simple plastic tube gauge (can be bought online or from a hardware supplier, and does not need a plumber to install) so children can see how much water is in the water butt, and you could also mark it up with numbers to show how water can be measured.

When you make your purchasing decisions, it's worth knowing about embedded water – the amount of water used to grow the food we eat and the products we consume. You might want to choose different things when you consider the need to conserve water, for example a cotton t-shirt takes 4000 litres, a plastic bottle of water takes 6–7 litres to produce, a slice of bread is 40 litres, a beef steak is 5000 litres, a car 175,000 litres, and a phone 13,000 litres.

In the UK we all use around 140–150 litres of water a day, but only drink about 2 litres. We cannot continue to consume at this level. It's not sustainable, and is increasingly unsustainable as the population increases. When you think of it that way, water is seriously underpriced, and therefore we don't value the most precious commodity on earth.

The water companies/governments and ourselves must stop more leaks. It is well worth you checking your water consumption – leaks on your side of the mains are just added to your bill and may never be repaired unless you do it. I heard from South West Water that a local hotel recently saved £100,000 in water bills by repairing three major leaks. What is your water bill, and what do other nurseries in your area pay? Are you in line?

A good water care company will help with this by auditing your water use. For example, they could install a water logger – which would identify whether you are using any water overnight for example (when your business is closed); if you are, you've got a leak! They will also check for meter inaccuracies, water storage leakage and overflows, recycling and re-use options, check your systems for legionella, temperatures on water heaters (should be above 55), clean and descale showers and hoses, and do annual servicing of annual thermostatic mixing valves (TMVs) – needed on all children's basins to prevent scalding.

Conclusion

I believe we can stretch our funding further while making frugal and sustainable decisions with our resourcing and power and water use. It's good for our reputation to communicate why and how we are doing this to our customers and to our suppliers, but do watch out for greenwash and for things just changing with innovations and science. Having a good relationship with a few suppliers, doing due diligence over their products, deliveries and sourcing, is a good way to reduce your workload. Sustainability isn't just about carbon footprint; you can become more sustainable environmentally, economically and also socially.

Notes

1. Turner, A. (2018). Concentration and Migratabilities of Hazardous Elements in Second Hand Children's Plastic Toys. *Environmental Science and Technology*, 52(5), 3110–3116.
2. See https://greenglobe.com/ for more information.
3. www.communityplaythings.co.uk/.
4. Rainforest Relief. (2007). *Avoiding Unstainable Rainforest Wood* [online]. Rainforest Relief. Available from: www.rainforestrelief.org/What_to_Avoid_and_Alternatives/Rainforest_Wood.html.
5. https://friendsoftheearth.uk/.
6. www.unenvironment.org/.
7. www.teebweb.org/.
8. Soil Association. (2018). *Unwrapping Organic Packaging* [online]. Soil Association. Available from: www.soilassociation.org.
9. www.merriam-webster.com/dictionary/biodegradable.
10. See www.sciencelearn.org.nz/resources/1537-biodegradability.
11. Science Learning Hub. (2018). *Biodegradability, Compostability and Bioplastics* [online]. Science Learning Hub. Available from: www.sciencelearn.org.nz.
12. See www.vegansociety.com/your-business/vegan-trademark-standards for more information.
13. www.bbc.co.uk/iplayer/episodes/m0005xh7/war-on-plastic-with-hugh-and-anita
14. www.worldhappiness.report/ed/2019/.
15. www.aplasticocean.movie/.
16. https://rapanuiclothing.co./.
17. www.kiteclothing.co.uk/.
18. www.carbonfootprint.com/carbonoffsetprojects.html.
19. https://orsted.co.uk/.
20. http://bespoke-energyltd.com/.
21. www.goodenergy.co.uk/.
22. https://octopus.energy/.

14 Transport and trips

When we work with children, we like to get out and around the community, and we also have to cope with the impact of others travelling close by our buildings and the impact that that has on our children and on the environment.

With each trip, there are environmental factors we must consider and choices that we make as individuals and as adults working in the early years sector. This chapter is about air pollution, walking, cycling, public transport and different types of vehicles, in order to help you weigh up your choices through understanding the risks and benefits of those choices. It also provides some guidance on sharing sustainable travelling information with your colleagues and parents through a sustainable travel plan.

Air pollution

Air pollution from traffic fumes, petrol vapour, tobacco smoke and chemicals affect our children outside on trips. Breathing in polluted air is bad for the children's lungs and can cause asthma and lung disease. Pregnant women can risk premature birth, low birth weight and altered lung development if exposed to a lot of air pollution. If children are exposed to high levels of air pollution over a long period, they might be at risk of their lungs not working as well as they grow older, worsening asthma, wheezing, coughing, lung cancer and pneumonia.

What can we do about air pollution?

We can avoid very busy roads and junctions, and any other areas that are high in pollution. We can identify these by contacting our local Department for Environment. In the UK this is DEFRA, and their website[1] has an air pollution forecast for today, tomorrow and the outlook ahead. There is a daily air quality index which ranges from 1 (low) to 10 (very high) with colours that are green for low, going through amber, red, maroon and purple at 10. You can put in your postcode to check your air quality, and you will notice that the best numbers are, of course, on the coast.

We took part in UNICEF UK's diffusion tubes monitoring activity in March/April 2018 in their campaign to protect children against toxic air where they live, learn and play. We had attached a tube at child height outside several nurseries for a month and then sent them of the independent laboratory that UNICEF had commissioned. The diffusion tubes measured the average air pollution levels during the time they were placed. Air pollution levels are likely to have been higher during peak times than the results indicate. The result gave risk ratings for each location – low 0–20 µg/m³, medium 20–30 µg/m³, or high 30+ µg/m³ in accordance with the World Health Organization (WHO) recommended limit of 40 micrograms per cubic metre (µg/m³) as an annual mean value. We received three results out of the five sent as there were various problems with the post system and 'use by' dates provided by UNICEF. Of those three, one was low and two were medium, despite the nurseries being near the coast.

UNICEF have recently published a new report to urge the UK government to tackle air pollution wherever children learn and play. You can access this here: www.unicef.org.uk/clean-air-child-health-air-pollution/.

Unarguably, vehicles and the burning of anything exacerbates pollution, but there are a number of other things we can do to help.

Walking

Provided the air pollution is not serious, walking with the children is the best form of transport, as it doesn't increase the air pollution. Risk assessments need to include the risk of children running into the street. Some settings do use straps around children's wrists so the children are effectively on leashes, and parents sometimes use harnesses. We don't use either device, but this is a matter for each setting to decide with reference to their local laws, customs, and culture. We do try and head to the fields, forest or beach as soon as possible so that the children can be free to run and climb rather than try to walk in a formation, and they are more likely to have fresh air away from the roads. Double and triple buggies help us take the youngest children out and can minimise the need for large rucksacks of spares by attaching bags to the buggies. Some nurseries have little wagons to pull along with either bags or tired toddlers in them!

Walking trains or crocodiles

Walking trains or crocodiles are when pairs of children walk along behind each other, with adults at the front of the chain, to the sides and the back. This is a way of getting a group of children from one point to another, perhaps from breakfast club to school, or on a trip when trying to move dozens of children with only a few staff. In day nurseries, we have much smaller groups, maybe six children with two staff, because it is much more difficult to lead a group of 2–4-year-olds. Younger children understand hazards less than a school-aged child does. Conditions such as attention deficit disorder may not have been diagnosed yet, and the whole experience could be completely new for a child who has been carried from house to car to nursery, and back again at the end of the day. The rope bus is a good method to use when walking through car parks, going down slopes, or along roads. You just use a rope and ask the children to hold onto it, but spread them out so they don't trip over each other's heels. You can knot, mark the rope, or tie coloured string around it to help children avoid bunching up. You can easily supervise eight children on one rope with one member of staff. Swapping the leader, stopping for animals or pre-planted photographs of models of animals can add interest if necessary.

Cycling

Children aged 0–4 are not generally competent to ride a bike to and from nursery or on trips; cycling is something we do in the playground to practise. It's far more likely adults would have a child on the back or front of a bike in a child's seat, but that is too adult-intensive (generally one-to-one) to be practical for a day nursery. We do, however, have several day nursery bikes and carts in our area. Normal bikes for adults cycling in and out of work are very popular in our workplaces and we just need to provide safe parking where the bikes can be locked up, and ideally a shower room and lockers. The UK 'cycle to work' scheme[2] enables loans of up to £1000 per year to be made from pay to any member of staff before tax, saving around 30 per cent of the spend. The money can be spent on bikes (including for the members of staff's children), jackets, padlocks, child seats, paniers, lights, and any other relevant equipment for any member of staff taking this up. The payback period can be up to a year without interest. This is a significant perk for people whose employers engage in the scheme, which is good for staff retention as well as encouraging a sustainable way to commute. The more people on bikes instead of in cars, the better it is for air pollution and, therefore, for children and adults.

Bikes and carts

Bikes can be attached to a cart that can hold around six small children. The member of staff has to work very hard to cycle along, and the children get to sit comfortably looking at the scenery. This does nothing to combat childhood obesity, but it helps keep the staff fit and is a fast, effective way of travelling maybe half a mile from the nursery building to the forest or beach on a flat road. Having a little electric motor on the bike would make it a lot more pleasurable for the staff member!

Electric bikes

We were fortunate to be successful at applying for a grant for four electric bikes from our local council, which was keen to promote sustainable transport. The bikes came with locks, batteries, helmets, front and rear lights, and servicing after a year. We invested in an undercover bike park and spread the information out to colleagues to try and get them used. The big advantage with electric bikes is that you can avoid breaking into a sweat on the way to work, and therefore having the inconvenience and time consideration of having to take a shower when you get to work, or being an anti-social work colleague. We had to work hard to encourage people to try them, but currently have three out of four loaned out. When you consider they are worth over £1000 each, this is an attractive opportunity. I tried one myself, to show willing. I do own, and ride, a regular

Figure 14.1 Colleagues at Hadland Care Groups with electric bikes

hybrid bike and I have a flat ride to work, so I really didn't need an electric bike, but it's important to set a good example. If a granny like me could ride one, I thought it would be a good motivator amongst colleagues. It was much heavier to ride than my own bike, and it was also less manoeuvrable, but I got used to it in a few minutes. Several colleagues started riding them between local meetings at work, and we also allowed people to take them home for the weekends to enable them to engage in family bike rides and trips in ways they hadn't been able to before.

One of the issues with some electric bikes is that some are far too heavy to carry up the stairs and put in your flat's hall, too big for most small home entrances, and some of the local areas are just too prone to theft to leave outside the front on the pavement. However, we have recently taken receipt of a foldable, lightweight electric bike and that is proving more popular for exactly these circumstances.

Public transport – buses, trains, trams

On the Stagecoach website[3] it says that the choices each individual makes every day affects the planet. We can see how fragile the earth has become by looking at climate change. Stagecoach buses and trains have been reinvented to become part of the solution by reducing their environmental impact, improving their energy efficiency, conserving water, and increasing their recycling. With a little research, I found that they had cut the carbon intensity of their businesses in the UK and North America by 30 per cent from 2009 to 2014, and they have ambitious targets to reduce buildings' carbon emissions. They have cut fleet transport carbon emissions, lowered their water consumption and achieved a waste recycling rate of 83 per cent. They have also been awarded the prestigious Carbon Trust Standard[4] for measuring, managing and reducing their global carbon footprint. They have a cute 1:38 video on their website, talking about what being green means, for them. They engage their customers and colleagues in a green week and want to help everyone to have a greener lifestyle to make communities cleaner and healthier. If you are going to take public transport, Stagecoach is probably the greenest way to go.

Some areas have a 'park and ride' scheme where colleagues and parents drive to an out-of-town car park and take a bus into work. This works well, although we have had problems with them not opening early enough to enable colleagues to arrive at work before the first shift workers arrive. Another problem can be having the correct car seats for the children on the bus or indeed even being allowed to bring children onto the bus, although there is no reason that this cannot be surmounted.

Diesel cars

Greenpeace[5] has always been clear that diesel's big advantage – lower carbon dioxide emissions compared with petrol engines – doesn't outweigh the health-threatening nitrogen oxide (NOx) emissions. The key issue is the gas released through exhaust pipes as a result of the engine powering the car. Diesel vehicle exhausts emit nitrogen oxide, which is the more toxic gas in terms of pollution and human health, but petrol vehicles have more carbon dioxide (CO_2) fumes, which is a greenhouse gas causing global warming, and also therefore dangerous for human health.

Diesel cars are 'more polluting than thought' according to an analysis by Transport & Environment reported in the *Financial Times*,[6] which found that a typical diesel car emits 42.65 tonnes of NOx over its lifecycle, or 3.65 tonnes more than a petrol car. Professor Sir David King, the government's former chief scientific advisor, has said companies producing or encouraging the use of diesel cars have blood on their hands. He argues that 'the number of early fatalities in Britain is very very very large due to NOx (nitrogen oxides) in the air, with governments across Europe encouraging diesel on the basis that the catalyst traps worked.'[7]

Campaign groups blame EU rules – such as a 100 per cent discount on the London Congestion Charge, favourable car tax and company car taxes – for the high use of diesel cars in Europe. In the EU, approximately 52 per cent of cars are diesel; in Russia it's only 8 per cent. Cities are beginning to ban old diesel cars because they are 20 times as toxic as a modern diesel car! Hamburg was the first German city to ban old diesel cars in May 2018, and manufacturers in the EU are reporting falling diesel demand.

If you want to check out a car's emissions, see Next Green Car.[8] Ultra low emission vehicles (ULEVs) are defined as cars and vans with tailpipe CO_2 emissions of 75 g/km or less. My diesel Audi A6 (which I recently replaced with a Hyundai Kona) produced NOx 52 mg/km and 118 mg/km CO_2 but achieved over 50 miles to the gallon. Tops Day Nurseries is in the process of moving over to electric vehicles with an 85% electric fleet in 2019.

Governments are beginning to limit diesel as a fuel despite some, such as the UK, favouring them in the past, so companies are beginning to turn away from buying diesel cars. On the other hand, there are ways to clean up diesel emissions, so modern cars with these expensive filters fitted are perhaps not the devil that we are being told they are. They are fuel-efficient, typically averaging over 50 miles per gallon compared with petrol at 40 miles per gallon, and the engines last longer than petrol cars too. Car models that have been awarded certification for their low carbon emissions are sometimes eligible for reduced road tax, making them more cost-effective as well as better for the planet. Nevertheless,

UK diesel car sales fell almost 40 per cent in the year to April 2018 and a diesel ban is being considered by 2040. Diesel car sales in the US, while already minimal, are falling lower still, although diesel truck sales appear to be holding steady.

Petrol cars

The amount of CO_2 produced by a petrol car is directly connected to its fuel consumption. The bigger the car, and the faster it is driven, the more greenhouse gas it produces. Once you know this, you realise that speeding is not only dangerous (and illegal in some countries/at some speeds), but also worse for the planet. Petrol cars also produce carbon monoxide, a toxic gas that interrupts our intake of oxygen, so we can only tolerate it in very small amounts.

Hybrid cars

A hybrid car has two engines, a normal petrol/gasoline one and an electric engine. This secondary engine can help when additional power is required, such as when accelerating or hill climbing, or can supply all the required power when operating at low speeds, as in city driving. This massively reduces the amount of fumes in the city, which is where the accumulation of toxins is most serious.

Hybrid cars use less fuel in theory, although an efficient diesel vehicle *could* still claim the title of least fuel usage, and the new diesel cars turn themselves off when stopped at lights and junctions, which obviously helps as well.

There is only a small battery on a hybrid car which is generally charged by the car in motion, but some also have a plug-in charge facility. It is topped up either by braking or by engine motion, so the all-electric range is just a few miles in a hybrid.

Electric vehicles

Electric vehicles have zero tailpipe emissions as they are fuelled by electricity and they all have a rechargeable battery on board to power the electric motor which turns the wheels. The battery is charged by plugging the car into a power source such as a mains socket, home charging unit or public charge point. I trialled the Nissan Leaf and we now have a small fleet of these for the day nurseries. They take most of the night to charge up at the nursery and can then drive for about 120 miles (less if you speed or if it's cold), but if you lease one, you can have a charging unit installed at work or at home, which then drops the charge time to around four hours. There are also some public high speed charge points which only take 30 minutes. When I first drove the Leaf down to our nurseries in Taunton (about 60 miles each way) I thought I could drive down, have my meeting and drive back no problem. It didn't work out that way and I suffered from 'range anxiety' on the way home. I was obliged to stop short of getting home for a charge, despite driving slowly, with the radio and air conditioning off, not being able to charge my phone and stressing for the last 30 miles as the charge gradually went to zero. In a diesel or petrol car, I could have driven much further, had a can of fuel in the boot as a back-up, and taken a tow from another car if necessary.

With an electric car you do have to plan longer trips, and stop for coffee where there's a high speed charger and Wi-Fi in order to have a productive day! An extended-range electric vehicle (EV) would be better, such as the Tesla, with the car capable of being used as a conventional EV, but with the added safety net of the on-board generator extending the car's range. There are generous discounts and tax savings for companies wanting to buy or lease a Tesla, including exemption from the London congestion charge and significantly lower benefit-in-kind (BIK) for company car drivers, but they are still beyond the budget of most day nursery owners. My new electric car, though, a Hyundai Kona, has the best practical range of all electric cars on the market according to *Which?* Magazine.[9] In practice I can get 315 miles in the summer by driving eco+ (no faster than 60 mph, no fast accelerating and no air conditioning!).

Electric cars are easy to drive, quiet and powerful (high torque electric motors) and braking is generally gentler than a petrol or diesel vehicle. People do have a worrying habit of stepping out in front of the car because they don't hear it coming, though.

Sadly, electric cars are currently more expensive, there may be a long waiting list for them, and finding a second-hand one is very difficult, so we still have some old vehicles that we would like to replace but are just unable to currently. Hopefully this will change in time. There is another downside to the electric car – the batteries. The batteries are made using a lot of lithium, which is not in abundant supply, and there are mines that use slave and child labour (only about 2 per cent of lithium), but it's hard to identify which lithium is from those mines and which is fine. Clearly it would be unethical to be involved in enabling anyone to use child or slave labour. But how can you tell where your lithium is coming from, and also how can you be sure that it will be recycled properly at the end of its life? I don't have the answers to this. And this is the reason that not everyone is enthusiastic about EVs – along with the concern that if everybody moved to electric cars now, there would not be enough electricity in our national grid. One also has to ensure that the electricity comes from a renewable source, and not burning fossil fuels, for this to be a more sustainable choice. Electric cars

Figure 14.2 Electric car in use for delivering meals and transporting children to and from school

are therefore not a perfect solution, but most would argue that they are better for our climate and our air than burning fossil fuels to propel our vehicles.

Here are some calculations we did recently in the company comparing petrol/diesel cars with electric cars: in round figures:

- 1 litre of petrol = 9.1 kWh of energy.

- 1 litre of diesel = 10 kWh of energy.

- 1 litre of petrol will take you about 8–9 miles.

- 1 litre of diesel will take you about 10–11 miles.

- Therefore, 1 kWh of petrol/diesel will take you about 1 mile.

- 1 kWh of electric power will take you about 4 miles.

- **That is, electric cars use energy four times more efficiently than petrol/diesel cars.**

- The cost of petrol/diesel is £1.30 per litre, or about 13p–16p per kWh.

- The cost of electricity is around 15p–16p per kWh.

- That is, the cost of energy is broadly similar.

This is a very good argument for using electric vehicles, in the right circumstances.

Car-sharing

In order to help our colleagues car-share, it is useful to plot where all colleagues live and communicate that information to the rest of the colleagues – subject to their permission to do so, of course. Where nurseries have shifts that start at the same time rather than having staggered hours, there is a better opportunity to share cars. Obviously, car-shares not only limit polluting the planet but also reduce costs, and many companies offer beneficial parking opportunities and other discounts. You could go one further and plot where parents live to enable parents to share cars also – but you must plot them anonymously if you are going to post a chart with this information and then seek individual permissions from parents if they ask who it is that lives close to them in order to avoid falling foul of data protection. This will give you or your administrators additional work, but if it reduces the pollution from your car park or drop-off zone, it would be very good practice in terms of sustainability and fighting air pollution.

The future: hydrogen cars

At a Green Wheel show in Hampshire, I was fortunate enough to see a selection of green vehicles, including the Tesla electric car, but also a Toyota Mirai, the world's first dedicated mass-produced hydrogen fuel cell vehicle.

Basically, instead of filling up with petrol, diesel or electricity, you fill up with hydrogen, which is pumped in, under pressure – much like you'd fill a tyre through a valve and in a similar place to where you'd fill up with diesel or petrol. There is a large tank under the seat, which is much less explosive or flammable than diesel or petrol – the salesman said this was an improvement in terms of safety wise. (I was thinking of hydrogen balloons blowing up in the blitz and hydrogen bombs, but I was told this wasn't a risk from hydrogen cars, or at least less of a risk than from petrol – but you might want to satisfy yourself on this point as I didn't really understand the explanation myself – sorry!)

Currently, a fill of hydrogen will cost about £60 and take you about 300 miles, so this is not a cost saving – unlike electric cars. A hydrogen compressor can be sited just about anywhere, such as at petrol/diesel stations, but you wouldn't have one at home or at a single nursery. Currently, there is one in a bus depot, for example. There aren't enough places to fill up for the public; you'd have to be running a fleet from one base – like said bus depot. They are also beginning to run trains on hydrogen. The car itself costs about £61,000 – which, again, is expensive, but the prices will come down with more volume.

The massive advantage with hydrogen cars is that the only emission is water, which is mostly vapour with a few droplets, and there is no need for huge

batteries like with electric cars. Five kilograms of hydrogen is pumped and filtered from water, giving about 500 miles range in a car, and delivers 50 litres of water back into the atmosphere. No waste, no pollution. The power needed to separate the hydrogen from the water is electric, so would be better powered by renewables such as wind, solar or hydro rather than fossil fuels or gas – as with any electricity that we need. The hydrogen can be stored in tanks; no need for expensive, resource-heavy, toxic batteries. The engine has hardly any moving parts to service and it looks identical to the electric engines we are seeing in electric cars. Many think the future of road transport to be hydrogen cars rather than electric cars. Unfortunately, they just aren't ready to be ordered yet, nor are the hydrogen pumps yet available. You might want to rent your electric vehicles for three years and then re-evaluate when the scientists, engineers and manufacturers are further along.

There is something else to bear in mind:

Tyres

We think of tyres as being rubber, but they aren't. Synthetic rubber is a variant of plastic, which makes up around 60 per cent of the rubber in tyres. In 2017, the International Union for Conservation of Nature (IUCN) report[10] said that 15–31 per cent of plastic pollution came from primary microplastics, of which the biggest contributors (almost two-thirds) were abrasion of synthetic textiles, while washing, and abrasion of tyres, while driving.

As the tyres wear, the microplastic particles wear onto the road and are then washed down the sides of the road into the water system, and from there to the sea. Microbeads from cosmetics only contributed approximately 2 per cent of global ocean pollution, yet we've reacted to those and not to tyres and clothes. People are beginning to make clothes with less plastic in them and also producing filters for washing machines, but I've heard nothing about how to reduce tyre wear. Is the tyre-making lobby so strong that no suggestions are being made at all on how to reduce this?

What happens to tyres that are no longer legal to use on cars? Shredding tyres is a lucrative business, but there are still mountains of tyres around the world polluting the environment because they will last for hundreds of years, or make an incredibly toxic fire. Our day nurseries have been doing what we can by repurposing some tyres in the gardens, for balancing on, for planting in and for climbing through. Ultimately, this has to be an area the government and tyre companies lead on. Making artificial reefs from tyres has not been a great success; it has basically put a lot of plastic pollution underwater to gradually break up into microplastics.

The only other thing we can do is try and cut down our miles driven in cars – fortunately, modern technology is helping with this, with the option of online meetings, video conferencing and video calls. However, children need actual adults working with them, not machine supervision. This is one area where productivity is not a key performance indicator; fewer adult hours with our children, or larger groups of children per adult, can only mean poorer quality of education.

Sustainable travel policy

A sustainable travel policy is a document you would provide to every new colleague before they start. You might also provide one to every new family. After describing your ethos, you would describe all the sustainable options for getting to your building, so all the public transport options, including safe walking routes; whether you have a secure bike park, showers and lockers; whether you can offer electric bike or car connections; sharing vehicles; and anything additional that you might offer, such as cycle training, discounts arranged at local bike shops, or perhaps a 'bike to work' loan scheme. I've put one of ours in Appendix III to give you some ideas to start from.

Conclusion

Day nurseries can help with air pollution and climate change through making sustainable decisions themselves, and also encouraging staff and customers to make more sustainable choices in how they come and go from your building. Air pollution is a 'hidden' threat to children in particular, so providing information to colleagues and parents can help motivate an interest in reducing their impact.

Notes

1. https://uk-air.defra.gov.uk/forecasting.
2. www.gov.uk/government/publications/cycle- to-work-scheme-implementation-guidance.
3. www.stagecoach.com/sustainability.
4. www.carbontrust.com/what-we-do/assurance-and-certification/the-carbon-trust-standard
5. www.greenpeace.org/international/press-release/22240/greenpeace-report-on-electric-vehicles-offers-way-to-transition-away-from-diesel-and-petrol-cars/
6. *Financial Times.* (2017). Diesel cars are 'more polluting' than thought, study finds. *Financial Times.* 17 September.
7. Car firms have 'blood on their hands' over fumes scandal – former UK advisor. (2018). *Belfast Telegraph.* 30 January.
8. www.nextgreencar.com/emissions.
9. www.which.co.uk/reviews/new-and-used-cars/hyundai-kona-hybrid-2019.
10. Julien, B. and Friot, D. (2017). *Primary Microplastics in the Oceans: A global evaluation of sources* [online]. IUCN, Global Marine and Polar Programme. Available from: www.iucn.org.

15 Waste management

Introduction

Have a look outside at what bins you have. You may just have one large general waste bin that everything goes into, or you may have a range of bins because you have started sorting your waste to become more sustainable. This chapter describes some waste sorting and treatment of waste that you can do to make your nursery setting/service more sustainable.

General waste bin

We now have a small general waste bin into which we put as little as possible. The aim is to have smaller bins and/or less frequent collections. If you can get your waste collectors to provide you with the weight they collect each month, this can help monitor how successful you are in this regard. We had trouble getting this data despite the collection company having no problem telling us if our bin was overweight (which on one occasion I found out was because misinformed colleagues were throwing sand into the bin rather than cleaning it for re-use). We managed to halve our general waste quite quickly and we continue to work to reduce it further. We also communicate frequently with our waste collection company to reduce the bin size/number of collections and therefore the bill. We found that when we replaced some (not all!) of our plastic toys with wooden ones and upcycled/recycled items, we were left with a load of plastic toys we didn't know what to do with. In the end, we either gave them away to parents or took them to charity shops or car boot sales – far preferable to throwing them into the waste bin!

We have recently found a new waste organisation[1] which audits and monitors all our waste, providing us with data on how much of each type of waste we create. They sometimes audit the contents, letting us know if bins are found to have the wrong things in them. This is very helpful information to be able to feed back to nursery managers and their staff. This method also helped us identify an unforeseen issue with cleaners at our head office. Despite our care in separating our waste into the correct bins in our desk and canteen areas, the cleaner was then throwing the contents of all of them into the same bin outside, just through lack of proper training. We had to rethink induction, training and monitoring of cleaners!

Recycling waste bin

What can be recycled at each setting will vary depending on the local authority or organisation responsible. Generally, we can put quite a lot in the recycling bin, such as glass jam jars and rigid plastic bottles or containers and tins/metals. Only some waste companies (not kerbside collections) will accept plastic bags, polystyrene foam cups or containers, drinking cups or egg containers, broken or sharp glass or plastic toys.

It can help to know a bit more about what can be recycled:

One of the most common plastics used in food packaging is polyethylene terephthalate, or PET, used for soft drink bottles, trays and fruit punnets. It's one of the most recyclable plastics around, and the vast majority of UK councils will take it in recycling collections because it has a value of several hundred pounds per tonne. It is marked with a '1' in the green/white recycling logo.

Councils will take high-density polyethylene (HDPE), which is used for milk bottles, cleaning products, yoghurt pots and soap dispensers and is marked with a '2' in the green/white recycling logo. Councils will also take polypropylene (PP), which is often used for margarine tubs, meal trays and soup pots and is marked '5'.

Councils are unlikely to collect '3' (PVC) or '4' (LDPE). PVC is used for blister packs, meat trays, pipe fittings and window fittings. It can be recycled to make more PVC products but needs to be disposed of at a waste management site. LDPE is used for things like bread, toilet rolls and freezer bags – you can identify it because it's easy to poke your finger through it. It is recyclable with a bit of effort – it's rarely labelled correctly, but some large supermarkets will take it. In both cases you are more likely to put these things in general waste and hope someone recycles it for you, somehow.

Crisp packets, salad bags, wrapping paper and other 'crinkly' plastic bags are all difficult to recycle and not currently processed by UK recycling facilities, but Terracycle[2] do collect crisp packets for recycling.

Non-recyclable plastics tend to be combinations, meaning they are made up of multiple layers of different types of plastic and other products. These make them difficult to break down and re-use, but they are used a lot by supermarkets for packaging for anything perishable that needs to be preserved, as they offer air tightness. They are also used for take-away drinks and meals.

Composting

Despite our best efforts to cook meals that encourage children to clean their plates, we inevitably produce waste – both in the preparation of meals and with leftovers. We make compost with our organic, uncooked waste, so that we are both saving the cost of buying compost for growing plants and reducing the waste that needs to be collected by our local refuse collection company. This could also save us money if we can reduce the number of collections or bin size as a result.

We are also teaching our children and their parents, and quite possibly our colleagues, the techniques to do this at home. This is a win for everyone, except possibly the refuse collectors. Although, with increasing populations in most places, they may appreciate our efforts!

In order to grow vegetables, fruits, flowers and herbs in the garden with the children we need some compost to mix with the soil. Yes, we can buy it from any garden centre, or we have sometimes had it delivered, but it's simple to save money plus transport costs by making our own: surely a good idea? Compost is made by rotting down vegetable/compostable matter with earth microbes.

We can't compost all of the food we waste unless we are vegan, because putting dairy, meat products or cooked sauces in with the composting is a sure way to attract vermin and to produce an unpleasant smell – both of which produce hazards from which we need to protect the children. So, we have two types of food waste: that which can be composted, and that which cannot. You might want to put a list up near your bins at work.

These are the things that you *can* compost:

- animal manure and paper or sawdust/woodchip bedding from herbivores (not meat eaters like dogs or cats, but you might have rabbits or guinea pigs, hamsters or gerbils as nursery pets)

- cardboard rolls, cereal boxes, brown paper bags, paper towels

- shredded paper or newspaper pet bedding

- coffee grounds and filters

- cotton and wool rags

- dryer and vacuum cleaner lint

- crushed egg shells (but not eggs)
- fireplace ashes
- fruits and vegetables
- grass cuttings and hedge cuttings
- hair and fur
- hay and straw
- houseplants
- leaves
- nut shells
- seaweed (rinse off salt water)
- tea leaves and tea bags that don't have plastic in them
- toothpicks, lollypop sticks and burnt matches.

But *do not* compost these items because they produce odour problems and pests:

- meat, fish or poultry scraps
- dairy products
- fats, grease, lard or oils
- cooked sauces/food.

Nor can you compost the following:

- coal or charcoal ash (contains substances harmful to plants)
- diseased or insect-ridden plants (diseases or insects might spread)
- pet waste, e.g. dog or cat faeces, cat litter (might contain parasites or germs)
- bush/tree cuttings that have been treated with pesticides (might kill composting organisms)
- black walnut tree leaves or twigs (substances harmful to plants)
- also best not to put perennial weeds (such as dandelions, thistles, or weeds with seed heads in)
- never plastic, glass or metals.

Good practice is to layer the waste, like you do a lasagne; green waste (fresher and wetter material), and brown waste (autumn leaves, brown paper bags, hair, newspaper). It needs to be damp to start up the microbial activity, and you can help it along by putting some fresh, moist dirt in with the waste, or adding a compost-making additive. Compost makers help create rich, dark compost in weeks rather than months, and instructions are typically to scatter a couple of handfuls of compost maker on top of 15 cm of material and then after each additional 15 cm up to about 1 metre deep. Some suggest filling a plastic sack/bin/barrel with material to be composted and mixing in about four handfuls of compost maker while you fill it up (before you churn or turn the mixture). Compost activators generally contain an acid/alkaline corrector and enzymes. If using hands to add the compost maker, you and the children will need to wear gloves. We bought some very cheaply from Aldi, made by Gardenline.

The Eden Project in Cornwall, renowned for its green credentials, has published their top 10 tips for how to make a compost heat like theirs.[3] Their advice includes picking a level, well-drained spot for your compost so that excess water drains away. They also sell an Eden Project aeration tool with a long handle to help turn the compost over, which leads to faster composting.

Most colleagues will not have composted food before, so an element of initial training is required for staff. Then the correct facilities and equipment need to be provided to allow composting to become a regular part of the children's routine.

Figure 15.1 Composting at nursery

Start with a container inside, and a composter outside. On some sites, we had buckets with a lid that fulfilled the criteria for an inside composter; it could be plastic, glass or metal, as long as it can be carried easily to the outside composter. The more up-market inside composters have charcoal filters built in to prevent onion and garlic smells from leaking out, and of course they can be purchased in trendy colours if you so wish.

The outside composter can be a large bin or a rotating barrel, or just an area in the garden that is sectioned off with wood or sleepers. The advantage of the rotating barrel is that it just needs to be turned over once a week or so with the handle on the side, whereas the composter that is just a box needs forking over with a pitchfork or spade. The compost needs forking over to get air into the mixture, as this is a key to keeping it smelling fresh and to simulating the earth microbes that actively make the compost into good fertiliser. You also need to move the newer waste down into the middle of the compost pile because it will change into compost most effectively where it is warm and damp.

Adults and children might enjoy forking over the compost and it is undoubtedly good physical exercise. However, they may not be so keen, so this needs some reflection as to what works best for your setting. Who will be responsible for this process? Perhaps put it in the diary so that if responsible individuals are away, the management know that the task needs doing. Try and restrain yourselves from turning the compost too often, or overwatering it, or from spending a lot of money on expensive bins, thermometers or other equipment. You just need to let it develop quietly until you are ready to use it.

Making the compost is easy and fun. Children will love being engaged in peeling and cutting food and collecting food bits that they aren't going to eat. Adults just need to support this activity, and their kitchen staff, and then ensure that the organic materials are put into the composting container every couple of days, or even every day if the team prefer. It's important that everyone knows what can be composted and what cannot. You might want to design a poster or signage with the children.

If the wrong food goes into the compost, you could well end up attracting rats. You can help prevent encouraging rats into your garden by investing in a metal composter.

Compost that is ready is dark brown, almost black, almost soil-like at the bottom, with a spongy texture. It will be rich in nutrients for plants and will be great for improving soil quality in the garden, helping retain moisture and suppressing weeds. You shouldn't need to use additional chemical fertilisers or pesticides, making your garden truly organic.

There really is little excuse for not composting, even if it's just collecting waste pack lunch scraps in the classroom. It's easy, instructive and, of course, sustainable.

Wormeries

Wormeries are basically compost heaps plus worms that you put in specially. Do not use normal garden worms as they aren't the right type of worms! And do ensure your wormery has a way for the water to filter through it when it rains as you don't want your worms to drown. You might also need a lid if it's kept outside. Several varieties of tiger worms are suitable, but the best according to Wormery[4] and the Eden Project are Eisenia Fetida. It is the most efficient worm that simply thrives eating organic waste.

If you know anyone who already has a wormery, they may well let you have a few hundred worms for free. Most mature wormeries will have a couple of thousand worms so would be able to spare some! Opt for younger, smaller ones as they eat more.

Worms are not keen on onion skins or citrus, harsh spices or oily foods, but they do love cardboard, newspaper and wood chip, and even like a bit of pasta (not pasta with tuna or cheese in it, though!). Wormeries do not get through large quantities of vegetables, particularly in winter. You will need to drill some holes in the bottom and layer some cardboard across the base. Some purchased wormeries have separate boxes and a tap at the bottom to collect the liquid compost, which is a highly nutritious liquid plant food.

Vertical Veg[5] has a lot of questions and answers you might have about wormeries. Wormeries with a transparent side, so the children can see what is happening, are great fun to watch and to feed food scraps to – don't give them too much

Figure 15.2 Wormery at Tops Day Nurseries, Lakeside

or it'll turn rancid and the worms won't like that! Bear in mind that wormeries are slow to start up initially because the worms can't eat the nice fresh stuff; they need a few weeks of initial microbial decomposition before they can ingest the waste, as not even tiger worms have teeth. They reach sexual maturity after six weeks and start breeding, providing they are feeding well. Having distinctive layers really helps the children see the worm action. Some suppliers[6] sell kits all ready to go with instructions and resources to help children learn more about worms' importance in our ecosystem: couldn't be much easier!

If you aren't sure about wormeries or composters and none of your staff have done them before, you might want to experiment at home before starting at the nursery so that you are confident to show colleagues and children what to do.

Reducing waste

One of the best ways to reduce your waste is to monitor what you already produce. This can be achieved by reflecting on the plates at the end of meals, or more formal weighing of waste. If you don't assess your wastage, you will have no way of knowing if it is increasing or reducing. Some waste contractors will roughly weigh your bins each time they collect, but getting that data from them can be a challenge – other than extra charges for overweight general waste, which they will happy to invoice you for!

The other avenue is to work with your suppliers to reduce packaging. Complain if they pack one tiny box of pencil sharpeners inside two further boxes along with some inflated plastic bags; threaten to return the packaging or charge them for its disposal. Logically, they are paying for the packaging and we are paying to get rid of it, so it should be a win–win situation. The only people who lose out are the companies that make the packaging.

Some suppliers are undoubtedly working on this area. For example, Findel-Education[7] responded to my questions with:

> Unfortunately the nature of our business means that we have to ship boxes to customers. But our state of the art packaging machine has cut our CO_2 emissions by 46%. I would welcome the opportunity for you to visit our distribution centre, so you can see what we do to reduce our impact on the environment – as a business.

Another supplier welcomed our photographs of what I called 'stupid' packaging so he could take these back to his company to investigate and hopefully improve.

There are more packaging options available now, such as mushroom-based packaging which can go into the composter. If you have replaced plastic cutlery and plates with bamboo or leaf-based items, they will be able to go into the composting as well. Whenever you buy something you should be considering what you are going to do with the packaging and with the product when its end of life comes. Perhaps you could also consider renting the product and returning it to the manufacturer when no longer needed – an ideal way of dealing with it as the manufacturer can then take it apart, remake it and sell it again.

Which? magazine and the TV programme *War on Waste* did some work on comparing products sold in plastic bags and sold without packaging, and found that those in packaging were significantly cheaper. Retailers say that there is more food waste if food isn't packaged as the odd damaged apple, for example, will be discarded in the shop, whereas if it was part of a six-pack it would be taken home (and potentially wasted there instead, but at the householder's/local authority's cost, not the retailer's!). Also, packaging is cheap, so it makes sense for retailers to do this. Clearly, if plastic packaging was taxed to reflect its recycling or disposal and its cost to the planet, the balance would change and retailers might make more sustainable decisions.

Conclusion

Stopping or reducing waste is one of the keys to running a sustainable nursery, and it's worth spending some time and effort considering how to do this effectively in your setting and in your community – plus it could save you money. Colleagues and children need help with what goes in the recycling and what doesn't; with what can be composted and what can't – and it's not easy. Without government intervention to make retailers, distributors, and manufacturers more responsible for the packaging they produce, right through its lifetime, the onus lands on consumers like ourselves to make sustainable choices where it is practicable and affordable, and to work with suppliers who are making the effort, and to complain and take your account elsewhere when they are not.

Notes

1. www.1stwaste.co.uk/.
2. https://zerowasteboxes.terracycle.co.uk/.
3. Eden Project. (n.d.). *How to Make a Compost Heap: 10 top tips* [online]. Eden Project. Available from: www.edenproject.com.
4. Wormery: The Home of Wormeries, available at www.wormery.co.uk.
5. Smith, M.R. (n.d.) *How to Make Your Own Wormery* [online]. Vertical Veg. Available from: https://verticalveg.org.uk/how-to-make-your-own-wormery/.
6. For example, Spotty Green Frog at www.spottygreenfrog.co.uk.
7. www.findel-education.co.uk/.

16 Legal framework and relevant accreditations (not early years specific)

Introduction

There are a number of ways of evidencing and benchmarking your sustainability work to yourself, your customers and to other businesses. This chapter covers the Energy Saving Opportunity Scheme,[1] which is compulsory to all businesses employing over 250 people, but also considers some other structures for measuring and auctioning your work. It also refers to the new Environment Bill, which is currently in the UK Parliament.

The Energy Savings Opportunity Scheme (ESOS) UK

In the UK, the Environment Agency (EA) is responsible for ensuring the environment is protected and improved. They are focused on where environmental changes have the greatest impact, such as from flooding, not enough water for people and wildlife, quality of air, land and water, and applying environmental standards for industry. They act to reduce climate change and also help people and wildlife adapt to its consequences.

The EA is responsible for ESOS, which is an energy assessment and energy savings scheme established by the ESOS Regulations in 2014, now in its second phase. Most day nurseries and early childhood settings are not obliged to take part in ESOS because only large undertakings must take part. They have defined large as employing 250 or more people, or an annual turnover of 50 million euros (about £39 million) and an annual balance sheet over 43 million euros (about £34 million). Higher education institutions are excluded, but universities are not. If a company already has ISO 500001[2] covering all energy use certification, this counts as an ESOS assessment. As Tops Day Nurseries employs over 250 people and doesn't have any ISO standard, we did qualify for ESOS.

We had to do an energy assessment and have it externally verified and submitted to the government by 5 December 2015 or face a significant fine. We did do this, but large numbers of businesses did not, and apparently they are being sent compliance notices.

The reason I include ESOS is that it is actually one of the best places to start in your sustainable journey, whether it's compulsory or not, because this is a good structure to measure where you are and what the impact of your changes will be. As the infamous business maxim goes, you cannot manage what you do not measure – meaning that you can't know whether or not you are successful unless success is defined and tracked.

For ESOS, you have to undertake the following steps:

Measure your total energy consumption – combustible fuels, heat, renewable energy and electricity. This includes any vehicles, electricity and gas bills for all mileage, heating, ventilation, air conditioning, lifts, photocopiers, lighting, cookers, etc. You have to verify it all with invoices, meter readings and mileage claims. You have to gather your Energy Performance of Buildings Regulations certificates (graded A–G, A++ being the best). You then review your findings, and identify energy-saving opportunities, such as installing smart metres and energy monitoring tools, changing your opening hours, replacing driving with video conferencing, capital investment projects and behaviour change projects. With these in mind, you can then calculate how much you could save. You don't have to do any of them, but you would be a bit stupid to not make savings you have explicitly identified.

After the site visits, audit, and director sign-off, you advise the EA of compliance – and that's it.

Then you start putting together an action plan and start to work through that. Note that this is just about energy, so all your measures to reduce single-use plastic are not included in this action plan. However, rather than having several environmental action plans, we have one plan with everything in it. We have one overarching action plan, and one that is per site.

We split our action plan into things we could do for free (such as reminding each other to turn lights off); things that cost a small amount of money but we could make it back with the savings in one year (cost neutral from the finance director's point of view), such as light bulb changes and installing timers on the cold water dispenser; and things that we need to find the money to invest in because the return would take longer, such as solar panel installation.

We have had to do the process again because we are in ESOS Phase 2, the deadline for which was December 2019.

There are other international approaches to sustainability that contribute guidance that you might also like to consider:

Planet Mark sustainability certification (Eden Project)

'The Planet Mark is a sustainability certification which recognises outstanding achievements, encourages action and builds an empowered community of like-minded individuals'.[3]

The programme helps organisations to measure and then reduce their carbon emissions, energy and water consumption, travel, and the amount of waste they create. They aim to help organisations to engage their people in the process; help save money; build a stronger brand; and continue to thrive. It's aimed at all sizes of organisation, is worldwide and is clearly absolutely in line with what we need to do. The downside is that there is a hefty charge to register.

ISO 26000. Social Responsibility Guidance Standard

This is an international standard encouraging the responsibility and sustainability of organisations of all types. It was developed through a multi-year global process involving a wide range of stakeholders. It covers a very wide range of issues, including ethics, human rights, ecological sustainability and stakeholder engagement.

ISO 26000[4] was designed to be useful to as many different organisations as possible, including ours and NGOs. This is guidance rather than a management standard, so companies are not certified for this.

Global Reporting Initiative (GRI)

The GRI[5] is a multi-stakeholder international initiative which supports and drives best practice in sustainability and CSR reporting. It has a wide range of materials to support and help organisations to understand, analyse, respond and report on their environmental and social performance.

UN Global Compact (UNGC)

The UNGC[6] is a voluntary global programme for organisations to engage in a systematic approach to responsible management. Members are required to sign up and report their progress in implementing 10 universally accepted principles in the areas of human rights, labour, environment and anti-corruption. There are about 10,000 members globally.

Figure 16.1 Sustainable Development Goals

UN Sustainable Development Goals (SDGs)

The SDGs[7] are 17 goals, each split down into smaller objectives, developed by the United Nations to help countries establish their action plans. The key SDG for our sector is number 4 – Quality Education, but the goals are all inter-related, and most are relevant to us and our children/communities, e.g. Goal 1 is No Poverty, Goal 3 is Good Health and Well-being, and so on (see Figure 16.1).

The UN website (www.un.org/sustainabledevelopment/takeaction) includes 'The Lazy Person's Guide to Saving the World', which has some useful starting points that you might like to use with parents.

The Environment Bill 2019

The new bill[8] seeks to fulfil the government's ambition to establish a world-leading green governance body – the Office for Environmental Protection (OEP) – to provide advice, scrutiny, reporting and enforcement of environmental law once Britain has left the EU. The bill covers sectoral environmental regulation, such as standard-setting in areas such as air quality, wildlife and habitats, and better management of resources, water and waste (not climate change). With the delay in Brexit it is not clear what will happen to this. Some are concerned that the bill will not be tough enough; others welcome the opportunity to address issues such as importing shark fins into the UK not being illegal under EU law. Some are hoping that more demanding requirements could be made, whereas others (commercial fishermen) may want to place limitations on others. I think we can be sure that very little will be addressed through this bill immediately, but the hope is that once Parliament can stop focusing on Brexit, it might be able to focus on this and develop more challenging and appropriate policies for us in the UK. Certainly bans on single-use plastic products are being discussed, but it may take time for these to be made law and implemented. My impression is that we may have more influence over policy in the UK post-Brexit, so this will be an important time to be aware of what the legal framework is and to look out for ways to feed back our concerns as they arise (see Chapter 17).

Meanwhile, in countries across the world, in cities and states, legislatures are bringing in laws to limit plastic bags and other single-use plastics, to recycle bottles, and yet others are wanting to protect their plastic manufacturers and their employees, actually banning plastic bags being banned. Currently, plastic production is set to increase, not reduce.

Conclusion

Time will tell how legislation across the world and how the Environment Bill in the UK will affect us, compared with EU legislation, and how UN agreements are actioned. In the UK, only larger organisations (over 250 staff) are obliged to complete ESOS surveys, and no one is obliged to act on the results of the survey.

However, it makes good sense to measure your consumption/impact, and then to put an action plan in place to reduce your energy use because this will produce savings in running costs as well as reduce your impact/improve your sustainability.

I have described a number of schemes to choose from if you would rather have external accreditation or certification to offer independent evidence of your sustainability work, and there are further early-years-specific accreditations to achieve that are described in Chapter 18, or you may choose to use the simple sustainability checklist included in Appendix VI and adapt that for yourself. You might also find it helpful to visit the website GECCO.org.uk (registered charity focused on bringing you best practice in this area) for updates on this.

Notes

1. www.gov.uk/guidance/energy-savings-opportunity-scheme-esos.
2. www.iso.org/iso-50001-energy-management.html.
3. https://theplanetmark.com/.
4. www.iso.org/iso-26000-social-responsibility.html.
5. www.globalreporting.org/.
6. www.unglobalcompact.org/.
7. https://sustainabledevelopment.un.org/.
8. www.gov.uk/government/news/government-introduces-ground-breaking-environment-bill.

17 Advocacy

Introduction

Advocacy on behalf of our smallest citizens, in order to promote sustainability, is a many-faceted issue, with many stakeholders involved. There are some organisations that advocate for smaller organisations, where it's extremely hard to lift your thoughts beyond the immediate needs of small children. In some cases these will be state-funded or membership organisations, or they will be charities or a blend. However, some of us are able to involve ourselves, and I count myself lucky to be one of those – due to having a medium-sized team with a strong board of directors who can handle things very well in my absence. So, I share my knowledge in the hope that it will shorten your journey.

Advocacy includes involvement in politics, both national and local, with partner organisations and with parents and the community. Parents have a chapter all to themselves, so this is about politics and the community.

We are the ones looking after children with asthma, seeing plastic and rubbish on our beaches and parks, and seeing images of wildlife suffering, dying and becoming extinct, so there is no reason why we shouldn't make our views heard. We need to make it very clear what we would support in our politicians, so if you agree that we should bring sustainability into our early childhood institutions, day nurseries, centres, and families, then we need to speak up. This chapter is about who to speak to, where and when, and what to say.

How can we be heard by politicians?

Petitions

These are easy to spot. They come through social media all the time: official ones achieving 10,000 votes get a response from the government, and those with over

100,000 votes are considered for debate in the UK Parliament. It is also possible to sign Canadian and Australian petitions and even petitions asking our own governments to involve themselves in other countries' legislation. I personally sign all the ones I agree with, in the hope that another small cry might make a difference.

First, who are the politicians?

Do you have **local councillors** and do any of them have the portfolio for waste management? Do you have a **mayor**? Finding their details is easy on the internet – they want to be known. They will have contact details and visit schedules and possibly offices where you can arrange to meet with them or write to them.

Do you have a **Member of Parliament** or representative for a larger area that meets nationally? Similar to your councillors, it is very easy to find out who they are on the internet and their contact details. MPs generally only communicate with the constituents that live/vote in their area, but will also visit your nurseries for events to discuss your concerns. They usually like to be photographed being in the community, and a press-worthy event such as opening a new service, or celebrating a particular success, helps give you an opportunity that will be interesting and beneficial for their image as well, so everyone benefits. You can also go to Parliament and 'lobby' them – catch them when they go through the lobby and speak with them.

Politicians find it more convenient to listen to groups of individuals represented by a committee: it's a more efficient use of their time than listening to us one at a time. They also need facts and real stories rather than generalisations so they have evidence to take back to their colleagues and the civil servants, and are able to ask questions in Parliament. You can also go to party conferences; you can attend courses run by political lobbying specialists, often ex-MPs and their assistants, to learn more about this type of work; or you could hire a public relations specialist to guide you through – but that will not be cheap, hence usually being left to those with multi-million-pound businesses wanting to push or stop particular legislation rather than to a sector such as ours.

How do we work with politicians?

- Write to them or email them. Let them know you will vote for leaders who promote sustainability. Give them real stories and evidence.

- Attend their meetings or 'surgeries'.

- Attend marches or demonstrations if you are brave enough and there is one you can organise or join.

- Attend community events, carnivals and fundraisers and attract them to your stand or truck with your children and your lovely smile, and then speak up.

- Invite them to attend your centre. Politicians like photographs of themselves with small children (willing, smiley children who have written parents' permission as well as their own).

Use social media. Increasingly, this is being used for polls, surveys, petitions, blogs, and general communication and is a specialist skill in itself. I founded and then co-sponsored an **All Party Parliamentary Group (APPG)**[1] through the capable and expert hands of lobby professionals called Connect. Connect are professionals in the political world, and knew how to invite MPs to form a group to discuss early years settings separate from the government nursery schools. They help our voices be heard and gather some leading voices already representing the sector to contribute both with knowledge and financing. The MPs control the group now it's formed, but their administrators (Connect) do the groundwork – arranging the meetings and speakers. The sponsors are able to attend, giving us access to MPs that we wouldn't have had otherwise.

Figure 17.1 Cheryl Hadland hosting a visit from local MP

Figure 17.2 Cheryl Hadland and Amy Alderson (Tops Ops. Director) at the House of Commons, asking MPs to pledge their support for a sustainable early years education

Representative organisations

Do you have a representative organisation whose job it is to represent us politically? In the UK, we have the National Day Nurseries Association (NDNA), the Early Years Alliance (EYA) and PACEY. Their membership crosses over into each other's areas, but broadly, the NDNA represents private day nurseries but is part funded by the government, the EYA represents preschools (who could be private day nurseries and they also represent some childminders) and PACEY represents childminders. But the Early Years Alliance also represents childminders and is independent of government funding. Representation is fragmented in the UK, as indeed is the whole sector, with 23,000 day nurseries, 9500 preschools, 40,000 childminders and 400 grant-maintained nurseries, the vast majority of which are singles and groups of two and three. Having different representative groups giving conflicting ideas and opinions leaves the politicians confused and somewhat paralysed. There is one main research organisation, though – CEEDA – which offers additional surveys, questionnaires and analysis as well as benchmarking data for the sector, which is shared with the representative organisations and politicians. This at least helps to inform opinions within and externally. Due to huge financial pressures that threaten financial sustainability in the sector currently, there is negligible focus on environmental sustainability issues from the representative organisations so far.

National nursery chains

Some of the national nursery chains and smaller nursery groups are interested in sustainability and already have a direct line to politicians through lobbying. The biggest appear to be shy of representing the whole sector, in my experience, citing focus on expanding as being their reason (first-hand). The very largest of the national chains in the UK has only around 330 settings, less than 2 per cent of the whole sector.

Groups or voluntary organisations

Some nurseries have grouped together into groups or voluntary organisations such as Ofsted Big Conversation (OBC), Nursery Owners, Nursery Managers, Early Years Best Practice, and have meetings and/or Facebook groups to communicate and share best practice and experiences – a quick search of Facebook will offer many options.

Not-for-profits and non-governmental organisations

You might find one of the local, national or international charities, not-for-profit organisations or non-governmental organisations (NGOs) can help or can include you in their campaigns. For example, we have been working with UNICEF[2] on their clean air campaign. These organisations are set up by passionate people around a specific issue or sector, and they can be very informative, very effective at being heard and successful at putting pressure on corporations and politicians to change. Some have amazing track records and are doing very well. They can be very competitive with each other, as they are competing for funding to operate and function, much like a limited company. Though their objectives are more charitable in appearance, calling on your money to help with conservation, cancer or similar causes, they may well be paying a lot of your donations into their administration and marketing rather than the research you thought you were contributing to. It is always worth checking up on their accounts with the Charity Commission.

I had a meeting with a CEO of a four-strong group of nurseries in the Midlands recently. We were talking about charities and he related that he had checked on a charity that had tugged at his heart strings. He was going to donate to them until he checked their accounts to discover that the CEO was earning over £300,000 a year! Despite the wonderful aims and objectives of the organisation, he felt he couldn't engage. This was an educated choice I admired. I also saw him con-tribute directly and anonymously to someone he knew was in financial difficulty – every penny would be used by a particular family in need. It isn't easy, and it's about personal choice.

There is a very long list of NGOs, charities and not-for-profits, with more setting up all the time. I started an appendix listing the ones that I know about that are focused on sustainability and relevant to our sector, but there are so many and they change so often that I leave it to you to search the internet when you need to. Extinction Rebellion[3] activities have caught the attention of the media recently. Be aware that there are more unscrupulous organisations running that look like charities but are actually companies that do not declare their accounts, and just donate a tiny percentage of their profits to various charities and trade on the goodwill from that to sell their products, such as jewellery, as an effective marketing ploy.

B corps

You might also be interested in becoming a B corporation[4] – B corps are for-profit companies certified by the non-profit B Lab that have to meet rigorous standards of social and environmental performance, accountability and transparency. It is a growing community of companies in more than 50 countries with over 130 industries working together toward a unifying goal: to redefine success in business. B corps use business as a force for good.

Ethical Corporation

Ethical Corporation[5] is an independent business intelligence, publishing and networking company founded in 2001. They publish detailed studies and organise business conferences focused on sustainability every year in several cities across the world. Their 'Innovate, Collaborate and Transform the Value Chain' conversation in 2019 included tackling key climate impacts, gaining greater traceability and transparency, mainstream and scale circular innovations, and achieving a low-carbon supply chain.

Chamber of Commerce

You might find your local Chamber of Commerce[6] interested in supporting a war on waste, or a plastic-free zone or week, as some of ours have. This is a welcome involvement from a very powerful and influential organisation, and indeed group of organisations, as your local one will be affiliated to others in the area as well as nationally.

Where do politicians meet and where else can you raise your concerns?

Surgeries

MPs all run surgeries from their offices in the local area and it is possible to make an appointment to meet them there, and also to invite them to visit you in your local business.

Networking meetings

Networking meetings are sometimes organised by local solicitors or accountants, or are a business in themselves, and may invite MPs or other political figures to attend. These often have a speaker or two present to offer something additional to those attending. If you don't mind a bit of public speaking, volunteering to speak at networking meetings can be good for your business, but also for sustainability if you can communicate what you are doing, and what you would like from others, to benefit the future for our children. There are some networking groups listed in Appendix V.

Awards

Some organisations offer opportunities to sponsor or to win prizes, for example for the woman running the most sustainable business, or for the most sustainable idea, or for the environmental entrepreneur of the year, or sustainable business of the year, by area or nationally. In our sector, such awards also come from the National Day Nurseries Association, *Nursery Management Today* (NMT) magazine, and the Venus Awards, which focuses on women in business.

Conferences

Early years conferences are organised around the world, and are of course an opportunity to network, to hear about sustainability or to talk about sustainability. In the UK, early years conferences are organised by Broadway; Nursery World Conferences; *Nursery Management Today* (NMT); Childcare Expos; the National Day Nurseries Association (NDNA); the Early Years Alliance; and the National Association of Head Teachers (NAHT). Recently, I've also attended and spoken on sustainability at the International Early Childhood Symposium held in Sydney and the bi-annual World Forum Foundation events in Auckland (2017) and Macao, China (2019). I'm sure there are many others occurring around the world that I'm not aware of, but you might be – in which case, perhaps ask for sustainability to be one of the subjects covered, if it isn't already.

Businesses

Companies of all sizes are also increasingly interested in being perceived as performing on their third bottom line, corporate social responsibility, and may have an identified percentage of their profit that they commit to donating to charities or worthy community organisations – perhaps like yours!

If you can offer the opportunity for them, or their staff, to work with you to benefit the community, climate change, or other CSER goals, the partnership could be beneficial for all involved. Examples of this taking place include developing the children's garden or a community outdoor space, or as part of their circular economy (recycling their cable reels or pallets, for example, or giving them your food waste). They might also be able to share this practice with other businesses and their own political connections, and you spread the word that way. There are always some who would prefer to just pay lip service to their responsibilities, but business executives are increasingly realising that their staff are becoming more and more purpose-driven in their work. If they want to keep their staff, they need to contribute to society as well as selling a product or service. Some already acknowledge that a happy, prosperous life isn't just about an ever increasing income and turnover, but about quality and purpose. Some shareholders want ever-increasing returns on their investment, and ever-increasing productivity and growth rather than service.

Benevolent and generous benefactors and philanthropists are also making a real difference to children and the world, such as Warren Buffet, Bill and Melinda Gates, Oprah Winfrey, Roger Federer (tennis), Tom Cruise (actor) and many others.

We also have the Small Business Federation[7] and the Association of Employment and Learning Providers[8] who will also represent us when our agendas coincide, which they clearly could do on sustainability.

Nature reserves

We are fortunate to have nature reserves, sites of special scientific interest (SSIs), (SSSIs),[9] forests and bird sanctuaries to visit in our local communities. Let's learn the rules and behaviours required and visit them if we possibly can; what wonderful opportunities to teach the children – far better than taking them to marine parks and zoos, where animals are kept in captivity. It is hard for young children to distinguish between circumstances where creatures are kept in captivity for human purposes and those in order to protect them/breed because they are endangered in the wild. Farms are fabulous for introducing children to domesticated animals, such as chickens, lambs, piglets, foals, and even cats and dogs, because they may not have experienced animals in their home lives. We do need to be conscious of the treatment and killing of animals for humans; children need to learn that the lamb they are stroking could be killed for their Sunday lunch, in a way that is acceptable to parents who may be farmers or run abattoirs or a handbag shop, and other parents who will be vegan or vegetarian, or have religious or cultural rules that preclude eating meat(s) or fish/shellfish. It is not for us to judge parents, but we can educate the children so they can make informed choices about what they eat, and use, if options are available. There may be different options and rules at home compared with the early years service/day nursery, in this and in all areas.

What do we say?

In your communications, whether in writing or face to face, you have a real opportunity to show politicians you care about a sustainable environment for the children. Tell them about your policies, about your beach and park cleans, about what the children need in order to have a healthy environment to grow up in. Our smallest children need representation because they are not able to do it themselves yet. We and their parents are their voice. Remember, the politicians want to hear what they have to do to get our vote – so tell them!

Explain what help you want from them: tax relief for sustainable materials; manufacturers to be responsible for their products post-sale; true cost charges to be passed to companies using unsustainable products, such as plastic packaging or vehicles or animals or chemicals that pollute the air, sea or land. Give them ideas. They like to join in with successful and well-organised campaigns that are in line with popular policies.

You can also explain your experiences of greenwash and maybe show them where you feel products are being misrepresented to us or are keeping us in the dark on their impact – such as 'disposable' nappies, cups, balloons, straws, and '100% pure' baby wipes, all of which are mostly plastic that will last for 400 years. 'Biodegradable' balloons that can kill a turtle well before they biodegrade … I could go on! Your voice counts and we are seeing actions such as banning straws and cotton buds with plastic sticks planned to be law in 2020. Every single individual counts, so do not think that you can't make a difference just because you are one mum or childminder or nursery owner: you can!

When?

Members of Parliament are only free to visit their constituents in the UK on Fridays, so if you want a nursery opened or have a special event that you think they might like to attend, it needs to be on a Friday. Be aware that if there is an emergency and all MPs are recalled back to Westminster, or if there is a general election announced, they won't be able to attend. It's best to have a back-up plan if possible. Members of Parliament work long hours and often seven days a week, so you could see them at Parliament or at events at any time.

Timing is important. Press like to have information and photographs as quickly as possible, and tying in with themes relevant to your area, festivals or awareness dates such as Waste Week, Recycle Week, National Honey Bee Day, Plastic Free July, etc., will help you gain publicity. Even if you don't achieve much publicity, these are all wonderful opportunities to learn with the children and the families you serve – any excuse for a party and some fun in our sector!

There are many more awareness days you could celebrate, but some starters are listed in Appendix IV.

Conclusion

Owners and managers of day nurseries lead a very busy life, with heavy demands on them, and it is very hard to find the time to take a more strategic view, never mind a national or international perspective, but we find we are a soft touch compared with our unionised colleagues in the schools sector, and often things are done *to* the sector rather than with us. Offering some information may help those who can find the time and know how important it is to be heard, to use their voice to advocate for our children and sustainability.

Notes

1. https://publications.parliament.uk/pa/cm/cmallparty/190102/childcare-and-early-education.htm.
2. www.unicef.org.uk/clean-air-child-health-air-pollution/.
3. https://rebellion.earth/.
4. https://bcorporation.net/.
5. www.ethicalcorp.com.
6. www.britishchambers.org.uk/.
7. www.fsb.org.uk/.
8. www.aelp.org.uk/.
9. https://data.gov.uk/dataset/5b632bd7-9838-4ef2-9101-ea9384421b0d/sites-of-special-scientific-interest-england.

Standards, curricula and accreditation specific to early years

18

Introduction

In this chapter we look at some frameworks for early years, some of which have sustainability integrated within them, and some do not. Some countries such as England have a curriculum that is used by other countries who do not have their own system. Scotland has its own curriculum separate from England. Detail on the English curriculum is below, and I also mention Australia and New Zealand because sustainability is integrated in their curricula and has been for many years. I have deliberately used 'framework', 'standards', and 'curricula' interchangeably, rather than enter that debate at this point.

In addition, Eco-Schools is the largest international accreditation scheme, and the Children's Environmental Health Network (CEHN) is an American multidisciplinary organisation whose mission is to protect the developing child from environmental health hazards, promote a healthier environment and have a detailed set of criteria. And, the new charity on the block in the UK to engage in this area is Surfers Against Sewage with their 'Plastic Free Schools' accreditation – which is actually focused on dropping single-use plastic.

The Early Years Foundation Stage (EYFS)

EYFS are UK Standards from the Department for Education, as inspected by Ofsted.[1] They currently do not include specific reference to sustainability. However, there are a number of areas where this agenda can contribute to children's spiritual, moral, social and cultural development, and indeed potentially contribute to an outstanding grading, being above and beyond what is expected (see Table 18.1).

Examples of how sustainability contributes to the EYFS are shown in Table 18.2.

Table 18.1 EYFS links to sustainability: spiritual, moral, social and cultural

Examples of sustainability actions that could contribute to an outstanding grading:	
Understanding of the consequences of their behaviour and actions	Understanding that reducing, re-using, recycling helps to reduce the impact of waste on our environment
Interest in investigating and offering reasoned views about moral and ethical issues and ability to understand and appreciate the viewpoints of others on these issues	Discussing sustainability while they are working, playing and in circle times
Use of a range of social skills in different contexts, for example working and socialising with other pupils	*While* gardening, growing food, preparing it and eating with others
Willingness to participate in a variety of communities and social settings, including by volunteering, cooperating well with others and being able to resolve conflicts effectively	Helping with putting the waste food into the wormery, into composting, tidying up, gardening
Acceptance and engagement with the fundamental British values of democracy, the rule of law, individual liberty and mutual respect and tolerance of those with different faiths and beliefs; they develop and demonstrate skills and attitudes that will allow them to participate fully in and contribute positively to life in modern Britain	Talking about vegetarians, vegans, Hindus, Muslims, Jews who refuse meat or various meats, shellfish, cruelty to other animals Taking part in their community, e.g. beach cleans, carnivals
Interest in exploring, improving understanding of and showing respect for different faiths and cultural diversity and the extent to which they understand, accept, respect and celebrate diversity, as shown by their tolerance and attitudes towards different religious, ethnic and socio-economic groups in the local, national and global communities	Learning about vegetarians, vegans, different faiths and cultures, and discussing how precious water and minerals and oil is in different countries and what we can do to help conserve them Global communities suffering rising water levels due to global warming – caused by our greenhouse gases – and what we can do to reduce this Global communities and ourselves suffering poisoning of our oceans, and fish, caused by our plastic and chemical waste – and what we can do in our nurseries to reduce this

Table 18.2 EYFS links to sustainability: physical, PSE, understanding of the world

EYFS states	Examples of how sustainability contributes
Physical development: Children must also be helped to understand the importance of physical activity, and to make healthy choices in relation to food.	When watering the plants, digging in the garden When choosing fruit and vegetables, water instead of sweets and biscuits
Personal, social and emotional development: To form positive relationships and develop respect for others	To respect others' opinions – turning off lights, turning heating down, putting rubbish in the bin, sorting recycling
Understanding the world: Guiding children to make sense of their physical world and their community through opportunities to explore, observe and find out about people, places, technology and the environment Similarities and differences in relation to places, objects, materials and living things, talking about their own environment and different environments, observing animals and plants and explaining why some things occur and talk about changes Technology; children recognise that a range of technology is used in places such as homes and schools. They select and use technology for particular purposes Exploring and using media and materials They safely use and explore a variety of materials, tools and techniques, experimenting with colour, design, texture, form and function	Learning about the environment, outside in particular, about recycling, re-using, wormeries, composting, glass, plastic, metal, paper Learning about change in animals: caterpillars into butterflies, eggs into chicks/chickens, growing plants, frog spawn into tadpoles and frogs What happens to our waste – water, recycling bins, generate waste, food waste Selecting technology for particular purposes, using YouTube to learn more about the world and its resources They are made aware of the sustainability of materials, tools and techniques – where they come from, what happens to them next – re-use or recycle

Development matters in the EYFS

This non-statutory guidance material supports practitioners in implementing the statutory requirements of the EYFS.[2] The themes of 'A Unique Child', 'Positive Relationships' and 'Enabling Environments' add up to 'Learning and Development', and the document goes on to describe the **characteristics of effective learning**:

- Playing and exploring – engagement: finding out and exploring, playing with what they know, being willing to 'have a go'.

- Active learning – motivation; being involved and concentrating, keep trying and enjoying achieving what they set out to do.

- Creating and thinking critically – thinking; having their own ideas, making links and choosing ways to do things.

There is no advice specific regarding sustainability.

OMEP-UK

OMEP-UK[3] is a partner in the World Organization for Early Childhood Education and has recently launched the Early Childhood Education for Sustainable Citizenship Passport Award Scheme. Each child has a passport that not only summarises the provisions of the United Nations Convention on the Rights of the Child (1989), but defines sustainable citizenship as a lifelong emergent capability. The passport may provide discounts at wildlife conservation parks and other related community resources and services. Each child can collect up to 15 award stickers for their passports to show their relevant achievements at bronze, silver and gold level. The organisation supporting this also receives an award if 60 per cent of the children attending achieve their awards. Typical achievements include identification of three wild birds, wildlife habitats, recycling waste materials, and the recognition of cultural and linguistic diversity.

Education for sustainable citizenship (ESC) in early childhood

Siraj-Blatchford and Brock offer an 'emergent curriculum perspective' in their guidance for educators. The perspective recognises that in order for young children to make sustainable balanced decisions, there are attitudes, skills, knowledge and understandings that are required first. Further, the children learn sustainable citizenship through play (free flow supported by adults providing focused activities and appropriate resources in line with the schemas and schemes observed or modelled; see the SchemaPlay Zone of Proximal Development Flow model.[4] Thus children learn empathy and interdependency about society and culture, about the environment, about economics, and they develop literacy and numeracy.

Adults need to set a good example, showing that we enjoy and are proud of our own sustainable actions. And adults must provide experiences and opportunities for children to learn about the basic 'pillars', economic exchanges, diversity and respect that must be shown to other peoples and cultures, as well as the need to learn about the natural environment and the importance of us all accepting responsibility in caring for it.

This model ties in well with the new Ofsted Inspection Framework (September 2019), where the impact of the adult teaching, role-modelling and adjusting the environment in order to support each individual child's development as well as understanding and demonstrating cultural capital are important components.

United Nations Convention on the Rights of the Child

This is our human rights treaty which sets out the civil, political, economic, social, health and cultural rights of children. Many nations ratified this convention, including the UK and 195 other countries. The rights are as follows, a number of which are relevant to the sustainability ethos (which I have emphasised in bold below):

- The Right to Live in a Family Environment: Every child should be able to live in a family, either with their parents or in an attachment-based, family-styled environment while experiencing a sense of belonging.

- The Right to a Stable, Loving and Nurturing Environment: Every child should be able to experience attachment with its caregiver through a stable, loving and nurturing family environment.

- The Right to Healthcare and Nutrition: Every child will receive regular and high-quality medical attention at all times. We will inculcate in them **good health and hygiene habits. They will be provided with healthy, nutritious and delicious food in every meal**.

- The Right to Clean Water, Electrical Power and a Safe Environment: Every child will receive **consistent access to clean water and electrical power in a safe environment**.

- The Right to a Quality Education: Every child will receive quality education appropriate to their abilities and interests, supplemental enrichment programmes, and will have access to higher education and/or vocational training.

- The Right to Equal Opportunities: Every child will receive the same opportunities regardless of gender, race, ethnicity, origin, economic status, religion, creed and/or handicapping condition.

- The Right to Guidance from a Caring Adult: Every child will be actively supported by caring, trained adults who will invest in the child's success.

▓ The Right to be Heard and Participate in Decisions that Affect Them: Every child will have the right to express their views freely in all matters affecting them. They will be encouraged to develop and express independent thought.[5]

▓ The Right to be Prepared for Active and Responsible Citizenship: Every child will **be taught responsibility, a sense of community, and given the opportunity to give back**.

▓ The Right to be Protected from Abuse and Neglect: Every child will receive effective protection from harmful influences, abuse (physical and mental), neglect, corporal punishment and all forms of exploitation.[6] Additionally, every child is provided opportunities to make complaints to an identifiable third party. Those caring for children are trained and given appropriate discipline techniques.

▓ The Right to Dignity and Freedom: Every child is treated with respect and lives in adequate conditions with sufficient belongings that foster a sense of dignity and freedom.

▓ The Right to Spiritual Development: Every child is provided opportunities to develop a religious affiliation that promotes spirituality and moral development.

Modern Educational Movement (MEM)

This curriculum model is being applied in many preschools in Portugal. Folque[7] describes how the MEM model is increasingly being applied in Portugal to achieve aims that are broadly consistent with sustainability teaching. For example, their projects include cultivating vegetables for the children to eat and campaigning for better access by walking rather than using cars.

Australia and New Zealand

In Australia, the Early Years Learning Framework is an early childhood curriculum which is delivered in learning programmes around the country. Sustainability has been part of that for the last decade.[8] The Eco Smart System, developed by the Australian ECEEN, includes amongst their aimed outcomes for children to become socially responsible and show respect for the environment. Another aim is for children to resource their own learning through connecting with people, places, technologies, and natural and processed materials.

Yet, when I visited day nurseries in Sydney this year, I found them using glitter and washing the micro-plastic into their water supply, using single-use plastic gloves and aprons, and yet not being allowed to eat the food they grew in their gardens. They did demonstrate lots of positive actions, also, such as re-using and upcycling a high percentage of their resources. The children had many activities available that related to animals, both on land and in the ocean, and they hadn't used food materials to play with for a very long time – unlike the UK, where some nurseries are still using pasta and rice as an alternative to sand. In the UK, playing with food has been taught as good practice, whereas the Australians consider it disrespectful to those without enough food to eat.

In New Zealand, Te Whariki[9] is the early years curriculum, set up in 1996. There are three education for sustainability professional development pro-grammes (Enviroschools Programme, the National EfS Team and Matauranga Talao) and they have been found to be achieving great inclusion of sustainability content and more integrative teaching across the curriculum. Sustainability is now embedded in the New Zealand curriculum and they have progressed to iden-tifying that sustainability leadership calls for collaborative rather than top–down management. This means that anyone can become a leader, be it centre owners and managers, teachers, student teachers, or children. Such leaders are deeply aware of the impact of their actions on the environment and those around them.

Education for sustainability is not mandatory in New Zealand. However, the principles, strands and goals do implicitly provide guidance for teachers to include sustainability practices within their centre curricula. Anita Croft's research makes an interesting case both for and against the efficacy of teaching sustainability to the very young and is well worth a read.[10] She shares many of our concerns that today's children are not having the opportunity to connect with the natural environment as we have in the past. This is a growing concern as the children need sensitive adults who can share their sense of wonder and support their growing understanding of the world around them if teachers are not ecologi-cally aware.

Eco-Schools

Eco-Schools' own website describes Eco-Schools as a global programme that engages 18 million children across 64 different countries.[11] It is operated by the Foundation for Environmental Education (FEE), which was launched in 1994 in response to the 1992 UN Rio Earth Summit. South Africa was the first country to join when it went global in 2001. It is the largest international network of teach-ers and students in the world and extends to EcoCampus at university level.

Environmental charity Keep Britain Tidy is the Eco-Schools National Operator for England, where more than 18,000 schools are registered and 1200 schools currently hold the internationally recognised Eco-Schools Green Flag.

The programme involves nine topics: biodiversity, energy, litter, global citizenship, healthy living, school grounds, transport, waste, and water. Strangely, the international themes also include marine and coast, and climate change.

The programme is pupil-led rather than adult-led, which doesn't make it a perfect match for the early years, where we need staff and parents to engage, teach and role-model what an eco-community is all about, but we are engaging with the system nonetheless, as are many other early years centres, day nurseries and preschools in the UK.

There is a section on early years resources in each of the nine areas, but the focus is mainly on primary-aged children as activities are suitable for ages 7+. A rare 5+ activity is to create a wildlife garden poster. There are none for the under-3s, although Chester Zoo have provided some, including making a yoghurt pot bird feeder (with a plastic yoghurt pot and lard or olive spread). Another is making a 'Toad Abode' with a water-based acrylic paint, unspecified glue, and a terracotta pot, as well as an idea for a wildflower wellie, using an old wellie, compost, seeds and gloves. None of these have teacher notes, which is a missed opportunity to discuss the desirability and sustainability of using plastic, acrylic paint, PVC glue, and gloves when other options are available.

Both the bronze and silver stages are free to engage in. The programme has a methodology of seven steps, starting with the establishment of the Eco-Schools Committee, then environmental review, action plan, monitoring and evaluation, curriculum linking, informing and involving the wider community, and finally producing an Eco Code. The International Green Flag is accessed through the FEE, so there is a charge, but it's something to be proud of. It demonstrated that the school has engaged with becoming more eco, but it is very important that this isn't reduced to a box-ticking exercise.

The self-evaluation questions are very basic, and they don't seem to have evolved to include what we know about the destructive impact of plastic. Going through the process led to some creativity in colleagues and finding resources such as the WonderGroveKids video entitled *Save Water to Help the Earth*,[12] which shows kids talking to other kids about saving water while they brush their teeth, for example (and includes jokes such as 'what did the ocean say to the shore? Nothing, it just waves'). It is a bit American and uses words such as faucet rather than tap, but the number of videos available on their YouTube channel increases every day, so you might find they add a useful dimension to your teaching, when shown occasionally.

Plastic Free Schools

Another initiative we are seeing in the UK is Plastic Free Schools,[13] although the name is rather misleading, because the mission is to tackle single-use plastic rather than all plastic. The scheme is around having a Plastic Free Committee group and working together to discuss and action what to do about plastic pollution. These may be some good questions to consider for a first meeting:

- Is plastic pollution/litter a problem at your school?

- Where is plastic pollution escaping from in the school grounds?

- What can we do to eliminate single-use plastics from our school?

Ongoing meetings are expected to come up with at least three actions straight away, and working on a further three, such as boycotting one-use water bottles, straws and plastic bags, but also to take part or organise rubbish clean-ups, write to MPs, get photographic evidence of manufacturers' products causing the littering, and then writing to those companies and boycotting those products.

Surfers Against Sewage (SAS) are now rivalling the Marine Conversation Society for their work to protect the oceans, and I noticed that they were also one of the small group of charities chosen to benefit at the recent marriage of Prince Harry to Meghan Markle, now the Duke and Duchess of Sussex.

Children's Environmental Health Network (CEHN)

CEHN is an American multi-disciplinary organisation whose mission is to protect the developing child from environmental health hazards and promote a healthier environment. CEHN has been working since 1992 on education, protective policy and support of research vital to children's environmental health protection. Their website[14] provides significant information on their research, children's environmental health and resources.

CEHN began managing the Eco-Healthy Child Care Program in October 2010. This American national environmental health training and assessment programme has already endorsed 1000 child care providers in 44 states and continues to expand. The EHCC checklist provides 30 easy-to-follow steps to reduce environmental health hazards in nursery settings. Childcare providers in the US who comply with 24 of these steps can become EHCC endorsed (with appropriate payment, etc.).

I think it's worth sharing the areas of their work as it goes further than ours in some areas, such as no fitted carpets. References to where waste can be recycled are, of course, American, but this does provide the opportunity for reflection and potentially action. This is, after all, a work in progress for everyone. This is what they would want us to sign up to:[15]

Pesticides and pest prevention

1. We use non-toxic techniques inside and outside of the facility to prevent and control pests (both insects and weeds). If a serious threat remains and pesticide application is the only viable option, parents and staff are notified in advance and a licensed professional applies the least toxic, effective product at a time when children will have the least exposure to the application area for at least 12 hours (see manufacturer's instructions to ensure 12 hours is enough time).

2. We thoroughly wash all fruits and vegetables to avoid possible exposure to pesticides, and we take the opportunity to educate children about the importance of doing so.

Air quality

3. We avoid conditions that lead to excess moisture, because moisture contributes to the growth of mold and mildew. We maintain adequate ventilation (which can include exhaust fans and open screened windows). We repair water leaks and keep humidity within a desirable range (30–50%).

4. We do not allow vehicles to idle in our designated parking areas.

5. We do not use scented or unscented candles or air fresheners.

6. During operating hours, we prohibit smoking, including the use of e-cigarettes or 'vaping', anywhere on the premises or in sight of children. (Note: For the healthiest environment for children and staff, smoking should not be allowed on the premises at any time.)

Household chemicals

7. We use fragrance-free, 3rd party certified (www.ecologo.org, www.epa.gov/saferchoice, OR www.greenseal.org) least-toxic cleaning, sanitizing and disinfecting products. When sanitizers and disinfectants are required, they are used only for their intended purpose and in strict accordance with all label instructions.

8. We use chlorine bleach only when and where it is required or recommended by state and local authorities. We use it prudently and never use more than necessary.

9. We do not use aerosol sprays of any kind.

10. We use only no-VOC or low-VOC (volatile organic compounds) household paints and do not paint when children are present.

Lead

11. We use only cold water for drinking, cooking and making baby formula; we flush all cooking and drinking outlets after long periods of non-use; and we clean debris from our outlet screens or aerators on a regular basis. If we suspect that there could be lead in our drinking water, we have our water tested and, if appropriate, use water filtration devices that have been certified to remove lead for additional treatment of drinking water at the outlet.

12. Our building was built after 1978 OR 1) We maintain our facility to minimise lead hazards AND 2) We follow the Federal requirements in EPA's Renovate Right brochure before painting, remodelling, renovating, or making repairs that disturb paint.

13. To avoid possible lead exposure, we do not use imported, old or hand-made pottery to cook, store or serve food or drinks

14. To reduce possible exposure to lead-contaminated dirt, we supply a rough mat at the entrance of our facility and encourage the wiping of shoes before entering – or – we are a shoe-free facility.

15. We screen our toys for lead by searching www.cpsc.gov.

Mercury

16. We do not use any mercury-containing thermometers or thermostats. Instead we use digital options.

17. We securely store all used batteries and fluorescent and compact fluorescent light bulbs; we then recycle them at a hazardous waste facility. Visit www.earth911.com to find locations.

Furniture and carpets

18. To avoid possible exposure to flame retardants, we ensure furniture is in good condition without foam or inside stuffing exposed. Stuffed animals, carpet padding, nap mats, pillows, and other foam items are also intact

19. Furniture is made of solid wood or low-VOC (volatile organic compounds) products, with few items made of particleboard. When purchasing furniture or renovating, we choose either solid wood (new or used) or products that have low VOCs.

20. We do not have permanently installed carpeting where children are present.

21. Area rugs are vacuumed daily and cleaned at least twice a year and as needed using fragrance-free, 3rd party certified (www.ecologo.org, www.epa.gov/saferchoice, OR www.greenseal.org) cleaners.

Art supplies

22. We use only non-toxic art supplies approved by the Art and Creative Materials Institute (ACMI). Look for ACMI non-toxic seal 'AP' at www.acmiart.org.

Plastics and plastic toys

23. We avoid products made out of PVC (such as: soft vinyl dolls, beach balls, and 'rubber ducky' chew toys). We use only those products labeled 'PVC-free' or 'phthalate-free'.

24. When using a microwave, we never heat children's food in plastic containers, plastic wrap or plastic bags.

25. When choosing baby bottles, sippy cups or drinking cups, we only use safer alternatives: products made of glass, covered with a silicone sleeve (a silicone bottle jacket to prevent breakage), OR those made with safer plastics such as polypropylene or polyethylene. We encourage the families we serve to purchase and provide the same.

Treated playground equipment

26. We do not have playground equipment made of CCA treated wood (pre-2004) – or – if we do, we apply 2 coats of waterproof stain or sealant at least once a year.

Radon

27. We have tested our facility for radon. If elevated levels of radon are found, we take action to mitigate. We have visited www.epa.gov/radon for resources, and have researched state requirements and guidelines to learn more.

Recycling and garbage storage

28. We recycle all paper, cardboard, glass, aluminum and plastic bottles.

29. We keep our garbage covered at all times to avoid attracting pests and to minimize odours.

Education and awareness

30. We create opportunities to educate the families we serve on eco-healthy practices.

For more information on any checklist items, visit www.cehn.org/ehcc/resources. I am on their mailing list and read what they are engaged in with interest; they are particularly engaged in fresh air initiatives at the moment.

Liverpool John Moores University developed some innovative resources for the early years sector in support of their contribution to the Early Childhood Education for Sustainability Development Framework (ECEfS), including a suite of resources in line with the EYFS to support early childhood education in environmental sustainability. These resources help settings with the challenges they face when trying to integrate environmentally sustainable practices and learning opportunities, and include an ECEfS Pedagogical Toolkit – Activity Resource Pack, an Early Years Settings Implementation Pack and an Early Years Settings Poster.[16]

What is really interesting is that the poster uses the same nine eco-themes that Eco-Schools have used, tied in with the prime and specific areas of the EYFS, as well as Fundamental British Values. Also, instead of the seven steps of the Eco-Schools, the ECEfS have eight rather different steps that are much more appropriate for early years practitioners:

- gain support

- keep it simple

- connect with other experienced, sustainable settings

- establish a support network of other settings in a similar position

- family and child involvement

- resourcefulness, creativity and streamlining

- communication

- celebrate and share.

They have some nice self-assessment matrices on each of their nine areas (see below), which also consider lower effort and/or cost to higher effort and/or cost. The university has produced a simple tick-box list you could also use.[17] As ever, we must make sure that changes in procedures and processes are consistently followed through:

Biodiversity

▦ Discussions with children and families to find out how they would like to make changes to the outdoor area to support local diversity and nature play.

▦ Borrow a bug, reptile or mammal collection.

▦ Put up posters of animals, birds and insects in your setting and try to identify visitors to your garden.

▦ Plant a range of plants in your garden to provide shelter, nesting and food for animals and birds that might be passing through your outdoor area. Include or retain trees and tall shrubs, dense or spikey lower shrubs, plants that provide fruit, nectar and seeds.

▦ Talk to your local [plant] nursery to select suitable plants for your outdoor area.

▦ Tell your families about the actions you've completed to increase your setting's biodiversity.

▦ Include tips in your newsletter. It might inspire families to look at what they can do in their own garden! Add mulch, logs, large flat rocks and stone piles for lizards, animals and insects.

▦ Add a nesting box to your outdoor area to replicate natural shelters such as tree hollows. They are fun, cheap and easy to make.

▦ Create a frog pond that is safe for your children at your setting to access.

Energy

▦ Maximise the use of natural light and ventilation during the day.

▦ Turn off lights each day during rest time.

▦ Place signs near all light switches, power points to act as reminders to turn off when not needed.

▦ Use a check list at the end of each day to make sure all lights and appliances are turned off.

- Use fans where possible instead of air conditioners.

- Use correct temperature settings on air conditioners and section off rooms when heating or cooling.

- Make sure children are appropriately dressed, requiring less use of heating and cooling appliances.

- Tell your families about the actions you are taking to reduce energy use.

- Include energy saving tips in your newsletter.

- Always use cold water for washing, wait for a full load and use the eco cycle.

- Minimise the use of clothes dryers. Use the clothes line instead.

- Conduct an energy audit to eliminate unnecessary power use.

- Switch to more energy-efficient lighting.

- When purchasing new appliances, consider those with high energy star ratings.

- Install sensor lights in infrequently used areas.

- Consider installing a solar hot water system.

- Consider installing a solar power system.

Healthy living

- Discuss with families, children and staff your plans to become a healthier setting and ask for suggestions as to how this can be achieved. The more involved families feel, the chances of them adopting healthier habits increases.

- Encourage a walk to setting day for families and staff.

- Increase the physical activity levels of all children and staff.

- Ensure staff understand the long- and short-term benefits of adopting a healthier lifestyle.

- Ensure staff act as positive role models for children and are observed making healthy food choices and keeping active.

- Encourage staff and children to eat together.

- Invite families into the setting to share a healthy picnic and ask them to bring in a healthy food choice.

- Encourage breastfeeding and regularly hold information sessions for families.

- Buy local/organic/fair trade/produce where possible.

- Consider installing a vegetable garden/salad patch.

- Plant fruit trees.

- Invite families into the setting for a themed healthy food tasting session. For example, this event can be a regular occurrence, choosing different healthy foods from around the world or different fruits from around the world.

Transport

- Consult your families and staff and discuss ways to reduce your settings' carbon footprint.

- Carry out an audit of staff daily journeys and consider offering car-share options.

- Encourage families to walk to the setting by establishing initiatives.

- Introduce awards for the children who walk to the setting on a regular basis.

- Train staff on the impact of heavy vehicle use on the environment.

- Invest in a variety of alternative modes of transport for the children, including bicycles, trikes, scooters, balance bikes, wheelbarrows.

- Carry out a transport audit and consider the number of deliveries that arrive at the setting. Can any of these be reduced? Once a week to once a fortnight or once a month?

- Visit a train station, fire station or farm to allow children to experience modes of transport in their natural environment.

- Communicate with families through your newsletter the various ways you are striving to reduce the setting's carbon footprint and encourage them to adopt the same strategies.

- Invite transport operators into the setting, e.g. fire engines, ambulance, refuse collection, milk float, allowing children to experience a wide variety of transport.

Waste and litter

- Use re-usable shopping bags every time you shop instead of plastic bags.

- Ask staff to be aware of packaging waste and encourage them to seek out products with little or no packaging.

- Ask families to bring in recyclable items for children's activities and set up a useful box in each room to store them in.

- Encourage children to build and create using the recyclable items.

- Set up paper collection points in each craft area and encourage children to re-use one-sided paper.

- Encourage families to reduce food packaging by introducing a package-free lunch box initiative.

- Train staff on how to recycle more effectively.

- Place colour-coded bins in each room or in a central location.

- Assess whether you need to increase the number of recycle bins.

- Identify families who will take home excess organic waste for their own compost or worm farm.

- Introduce a worm farm/compost bin to your setting and provide training for all staff.

- Use worm castings and juice from your worm farm on your own veggie garden.

- Reassess the number of general waste bins and frequency of pick-up following the introduction of measures to reduce waste.

- Look for opportunities to use recycled materials from parents when planning new spaces.

- Move to online assessments and parental notifications so that documentation and newsletters are not printed out.

School grounds

- Introduce more plants, both indoors and outdoors.

- Ensure all staff know the watering, light and feeding requirements of the plants you purchase.

- For the outdoors, look for varieties that are low maintenance and have less watering requirements. These will also create habitat for local wildlife.

- Incorporate stones and other natural materials including shells, pebbles and pinecones into both the indoor and outdoor learning environments and encourage imaginative play.

- Create a mud pit or sand pit.

- Create a mud kitchen.

- Create a permanent display table with interesting natural and sensory elements, such as leaves, seeds and shells.

- Construct a tepee using bamboo and grow climbers such as beans over the frame to create unique and interesting spaces.

- Consider incorporating pets into your outdoor space, e.g. rabbits, guinea pigs, chickens – these can make excellent pets for young children.

- Undertake discussions with your children and families to find out what they would like to see in their outdoor area.

- Talk about how you could incorporate more natural elements, e.g. logs, stepping stones, seating and balance beams.

- Replace soft fall areas with sensory gardens and textured pathways.

- Hold an activity day, inviting parents to help develop outdoor areas.

- Consider investing in a bee hive and equipment.

Water

- Use the eco cycle on washing machines and dishwashers and only when full.

- Use a full sink of water to wash or soak items such as art supplies rather than use running water from the tap.

- Tell your families about the actions you are taking to reduce water use.

- Include water-saving tips in your newsletter.

- Investigate the opportunity to label bed sheets so they can be used on the same child for consecutive days.

- Increase mulching of gardens to prevent evaporation to reduce garden's watering needs.

- Conduct a water audit to eliminate unnecessary water use, and compare water bills when available – this is very motivating for staff and children.

- Locate your water meter and take manual water readings.

- Consecutive readings at the beginning and end of each day will highlight if water is being lost outside business hours.

- Ensure timely repairs of leaks.

- When purchasing water-using fixtures and appliances, select those with the highest water efficiency rating.

- Install low-flow taps including push taps to prevent water wastage through taps being left on.

- Ensure all toilets are converted to dual-flush toilets with hippos fitted.

- Install a rainwater tank with a gauge and connect to toilets and washing machine.

- Monitor the gauge.

- Consider installing a water butt.

- Install a water wall for children's play area.

The Eco Wheel (Figure 18.1) has been developed by Nicky and Fred Edwards, both engineers, who now run a small group of nurseries in Bristol. Their wheel offers a structure for day nurseries or other child care providers, including childminders, to work on their sustainability. Their membership-based website offers news and information as well as the self-assessed wheel (www. ecowheel.org).

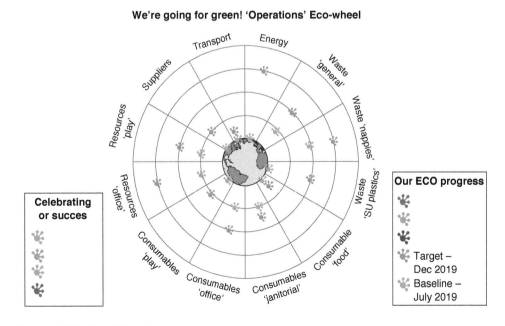

Figure 18.1 Eco Wheel

Conclusion

You may be required to work to certain curricula or framework, depending on your country and location, and indeed you are likely to need to achieve top results in order to maintain your reputation and even registration, so obviously those need to come first before considering sustainability and how to integrate or add this into your practice.

If your framework does not include sustainability, though, you can choose from one or more of the above to help structure your work as appropriate. And if you feel you would benefit from this connection or accreditation, you could work towards them (there is a charge for some) and could use this to celebrate, differentiate and market your service.

Notes

1. www.foundationyears.org.uk/files/2017/03/EYFS_STATUTORY_FRAMEWORK_2017 .pdf.
2. www.foundationyears.org.uk/files/2012/03/Development-Matters-FINAL-PRINT-AMENDED.pdf.
3. www.omep.org.uk/.
4. Siraj-Blatchford, J. and Brock, L. (2017). *Education for Sustainable Citizenship in Early Childhood.* Poole, Dorset: SchemaPlay Publications, p16.
5. http://se-ed.co.uk/edu/wp-content/uploads/2014/02/Report_-ESD-in-the-UK_2010_UKNC-UNESCOv4.pdf.
6. www.unicef.org.uk/what-we-do/un-convention-child-rights/.
7. Folque, A. et al. (2016). Education for sustainable development in Portugal. In Siraj-Blatchford, J., Mogharreban, C. and Park, E. (eds) *International Research on Education for Sustainable Development in Early Childhood.* Switzerland: Springer, p103.
8. This is well discussed in Elliott, S. (2014). *Sustainability and the Early Years Learning Framework.* New South Wales: Pademelon Press.
9. www.education.govt.nz/early-childhood/teaching-and-learning/te-whariki/.
10. Croft, A. (2017). Leading the change toward education for sustainability in early childhood education. *He Kupu: The Word* 5(1).
11. www.eco-schools.org.uk/aboutus/.
12. WonderGroveKids. (2014). *Save Water to Help the Earth.* YouTube.
13. www.sas.org.uk/plastic-free-schools/.
14. https://cehn.org/.
15. EHCC. (2018). *Eco-Healthy Child Care Checklist.* CEHN.
16. See Liverpool John Moores University. (n.d.). *LJMU Early Years Resources* [online]. Available from: www.ljmu.ac.uk/microsites/early-childhood-education-for-sustainability/ resources.
17. Available at: www.foundationyears.org.uk/wp-content/uploads/2017/11/Pack-1.pdf.

Summary

I believe we cannot wait for others to make space ships to take us to a second world, or to improve technology enough to get rid of all our waste plastic, nor for big retailers to change their ways, or even for governments to change the laws. We need to change our own ways as quickly as we can and to inspire others to do the same, for our children's sake.

And as Johann Arnold, of Community Playthings fame, quoted Doris Day as writing: a 'sense of futility is one of the greatest evils of the day'.[1] People say, 'What can one person do? What is the sense of our small effort?' Can they not see that if we just lay one brick at a time, take one step at a time, **we can** be responsible, we can be the change?

So what can we do, one thing at a time, as early years professionals and as small businesses? First, we have to accept global climate change as fact, and understand that plastic, vehicle fumes, aerosols and toxins are poisoning our food and our air, and making our children sick, and maiming and killing innocent creatures and plants around the globe. Only then can we motivate ourselves and establish what we can do as individuals, and as people working within the early years sector. We can join together as responsible people, and make the effort to live and work sustainably so that our children may go on to live healthy, sustainable lives.

As someone travelling this road already, but only for a few years, I've taken the opportunity to suggest a draft action plan. It's easy to implement – you need only put it into Word or Excel or similar; fill in the dates and who in your organisation is going to be responsible for each action. The vast majority of these actions incur no cost other than your time, and many even produce a saving; others are investments that you may need to work on:

1. Check out the facts yourself.

2. Inspire yourself and your colleagues, family and friends with documentary films such as *A Plastic Ocean*, *Blue Planet 2*, *Cowspiracy*, *Chasing Coral*, or *End of the Line*, or the TV series *War on Plastic* – follow your interests.

3. Measure – your energy use, your single-use plastic use, your food and consumables invoices, your waste. Work out your starting point so you can track progress.

4. Engage in one or more systems as described in the book, or decide on your own key performance indicators for you to track and celebrate your successes.

5. Develop your action plan into a SMART one. Sustainability is such a vast concept, you have to pick what is the most important area for you to work on, and in which order.

Just for example and in no particular order (there is also a checklist in Appendix VI):

- Reduce your energy use/bills.

- Cut your single-use plastic/consumables bills – stop or reduce purchase of anything single-use, such as glitter, balloons, aprons, straws, cling film, plastic bags, nappies, baby wipes. Replace these with sustainable alternatives.

- Offer a lower meat/dairy/fish-based diet and replace with plant-based.

- Stop using pasta and rice as an alternative to sand and water play.

- Start composting and start a wormery.

- Increase your vegetable and herb growing.

- Use scrap stores, charity shops and car boot sales for more of your resourcing.

- Plan activities to teach the children about sustainability, such as beach and forest trips, eco stories, recycling games on computers, pet care, etc.

- Make sure your staff can role-model sustainable practice (turning the lights off, heating down, reducing laminating, recycling with the children).

- Invest in your building (insulation, solar panels, heat exchangers).

- Change electricity supplier to one that sells renewable energy instead of fossil fuel energy.

- Run a more effective potty training system to have children out of nappies more quickly.

- Welcome or even introduce re-usable nappies.

- Find out where your rubbish goes, and change company if it goes to landfill. Can your company report on how much of your rubbish is recycled, and the weights of what you are paying them to dispose of? How do they recycle your rubbish – please don't accept sending it to Malaysia or some other country, where it will still go to landfill and end up in our oceans.

- Reduce your impact on air pollution by switching away from diesel cars, aerosols and toxic materials in paint and furniture.

- Join beach clean-ups and engage in citizen science, such as the big micro-plastic survey.

- Share your story with parents, other professionals, the community, local schools.

- Write to politicians, bureaucrats and influential people to implore them to lead change – promising to vote for them if they do.

6. Many responsible companies now have a sustainability policy, also called corporate social responsibility (CSR) or corporate social and environmental responsibility (CSER), to help communicate their vision and strategy. If you want a starting point, do look at our CSER on our website (www.topsday nurseries.co.uk) and feel free to copy whatever suits you and adapt as appropriate, for copying is the highest compliment you can pay.

This is a journey for us all, not a box-ticking exercise. The process can involve trading in some convenience and time-saving. Manufacturers, distributors and retailers will do their best to draw you into consumerism; however, pay more for quality goods that last or with people who will take your goods back at end of life to repurpose. You may choose not to give up all your one-use 'disposable' nappies or your latest model phone, or your holidays abroad, and it's okay not to be perfect. Just make sure you are basing your actions on careful reflection, not just following the crowd or because you can.

Decisions such as moving to electric cars, or even to glass milk bottles, are not black and white. You will need to make the best decision you can with the information that you have, your personal ethos, and your supplier options at the time. I believe we need to share what we learn so we can make the best decisions. This is why I've started a Facebook page and a website for our green early years charity, GECCO (Green Early Years Choices Champion Organisation), and started the GECCORealNappies project, and why we also share sustainable information, including supplier information, on our Tops Day Nurseries website. This significant cultural change will only be made by lots of people making many small changes, making a consistent effort to change.

Some investments are so significant that you may need a bank or a fund to support you – there are organisations that specialise in financial support and helping organisations measure their impact in terms of corporate social responsibility. Some investors are only interested in putting their money into organisations like ours, where we impact on people's lives and care about what we are doing – rather than those that produce cigarettes or pesticides. Examples of these are the Triodos Bank (www.triodos.com) and The Bridges Fund (www.bridges fundmanagement.com).

As George Monbiot wrote in his book *How Did We Get into This Mess* (which I'd recommend as instructive reading), 'Progressive change requires mass mobilisation.'[2] That means you, me, our children, our customers, and everyone we come into contact with. We need to treat the world with respect, reducing our impact on it to as close to zero as we can. We only have the one world. Never forget that there is no such thing as throwing stuff **away**. When we discard something into the waste bin, it doesn't just disappear. Try and make sure to only use resources that can be passed along to someone else after use, returned to the manufacturer, or upcycled or recycled.

Good luck and thank you so much for your time.

Notes

1. Arnold, J. (2014). *Their Name is Today: Reclaiming childhood in a hostile world*. New York: Plough Publishing, p159.
2. Monbiot, G. (2016). *How Did We Get into This Mess*. Verso Books: London, p151.

Appendix I
Suppliers' sustainability and eco-grading

Corporate social responsibility

Evidence should include the following:

- social enterprise

- B Corp

- registered charity

- staff members enabled to volunteer in the community

- charitable donations

- avoids use of one use plastic

- the 5 Rs policy (Refuse, Reduce, Reuse, Repurpose, Recycle) in place

- transport policy that focuses on electric or hydrogen vehicles rather than petrol or diesel

- delivery policy avoids single small items delivery in favour of grouping items or shared delivery

- use of renewable energy sources.

We would expect a CSR statement and evidence on the website or front of catalogue.

Product grading

1. locally sourced, regionally sourced

2. local artisans or providing local employment

3. made from renewable materials (e.g. bamboo, metal, FSC wood)

4. no toxic ingredients (e.g. bleach, formaldehyde, lead, mercury, BPA)

5. made from upcycled or recycled materials (e.g. recycled plastic, tyres)

6. durable (10 years minimum)

7. guaranteed to be returnable and replaced when broken or replacement parts provided

8. ethical (e.g. no slave or child labour, pay and conditions of workers checked)

9. packaging is home compostable or recyclable, collection and recycling offered by suppliers

10. renewable energy sources used in production.

We would expect each product to be graded by the producer or distributor, scoring 1 for each of the above, e.g. a desk could be a 10 or a 1, as eco description.

Appendix II
Tops Day Nurseries Corporate Social Environmental Responsibility (CSER) Policy

How we balance environmental, social and economic priorities over the long term.

Policy brief and purpose

Our Corporate Social Environmental Responsibility (CSER) company policy refers to our approach to do business while also being sustainable. We have responsibilities toward our environment, society, local community, the economy, the ecology, as well as our customers and colleagues. We consider the social and environmental consequences of our actions. Sustainability is one of our key company objectives and all strategies have sustainability embedded within them. For our CSER and Sustainability Action Plan please see Appendix A.

Scope

This policy applies to our companies. It also refers to suppliers and partners.

Materiality assessment – our business is in the service sector – the education and care of small children, and the training of adults, so the material issues are:

1. how we care for people

2. in the products that we buy and use to sustain this service

3. in the environment that we provide to deliver these services and

4. in the transport and communications systems that we use to support these services.

Context

We are a responsible business that meets the highest standards of ethics and professionalism.

Legality

Our company:

- respects the law
- honours its internal policies
- ensures that all its business operations are legitimate
- keeps every partnership and collaboration open and transparent.

Business ethics

We conduct business with integrity and respect to human rights.
    We promote:

- safety and fair dealing
- respect toward the consumer
- anti-bribery and anti-corruption practices
- supply chain checks to ensure that we do not benefit from slavery or unethical practices from those from whom we purchase any products or resources. (see purchasing guidelines policy, Appendix 2)
- we challenge suppliers to deliver goods with more respect for carbon footprint and clean air, and also with less packaging and waste.

Positive impact on people – children, parents, colleagues, learners, community

Our purpose is to provide care and education to children, to support their parents, and these impacts are measured through our KPIs, and in line with the United Nations Sustainability Goals. Our expectation is for all children to reach at least good levels of development, ensuring that children meet the grade descriptors within their age bracket.

Our purpose is also to provide meaningful careers to our colleagues and learners, and these impacts are also measured through our KPIs and in line with the United Nations Sustainability Goals.

We also promote our colleagues' and volunteers' health and well-being through a range of initiatives such as providing drinking water and fresh fruit at all locations, free snacks at meetings which take colleagues' allergies and intolerances into account as well as being vegan and plastic-free, free counselling (anonymous), financial contributions towards dental, opticians, prescriptions and medical health (see staff welcome pack). We provide advice on our website for a range of conditions and support needs, and demonstrate anti-discriminating and inclusive recruitment and retention policy and practices, as well as values that embrace British Values and family values (see the Company Vision, Mission and Values statements).

Our recruitment and retention policies, procedures and improvements are documented to evidence the many improvements being made – see 52 improvements in 52 weeks for 2019.

Protecting people

We ensure that we:

- don't risk the health and safety of our employees and community (see H&S Manual, Risk Assessments)
- avoid harming the lives of local people
- support diversity and inclusion
- take economic responsibility.

Human rights

We are a committed equal opportunity employer and will abide by all fair labour practices. We ensure that our activities do not directly or indirectly violate human rights in any country (e.g. forced labour). We engage in equality of gender pay, reporting and reducing any gaps if identified.

Donations and aid – philanthropic giving

Our company aims to preserve a budget to make monetary donations to our two charities, GECCO and the Employee Trust. These donations aim to:

- Alleviate those in need.

- Support sustainability education and actions. All our actions are viewed through an 'improving sustainability' window to ensure that we work to constantly reduce our impact and improve how we do business in order to continue to do this.

- We work in partnership with a range of different organisations such as hospitals and care homes (intergenerational childcare and education together with those on the elderly and dementia wards), sharing activities and music to benefit both generations. We also take part in local community events such as fetes, fairs and carnivals.

- We also have our own charity called GECCO, Green Early Years Choices Champions Organisation, which is a registered charity. The charity has been set up to support children, parents, and colleagues in the early years sector to encourage and educate people to be more sustainable for the future of the planet.

Colleagues wishing to arrange a fundraising event to support GECCO would contact one of the trustees.

We also support a range of relevant charities appropriate to the interests of the children and colleagues at each nursery and office.

Volunteering

Our company welcomes volunteers from other organisations in our establishments, such as children on work experience from schools, young people who are not yet ready to be employed, adults wishing to experience working with young children. We work with partner organisations, such as local churches, hospitals, and care homes, to encourage more intergenerational volunteers, recognising that 'retired' adults benefit as much as the children from spending time together in our settings.

Our companies enable colleagues to volunteer through flexible time arrangements. Colleagues can volunteer through programmes organised internally or externally if they so wish, but there is no pressure at all to do this. In fact, they are contributing to social impact through the work they do already, which is underpaid due to the culture of doing this in the community, local politics and national politics. Our companies may engage in social events organised by other charities, such as the Rotary Club, to fundraise for local charities and communities. Our colleagues may engage in initiatives led at nursery level, such as food banks and shared resources (such as nappies, craft materials, recycling collections).

Preserving and protecting the natural environment

As well as our legal obligations, our companies will proactively protect the environment. Examples of relevant activities include:

- stopping, or reducing, purchasing of resources, particularly single-use plastic (see purchasing policy)

- checking sustainability of all purchases, an embedded and integral part of any purchasing or resourcing decision

- refusing, recycling, re-using, reducing, returning waste; upcycling others' waste

- conserving energy

- using environmentally friendly and renewable technologies

- reducing our use of fossil fuels

- avoiding purchase or use of anything that will pollute the air we breathe

- working with suppliers in our supply chain to improve our impact, i.e. on our joint carbon footprint, air pollution, plastic pollution, if necessary changing suppliers in order to reduce our impact, if affordable

- monitoring the purchasing reports for any purchases that have not complied with sustainable purchasing policies so that mistakes can be rectified, training put in place to prevent these continuing, recognising that becoming more sustainable is a process, not a single result, and that technologies and processes can and must improve in order to address the climate change and extinction of species crisis

- working with colleagues, children and learners, customers and suppliers, and those in our networks, to learn together, to teach when there are opportunities to do so and to role-model a leading and inspirational example of sustainability in the early years and training sectors.

Our companies recognise the need to protect the natural environment. Keeping our environment clean and unpolluted is a benefit to all. We follow best practices when disposing of waste and using chemical substances and reducing green-house gases. Stewardship and role-modelling play an important role in our company.

Supporting the community

Our company supports colleagues wishing to engage in charities that are important to them in their private lives as well as in their work lives. We do not feel the need to publish these as company-supported actions; no list is maintained to record this impact.

Our company initiates and supports sustainability initiatives and education through our registered charity, GECCO, contributing 3 per cent of EBITDA per year.

Our company provides funds, 3 per cent of EBITDA per year, the infrastructure, and referral system for members of staff to engage with our Trust, both as contributors (from salaries and/or fundraising) and as beneficiaries.

Our company can provide support to non-profit organisations or movements to promote sustainable, cultural or economic development of global and local communities.

Our company engages with national fundraising and awareness events such as Jeans for Genes, Red Nose Day, and also with festivals from different cultures that are represented in our local communities/workplaces, such as Chinese New Year and Diwali. The upcoming events are announced once a month at the managers' meetings, and included in social media comment for cascading throughout the company.

Our company engages with charities such as Surfers Against Sewage (Plastic Free Schools, beach cleans); Eco-Schools (external accreditation); and Just One Ocean (microplastic surveys)

Learning and educating

Our expertise and reputation lies in our colleagues' expertise and performance, and therefore we actively invest in their continuous professional development, offering up to 32 days of training per year. We actively invest in R&D, such as in eyman and eylog, which helps to reduce our impact on the environment through effective and efficient IT. We are open to further suggestions and listen carefully to ideas. Our company tries to improve the way it operates continuously and to share good practice. We also share good practice in sustainability in our sector on our GECCO charity website.

Impact on child development is measured on eylog (early stages so targets have not been developed yet).

Impact on use of nappies and use of single-use nappies is also to be measured on eyman (in pilot stages).

Impact on staff of training – promotion records (early stages on eyman) – shows that progression from unqualified through the company, even to director-ship, is significant.

Training needs analysis is completed and updated for every nursery – showing progression and improvement in percentages of staff with key qualifications.

Financial impact of the company on those working – again early days on eyman, and we are expecting that these results will show that most staff are under the average wage, many on minimum wage, and many on less than living wage and therefore living in deprivation. We need the support of local and national politicians and press in order to improve this situation as the sector is underfunded, the second worst in the OECD, with insufficient investment being put into the early years – a serious misjudgement on the part of the governments of the day (hence our involvement with founding the APPG).

Our company is committed to the United Nations Global Compact. We readily act to promote our identity as a socially aware and responsible business. Management communicates this policy on all levels, see Facebook.

Managers are also responsible for resolving any local CSR issues but have support from area managers and directors, as well as strategically.

Sustainable transport policy

Every location that the organisation works from has a sustainable transport policy relevant to that location, including public transport such as bus routes, train stations, advice and information for walkers and cyclists, car-sharing opportunities, moving to electric rather than petrol or diesel, with the aim of reducing our carbon impact and air-quality impact on the community.

Leadership, accreditations and benchmarking

As well as leadership from the founder and directors, all colleagues are encouraged to take leadership roles to challenge and develop innovative and general progress towards a more sustainable, ethical, healthy and safe way of working.

We expect and work to be inspirational role models of sustainability in our sector. This is evidenced in speaking engagements undertaken, awards achieved, PR achieved, and our founding the All Party Parliamentary Group (APPG) for early years for Westminster MPs.

Board members are predominantly female, reflecting the composition of the company – there is no glass ceiling for females in this company.

Diversity is celebrated and there is a robust anti-discrimination policy, reflected in the composition of colleagues (see Gender Pay and Diversity reports), but specific successes are nearly 10 per cent male nursery practitioners against a 2 per cent national average and 5 per cent registered blue badge disabled colleagues at head office.

We have considered the Planet Mark (kite mark) but the costs appear to be extensive, ditto the ISO accreditations, and employment comparisons (*Times*).

We are in stage 2 of ESOS and have an action plan based on opportunities for improvement identified during the surveys.

We held IIP for over 15 years and continue to exceed the original standards, but did not apply for re-inspection or the Gold Standard due to the costs. We do our own questionnaires on Survey Monkey to guide improvements and engage in external surveys such as CEEDA to give us benchmarking information.

We hold the Matrix Standard in Aspire Training Team – which is mandatory and assesses information, advice and guidance given to potential learners/apprentices.

We have developed our own Eco Awards for those settings doing best across a whole range of sustainability initiatives.

Appendices

1. Action Plan – living document on S drive

2. Purchasing guidelines – in Operations Manual on S drive, frequently updated.

3. Sustainable transport policies (one for each site) on website.

Also referred to

1. Company Vision, Mission and Values Statements

2. Welcome pack for staff

3. Welcome pack for children/parents

4. Recruitment and retention policies and procedures

5. Gender pay and diversity reports

6. 52 improvements in 52 weeks for 2019

7. H&S manual

8. Risk assessments

9. Company KPIs – month reports – Ofsted/internal quality inspections

10. Company EBITDA – annual, audited accounts

11. Our websites:

    www.topsdaynurseries.co.uk

    www.aspiretrainingteam.co.uk

    www.hadlandcaregroup.co.uk

    www.GECCO.org.uk

12. External accreditation and comparisons:

    Eco-Schools: Bronze, Silver and Green Play

    Surfers Against Sewage: Plastic Free School Status

    ESOS

    Gender/Equal Pay Report (annual)

    Energy Performance Assessments – per site

    GECCO wheel

13. Real Nappy Campaign

14. Awards achieved

15. PR achieved (financial value) reports

16. Site summary – records impact on child development, single-use nappies, potty training, as well as EBITDA per site

17. Pay rates report – percentages on minimum wage, living wage

18. Promotion report – internal progression

19. Staff training report – per site, and impact of company on individuals

20. Charities

Signed on behalf of Tops Day Nurseries and Aspire Training Team.

Cheryl Hadland
Founder and Managing Director

Appendix III
Tops Day Nurseries and Aspire Training Team Sustainable Travel Plan and Policy

Address: 3 Wollaston Road, Southbourne, BH6 4AR

Please also refer to separate policies on Cycle to Work Scheme, Electric Bike Policy, Environmental Policy, Flexible Working, Vehicles and Driving Policy, Staff Handbook and CSR Policy.

Introduction

Measures to promote sustainable travel and strategies are in place to promote the use of public transport, car-sharing, walking, cycling, electric bike and electric cars/vans. The health benefits of walking and cycling are promoted to staff. Most staff live within the borough and already use sustainable travel to get to work.

Walking

Walking is the most sustainable method of travel, has a number of proven health benefits and is an important source of personal freedom. Walking is important for the vast majority of people, including those using public transport or without access to a car. It has the potential to play an important role in journeys to work, particularly for those living within two miles of their workplace. Walking is a form of active travel, which can offer a range of physical and psychological benefits to the individual.

Cycling

Cycling is cheap, offers reliable journey times and is environmentally friendly. Within the workplace, encouragement of cycling can lead to a healthier, more productive workforce.

A link has been identified between growth in the use of cars and obesity, with both trends increasing at a similar rate between 1985 and 2000. Travel plans offer substantial health benefits to individuals who are motivated to complete more journeys on foot or by bicycle. In turn, employers can benefit through increased productivity and reduced absence through illness.

The company operates the 'Cycle to Work Scheme', enabling employees to purchase bicycles and associated safety equipment through salary sacrifice. This means that employees are able to receive income tax and National Insurance savings on the retail price of their chosen bike and safety equipment package. The scheme is administered through a salary sacrifice agreement and is run in accordance with the government's Sustainable Travel Plan. Staff can select any model of bike up to a value of £1000 per annum through independent bike shops taking part in this scheme, thereby providing business to the local community.

The company also has a fleet of four electric bicycles which are currently lent to staff who do not have access to a bicycle at home. The company is considering increasing this provision by a further two electric bicycles.

The company encourages, supports and facilitates cycling by:

- providing a shower/changing room and lockers
- providing bicycle parking
- security – new bicycle parking in a covered enclosure
- bicycle loan/tax-free scheme for employees
- providing charging for electric bikes
- discounts on bicycles and accessory purchases
- marketing of cycling (e.g. health aspects).

And offers the following subject to demand:

- bicycle training
- bicycle buddy scheme
- cyclist events
- cyclist users' group.

Public transport access

Public transport remains important, particularly for journeys to work of more than 5 miles (8km). Its benefits include:

- no need to park

- traffic-free routes (with rail or bus priority existing)

- being able to relax, read or work (particularly beneficial for business travel).

Access to public transport is very good in the location of Wollaston Road. Yellow Buses and More Bus provide regular services with bus stops a short walk away.

The company will encourage and support the use of public transport for commuting to Wollaston Road by continuing with the following:

- subsidised bus season tickets – the company is a member of BTN

- bus season ticket loans.

Bus stops closest to Wollaston Road in Bournemouth:

- Church Road, Southbourne (2-minute walk)
  Bus no. 33 Bournemouth – Hospital – Christchurch
  Bus no. 1 Two Rivers Meet – Church Road – Bournemouth Triangle

- St Catherine's Road, Southbourne (3-minute walk)
  Bus no. 33 Bournemouth – Hospital – Christchurch

Access by train

The nearest station is Pokesdown Train Station, which is on the main line from Weymouth/Wareham to London, running close to a number of our nurseries, so it is convenient for learners and colleagues. The walk from the train station to 3 Wollaston Road is about 35 minutes, and by bus (M2 or 1) it is 13 minutes (four buses per half hour).

Managing car use

It is important that car use and parking are managed.

Where the only option is to transport by vehicle, mapping of staff journeys is used to aid implementing car-sharing. Car-sharing refers to a situation where two or more people travel by car together, for all or part of the car trip.

These initiatives work and greatly reduce car use, benefiting the health and well-being of staff and generally increasing quality of life with the added benefit of reducing the carbon footprint.

Expenses are not paid for students attending training for solo car use if they are able to share.

No parking is allowed in Wollaston Road by staff.

We have purchased four car parking spaces from the vicarage next door for directors to use. No additional payments are made to staff for car parking, as it is preferred that cars are not brought to work.

Additional car parks are available for a fee in the local Bournemouth Borough Council car park should they be needed; season tickets are available.

Colleagues are encouraged to use electric vehicles rather than diesel (air pollution) or petrol (global warming).

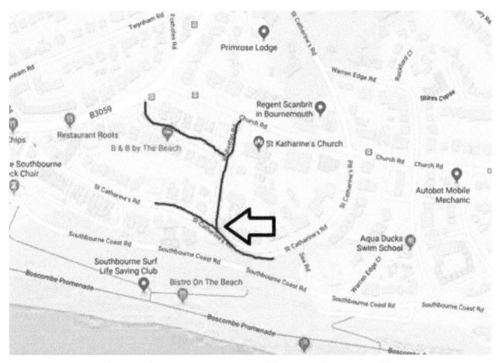

(Arrow = new office and training centre, red lines = **<u>do not park</u>**)

Van use

The landlords (Hadland Care Group) have an electric van used for maintenance, and a charging point at Wollaston Road. This van will normally be parked on site overnight but will often be visiting the other sites during the day. The parking space is to the left of the door and can also be used during the day by visiting electric vehicles as it is next to the charge point.

Accessibility

There is one parking space immediately outside the front door to the right that will be reserved for disabled use.

Signed:

Cheryl Hadland on behalf of Tops Day Nurseries and Aspire Training Team

Appendix IV
Environmental dates to celebrate

January

Big Energy Saving Week; National Bird Day; National Story Telling Week; World Religion Day

February

Fairtrade Fortnight; World Wetlands Day

March

Earth House; World Water Day; Waste Week; Vegetarian Week; International Day of Forests; World Wildlife Day; Earth Hour; World Book Day

April

The Big Pedal; Earth Day

May

National Walking Month; Compost Awareness Week; International Day for Biological Diversity

June

Volunteers Week; World Environment Day; Recycle Week; Empty Classroom Day; World Oceans Day

July

Oxfam Water Week; National Marine Week; Love Parks Week; Plastic Free July; Marine Day (Japan) (15 July: https://tokyotreat.com/news/umi-no-hi-celebrating-marine-day-in-japan); International Tiger Day (29 July: https://tokyotreat.com/news/umi-no-hi-celebrating-marine-day-in-japan)

August

National Honey Bee Day; World Breastfeeding Week

September

Waste Less, Live More Week; Read a Book Day; British Food Fortnight; Ozone Day; World Clean-up Day (15 September: www.worldcleanupday.org/); Respect the Aged Day (16 September: www.planettokyo.com/blog/japanese-culture/what-is-respect-for-the-aged-day/); International Day of Peace (21 September: https://internationaldayofpeace.org/)

October

Global Handwashing Day; World Animal Day (4 October: www.worldanimalday.org.uk/); World Food Day; World Habitat Day; Grandparents' Day (7 October: www.gransnet.com/grandparenting/what-is-grandparents-day); International Anti-slavery Day (18 October: www.antislavery.org/anti-slavery-day-2018/)

November

World Toilet Day; Universal Children's Day; Energy Month; Global Entrepreneurship Week; Giving Tuesday

December

Human Rights Day (10 December: www.un.org/en/events/humanrightsday/); International Volunteers Day; Mountain Day (Japan) (11 December: www.un.org/en/events/mountainday/)

Appendix V
Useful websites

Early years

www.gecco.org.uk Champions for Change in Early Years established to promote sustainability in early years childcare and education

www.early-education.org.uk British Association for Early Childhood Education

www.dorsetforyou.gov.uk Dorset Council supporting schools to become more sustainable

www.nurseryworld-magazine.co.uk *Nursery World* – early years magazine

www.nmt-magazine.co.uk *Nursery Management Today*

www.naht.org.uk National Association of Head Teachers and NAHT Edge

www.iecs.org.au International Early Childhood Symposium

http://worldforum.org Foundation that promotes the global exchange of ideas on quality services for children

www.broadwayevents.co.uk Conference creators active in early years

www.awarenessdays.co.uk Exact dates for important awareness days to celebrate

www.interfaith-calendar.org Exact dates for multi-faith festival dates

www.ecowheel.org A toolkit to support early years settings to become more eco-sustainable

Outdoor play

www.muddyfaces.co.uk Outdoor resources

www.janwhitenaturalplay.wordpress.com An independent consultant advocating and supporting high-quality outdoor provision for children from 0–5

www.bumblebeeconservation.org Established due to serious concerns about the plight of the bumblebee; great for resources

www.rspb.org.uk/youth/learn/earlyyears Teaching our young generation to provide homes for nature

www.naturedetectives.org.uk A Woodland Trust website to spark children's interest in the outdoors

www.woodlandtrust.org.uk/learn For people who want to see a UK rich in native trees and wildlife

www.lotc.org.uk Council for Learning Outside the Classroom (0–19), for Forest School training

www.outdoor-learning.org.uk Institute for Outdoor Learning – great for good practice, events, and bushcraft

www.playengland.org.uk/love-outdoor-play Resources and petitions to enable children to have the freedom and opportunity to play

www.bbc.co.uk/gardening Projects and fun activities for children

www.gardeningwithchildren.co.uk Interactive classroom, allotment plot and hobby garden

www.earthrestorationservice.org Free trees and materials for schools from the UK

Food

www.foodforlife.org.uk Making healthy, tasty and sustainable meals from normal ingredients

www.faceonline.org.uk Farming and Countryside Education – connecting children and young people to the countryside and where their food comes from

www.cwt.org.uk Caroline Walker Trust – great for sustainable food ideas

www.childrensfoodtrust.org.uk Eat Better, Start Better programme commissioned by the DfE

www.onegreenplanet.org Helps create a world where we eat delicious food and use amazing products that provide us with maximum benefit and have minimum impact on the planet

www.thebalancesmb.com The difference between organic and sustainable food explained

www.msc.org Marine Stewardship Council – provides information on sustainable seafood

www.soilassociation.org Resources to let us select food produces in a way that protects our natural world

Sustainability practice

www.eco-schools.org.uk Global programme engaging millions of children across 67 countries – the largest educational, environmental programme in the world

www.naee.org.uk National Association for Environmental Education – helps us to understand and act on the need to live more sustainably

www.se-ed.co.uk Sustainability and Environmental Education – supports and enables educators and young people to place sustainability at the heart of their work and learning

www.GECCO.org.uk Sustainability resources and information

www.war-on-waste.org War on Waste – recycling and general waste collections

www.sustainabledorset.org Central hub of sustainable activities across the county of Dorset

www.sas.org.uk Surfers Against Sewerage – protecting oceans and beaches through marine conservation, beach cleans, etc.

www.mcsuk.org Championing clean seas, sustainable fishing and care for marine wildlife

www.justoneocean.org An organisation established to raise awareness of some of the issues affecting our oceans

Plastic, toys and resources

www.childrensscrapstore.co.uk Making waste things play things

www.scrapstoresuk.org The diversion of clean, re-usable scrap materials from businesses

www.wrap.org.uk Information on the UK Plastics Pact

fashionheroes.eco/free-2-work free2work is a consumer information platform with barcode scanning technology that provides users with data on a brand's responses to forced and child labour

www.ethical.org.au/3.4.2/ Get the low-down on the environmental and social record of companies behind common brand names; shop with a clear conscience

www.goodguide.com Search for healthier food using scientists' information from analysing each product based on its composition – personal care, food, household, babies and kids

www.avoidplugin.com The Avoid Plug-in is a way to avoid products that are associated with the exploitation of children

http://apparelcoalition.org/th-higg-index Manufacturers, brands and retailers are joining together to identify and measure their sustainability impacts

www.abolishfoundation.com Say no to the use of forced labour in supply chains

www.soilassociation.org Resources to let us select food produces in a way that protects our natural world

www.rainforestrelief.org/documents/guidelines Avoiding the purchase of rain forest/endangered forest wood

www.inbar.int Resources for sustainable rattan and bamboo

www.fsc-uk.org/en-uk Forest Stewardship Council – an independent non-profit promoting responsible management of forests

www.pefc.org Programme for the Endorsement of Forestry Certification – guarantees wood comes from sustainable sources, is replaced after harvesting and is taken without harming the environment and neighbouring ecosystems

Information, advice and guidance

www.ltl.org.uk Learning through Landscapes – for grants and training resources

www.reepinfo.org.uk Religions and Environment Education Programme

www.foundationyears.org.uk Communication forum, resources, information on entitlements, knowledge hub and news

www.aelp.org.uk Association of Employment and Leaning Providers (UK)

www.ndna.org.uk UK charity that provides support, information, advice and guidance to the childcare sector

www.preschool.org.uk The largest and most representative early years membership organisation in England; offers information, advice, publications, and training

www.cache.org.uk High-quality qualifications for the care and education industry

www.mumsnet.com By parents, for parents – often some very good outdoor-focused posts

www.bbc.co.uk/programmes/b06nzl5q Hugh Fearnley-Whittingstall on a mission to find out why we waste so much

www.gov.uk/guidance How to comply with the Energy Savings Opportunity Scheme

www.carbontrust.com Carbon Trust

www.friendsoftheearth.uk Friends of the Earth

Business and politics

www.b.corporation.net B Corps are better companies – better for workers, better for communities and better for the environment

www.britishchambers.org Powerful and influential network of accredited Chambers of Commerce across the UK

www.wibn.co.uk   Women in Business Network

http://theathenanetwork.com   Networking for women serious about business growth

www.unicef.org/crc   United Nations 1989 Convention on the rights of the child

www.unenvironment.org United Nations Environment – the leading global environmental authority for sustainable development goals

www.findnetworkingevents.com To find local business networking events, groups and business clubs for women

Useful contacts

www.parliament.uk   What MPs do, and how to contact them

www.actionforchildren.org.uk Charity committed to helping vulnerable and neglected children and young people

www.care2.com   Petition website with causes such as animals, women, politics, food, LGBT, human rights, healthy living, etc.

Appendix VI
Sustainability checklists

Item	In use now? Yes/Don't know/ Not measured	Use Instead	Done?
Stop aerosols		Alcohol/essential oils with sticks, electric powered diffusers (natural essential oils)	
Clean air outside		Outdoor plants and trees – plant plenty	
		Stop cars idling	
		Reduce delivery frequency	
		Reduce waste collection frequency	
Clean air inside		Indoor plants – website check for non-toxic plants that clean air	
		Natural products rather than chemicals to clean	
		Steamer	
White goods		Buy best quality, A++, opt to return to manufacturer if on offer, check repairability, No CFCs	
Toxic and new paint		Low VOC, re-engineered paint	
Chipboard		Ensure it hasn't been made with formaldehyde, replace with solid wood (sustainably sourced)	

GECCO
Champions for Change in the Early Years
Sustainability Checklist – Climate Change Actions

Item	In use now? Yes/Don't know/ Not measured	Use Instead	Done?
Reduce fossil fuel use		Change supplier to 'renewable'	
Fluorescent or halogen light bulbs		Replace with LEDs	
Heating/hot water on		Timers – 7-day, 24 hours	
Lighting on		Movement/Light sensors	
Gas, Oil boilers		Infra-red, solar panels, renew – efficient, heat exchanger	
Diesel, petrol cars		Electric, hydrogen	
Idling outside nursery		Switch off policy	
Vehicle use		Sustainable travel policy – walking, bikes, car-sharing, lifts, public transport, government cycle scheme, secure bike park, showers, lockers, training	
Items being transported a long way		Buy local policy	
		Have fewer deliveries – daily to weekly to monthly	

GECCO

Champions for Change in the Early Years
Sustainability Checklist – Extinction

Item	In use now? Yes/Don't know/ Not measured	Use Instead	Done?
Toxic bug spray and weed killers		Grow organic fruit & veg on site	
Damage to habitat		Grow flowers for bees, bug hotel	
		Respect and care for nursery pets	
Lack of knowledge		Reading and telling stories, about sustainability – plastic pollution, recycling	
		Activities – sand, water, clay, mud	
		Learn about local flora and fauna	
		Support charities/NFPs that actively protect the environment or research (not bracelet sellers!)	

Visit **gecco.org.uk** for more information on sustainability
GECCO is a registered charity (no. 1171726)

GECCO

Champions for Change in the Early Years
Sustainability Checklist – Stop using one-use plastics

Item	In use now? Yes/Don't know/ Not measured	Use Instead	Done?
Nappies		Cloth (bamboo, hemp, cotton)	
Wet wipes including biodegradable and bio plastic		Cloth, home-made from kitchen paper & natural products	
Balloons, especially if helium filled		Cardboard, paper, clay, windmills	
Glitter/Sequins		Hole punch leaves, flowers, petals, paper	
Cutlery		Metal, bamboo – sporks	
Crockery		Washable eg pottery, porcelain, glass	
Clingfilm		Lids	
Gloves		Bare hands – wash, one hand only if essential (open wounds/infections)	
Aprons		Cloth – wash, PVC	
Shoe covers		Indoor shoes, slippers, bare feet	
Nappy sacks		Re-usable wet bags	
Plastic bags		Fabric, re-usable	
Bin liners		No liner – wash bin	
Water bottles		Re-usable bottles – metal, plastic or glass	

Visit **gecco.org.uk** for more information on sustainability
GECCO is a registered charity (no. 1171726)

GECCO
Champions for Change in the Early Years
Sustainability Checklist – Stop using one-use plastics

Item	In use now? Yes/Don't know/ Not measured	Use Instead	Done?
Fruit, vegetables in plastic bags		Greengrocers, deliveries in crates, re-use own bags	
Straws		Go without, paper, metal, pasta	
Milk		Glass bottles, re-usable lids	
Paper towels wrapped in plastic		No wrappers, recycled paper	
Toilet paper wrapped in plastic		No wrappers, recycled paper	
Washing liquids		Concentrated liquid in large bottles, re-use smaller bottles	
Liquid hand wash & don't use anti-bac		Soap on a rope, refillable smaller bottles	
Laminator sheets		Print on shiny card	
Plastic wallets		Re-use what you have, just hole punch	
Laundry liquids		EcoEgg	
Plastic toothbrushes		Bamboo toothbrushes	
Sanitary products		Into nappy bins for incineration, encourage alternatives that are reusable	
'Convenience' pack lunches		Pack lunch policy includes no one-use plastic.	
Party products		Party Hamper – hire to parents	
Packets of biscuits etc.		Bake your own	

Visit **gecco.org.uk** for more information on sustainability
GECCO is a registered charity (no. 1171726)

GECCO
Champions for Change in the Early Years
Sustainability Checklist – General Purchasing

Item	In use now? Yes/Don't know/ Not measured	Use Instead	Done?
New plastic toys		Wooden (FFC), metal, charity shop/second-hand	
Stuff that only lasts a little time		Invest in better stuff to keep for longer	
Plastic washing up brushes		Coconut husk, metal	
Washing up cloths eg j-cloths		Buy re-usable/washable – or cut up old towels	
Laundry powders		EcoEgg	
Laundry softener sheets		EcoEgg	
Meat and dairy		Reduce quantity & frequency, plant-based diet	
Packets of food – pasta, rice, cereals etc.		Buy from zero waste shop, use only when out of date or packaging damaged so can't eat, for play	
Photocopying		Reduce quantity – double screens, parent info by email, website, FB, software, reduce quality, use B&W	
Hand towels		Fabric, bamboo, electric hand drier	
Chipboard furniture (with formaldehyde)		Buy furniture from solid wood, second hand, cut down legs	
New furniture/storage		Buy second hand/charity shop, repair and upcycle	

Appendix VII
Children's books

Book Title	Author	Publisher	Date
The Nature Corner: Celebrating the Year's Cycle with Seasonal Tableaux	Van Leeuwen, M. and Moeskops, J.	Floris Books	2008
Where Does the Garbage Go?	Showers, P.	Perfection Learning Corporation	2015
Why Should I Recycle?	Green, J.	Demco Media	2005
The Three Rs: Reuse, Reduce, Recycle	Roca, N.	Barrons Educational Series	2007
I Can Save the Earth! One Little Monster Learns to Reduce, Reuse, and Recycle	Inches, A.	Paw Prints	2009
The Adventures of a Plastic Bottle: A Story about Recycling	Inches, A.	Little Simon	2009
The Adventures of an Aluminium Can: A Story about Recycling	Inches, A.	Little Simon	2009
10 Things I Can Do to Help My World	Walsh, M	Candlewick Press	2014
My Green Day	Walsh, M.	Candlewick Press	2012
Yucky Worms	French, V.	Walker Books, Ltd	2015
The Night Iceberg	Stevens, H.	Alison Green Books	2010
The Bee Tree	Polacco, P.	Putnam & Grosset Group	1998
What a Waste	French. J.	DK	
See Inside Recycling and Rubbish	Frith, A.	Usborne Flap Book	

Appendix VIII
Educators' resources

Book Title	Author	Publisher	Published
Loose Parts: Inspiring Play in Young Children	Beloglovsky, M. and Daly, L.	Redleaf Press	2014
Loose Parts 2: Inspiring Play with Infants and Toddlers	Beloglovsky, M. and Daly, L.	Redleaf Press	2016
Loose Parts 3: Inspiring Culturally Sustainable Environments	Beloglovsky, M. and Daly, L.	Redleaf Press	2018
Research in Early Childhood Education for Sustainability	Davis, J.	Routledge	2014
Global Childhoods: Critical Approaches to the Early Years	Edwards, M.	Critical Publishing	2015
Risk, Challenge and Adventure in the Early Years: A Practical Guide to Exploring and Extending Learning Outdoors	Solly, K.S.	Routledge	2014
Making a Mud Kitchen	White, J.	Muddy Faces	2011
Encounters with Materials in Early Childhood Education	Pacini-Ketchabow, V., Kocher, L. and Kind, S.	Routledge	2016
Education in Times of Environmental Crises: Teaching Children to be Agents of Change	Winograd, K.	Routledge	2016
Reduce, Reuse, Recycle: An Easy Household Guide	Scott, N.	UIT Cambridge	2012
Enabling Environments on a Shoestring: A Guide to Developing and Reviewing Early Years Provision	Eaton, C.	British Association for Early Childhood Education	2014
Reduce Your Carbon Footprint: A Beginner's Guide to Reducing Your Greenhouse Gas Emissions	Colson, A.	CreateSpace Indopondont Publishing Platform	2015

Book Title	Author	Publisher	Published
Homo Deus: A Brief History of Tomorrow	Harari, Y.	Random House	2016
The Rough Guide to Green Living	Clark, D.	Rough Guides Ltd.	2009
Silent Spring	Carson, R.	First Mariner Books	2002
Green Living for Dummies	Jeffery, Y., Barclay, L. and Grosvenor, M.	Wiley Publishing Inc.	2008
How to Live a Low-Carbon Life: The Individual's Guide to Stopping Climate Change	Goodall, C.	Earthscan	2007
How to Give Up Plastic	McCallum, W.	Penguin Life	2015
The Age of Sustainable Development	Sachs, J.	Columbia University Press	2015
Education for Sustainable Citizenship in Early Childhood	Siraj-Blatchford, J.	Schema Play Publications	2016
Zero Waste Home: The Ultimate Guide to Simplifying Your Life by Reducing Your Waste	Johnson, B.	Simon & Schuster	2013
Playing and Learning Outdoors: Making Provision for High Quality Experiences in the Outdoor Environment with Children 3–7	White, J.	Routledge	2013
Best Practice in the Early Years	Bryce-Clegg, A.	Bloomsbury	2015
The Toddler Brain: Nurture the Skills Today that Will Shape Your Child's Tomorrow	Jana, L.	Hachette UK	2017
Treasure Baskets and Heuristic Play	Featherstone, S.	A&C Black	2013
Communication Friendly Spaces: Improving Speaking and Listening Skills in the Early Years Foundation Stage	Jarman, E.	Basic Skills Agency	2007
Progress Matters: Reviewing and Enhancing Young Children's Development	Department for Children, Schools and Families	Department for Children, Schools and Families	2009
Continuous Provision in the Early Years	Bryce-Clegg, A.	Featherstone	2013
100 Ideas for Early Years Practitioners: Forest School	Maciver, T.	Bloomsbury Publishing	2018
Practical Guide to Nature-Based Practice	Buchan, N.	Bloomsbury Publishing	2017

DVD Title	Author	Publisher	Date
Two Year Olds Outdoors: Play, Learning and Development	White, J.	Siren Films	2011
Babies Outdoors: Play, Learning and Development	White, J.	Siren Films	2011

Website	URL
Early Childhood Environment Scale	www.ecersuk.org/4.html
Infant/Toddler Environment Rating Scale	www.ecersuk.org/4.html

Index

Page numbers in **bold** denote tables, those in *italics* denote figures.

absorbents 62–3, 142, 144
accreditations 165, 204–8, 251–2; Assured
    Food Standards 160; Lion Quality 160;
    RSPCA Assured 160
ACMI *see* Art and Creative Materials
    Institute
acrylic paint 226
additives 46, 52
advocacy 209–18
aerosols 77, 94, 239, 241
African snails 105–6
African violet 96, *98*
air conditioning 25, 138, 190, 205, 233
air fresheners 136–8, 140, 228
air transport 174
Alderson, Amy *211*
All Party Parliamentary Group 211, 251–2
allergies 112, 137, 140, 151, 247
alternatives and innovations 7, 11, 43–56,
    74, 126, 136, 138, 141–2, 144, 161, 163,
    177; compostable 50; growing 177;
    renewable 175; safer 230; sustainable 79,
    240
ammonia 94, 139, 141, 174
animal products 81, 177
animals 1, 3, 93–4, 103–5, 107–14, 116,
    155, 157–8, 177, 181, 185, 216–17,
    220–1, 229, 232; care and respect for
    103; domesticated 216; land-based 108;
    threatened with extinction 24, 45; water-
    based 108; *see also* farm animals
antibacterial soap 149–50
Appendix I 243–4, 266
Appendix II 245–51
Appendix III 254–8
Appendix IV 259–61

Appendix V 262–6
Appendix VI 267–72
Appendix VII 273
APPG *see* All Party Parliamentary Group
Art and Creative Materials Institute 230
art supplies 230, 236
Assured Food Standards accreditation 160
attitudes 19, 113, 220, 222
Australia 34, 52, 76, 107, 114, 178, 219,
    224; nurseries 52; petitions 210
awards 26, 28, 52, 164, 215, 222, 234,
    252–3; for the environmental
    entrepreneur of the year 215; for the
    most sustainable business of the year
    215; opportunities to sponsor or to win
    prizes 215; packages 164; popular with
    family, friends and the press 28; regional
    business and national 28; sustainability
    28; Venus Awards 215

babies 37, 53, 57, 59–60, 62–5, 68, 73, 88,
    105, 130, 139, 147, 164–5, 170, 264
Baby Boomers 21–2
baby bottles 43, 46, 230
baby wipes 66–7, 70, 174, 177, 217, 240
bacteria 1, 44, 46, 60, 74–5, 80, 143, 145,
    150, 176
bags 24, 43, 52, 55, 65, 73, 92–3, 169, 178,
    184; brown paper 197, 199; carrier 52;
    cloth 52; freezer 196; re-usable shopping
    234; wet 64–5; *see also* plastic bags
baking soda 74, 139, 141, 146–7
balloons 11, 27, 40, 45, 48, 72, 176, 217, 240
bamboo 53, 61–2, 81, 144, 148, 170, 172,
    177, 203, 236, 244; brushes 53–4; nappies
    62, 65, 145; toothbrushes 14, 22, *148*

banning 70, 188, 208; of garden hoses 74; of old diesel cars 188; of plastic 83; of wet wipes 70

bark, composted 92–3

baskets 36–8, 64, 92–3, 100–1, 169; *see also* treasure baskets

BATRRT *see* Best Available Treatment, Recovery and Recycling Techniques

bats 108

Bats Conservation Trust 108

batteries 119–23, 133, 180, 186, 189–90, 193, 229; cost-effective 133; installing 180; rechargeable 189; recycling 123; toxic 193

Beach Schools 113–14

beaches 12, 24, 40, 80, 84, 152, 167, 175, 184, 186, 209, 217, 240, 264

beds 21, 92–3, 110

bees 3, 98–9, 108–9, 112, 142, 153

beeswax 49, 78, 152

benefits 11, 22, 27, 31, 34, 87–9, 96, 101, 159, 210, 215, 246, 248, 250, 255–6; educational 112; Green Globe accredited hotels 172; psychological 254; retired adults 248; short-term 233; social 112, 157

Bespoke Energy Brokers 180

Best Available Treatment, Recovery and Recycling Techniques 120

best practice 24, 208, 212, 275; disposing of waste, using chemical substances and reducing greenhouse gases 250; providing open-ended resources for children 167; in sustainability and CSR reporting 206

bicycles 15, 84, 158, 185–7, 234, 255; and carts 185–6; electric 255; purchasing 255

big plastic bags *see* plastic bags

bills 9, 16, 70, 112, 130, 181, 195, 207–8, 216; online 14; single-use plastic/ consumables 240; stopping paper 14; waste disposal 70

bin liners 60

biodegrading 61–2, 67, 78, 81, 127, 129, 175–7, 217; different times taken for 43; nappies 60–1; PET plastic 44–5; PLA plastic 44

biomass 176

Biovation Company 65, 139, 143–4

birds 24, 46, 61, 80, 108–10, 114, 153, 232

bisphenol A 46, 244

bleach 74, 141, 244

board of directors 19–20; *see also* directors

boiling water 74, 141–2

Bonn Climate Change Conference 2018 5

bottles 48, 84, 139, 143, 149, 162–3; baby 46; glass 49, 91, 147, 161–3, 196, 241;

milk 162–3, 196; plastic spray 48; re-usable water 15; recycling facility for 45, 143

BPA *see* bisphenol A

brands 28, 64, 68, 137, 142–3, 147–8, 151, 169, 206, 264; causing birth defects, infertility and cancer 137; commercial 143; eco 143

Brexit 207–8

bricks 85, 108, 125, 239

Bridgewater College 113–14

British Forest School Movement 1993 113

Brock, Lynnette 25, 33, 222

brown paper bags 197, 199

brushing teeth *148*

Buchan, Niki 114

buckets 36, 64, 82, 152, 200; plastic ice cream 67; recycled 91

budgets 72, 82–3, 104, 121, 179, 190, 248

Buffet, Warren 216

bugs 75, 108, 153, 232

buildings 25, 27, 104, 124–5, 127–31, 133, 135, 137–8, 180, 183, 187, 194, 229, 240; design 124–35; freehold 133; German Passivhaus 124; leased 133; old 124; Passive Solar House 124; regulations 124, 205

bulbs 94, 130

businesses 9–11, 18–21, 116–17, 120, 169, 174, 180–1, 202, 204–5, 214–15, 245, 248, 255–6, 264, 266; food 159; local 15, 214; regional 28; responsible 246, 251; sustainable 160, 215

butterflies 98, 107–8, 221

car-sharing 192

carbon dioxide 75, 140, 143, 146, 165, 176, 188

carbon emissions 159, 187–8, 206

carbon footprint paint 135

cardboard 48, 53, 79, 143, 150, 169, 172, 174, 201, 231

care homes 91, 248

careers 21, 247

carpets 15, 44, 94, 127–8, 138, 142–3, 146, 229

cars 1, 6, 54, 170, 185, 188, 193–4, 224, 255, 257; diesel 93, 188–9, 191, 241; electric 7, 22, 133, 190, *191*, 192–3, 241, 254; hybrid 189; hydrogen 192, 192–3; petrol 162, 188–9

cartons 13, 161–2

catalogues 80, 98, 243; children's clothes 176; promoting organic products 178; standard supplier 144

caterpillars 98, 107, 221

cats 95, 105, 112–13, 197, 216

Ceesay, Isatou 84
CEHN *see* Children's Environmental Health Network
cellulose 43–4, 127
cement 125–6
CEOs *see* chief executive officers
certification 165, 172, 175, 204, 206, 208; awards 188; forestry 172, 265; organic 158; sustainability 206
cetaceans 109, 173
Chaitoff, Barbara 26
chalk 73, 76, **77**
change 2–3, 6–7, 19–20, 22–3, 26–8, 59, 66, 70, 103–4, 148, 213, 221, 232, 239, 241; behavioural 147; environmental 204; management 17; nappy 59; paperwork 28; personal 2; pilot 26; sustainable 22, 72
charitable donations 18, 32, 213, 243, 248
charities 4, 18, 31–2, 66, 91, 103, 209, 213, 215, 227, 248–50, 253; international 213; local 10, 15, 249; new 219; registered 208, 243, 248, 250
Charity Commission 213
charity shops 49, 79, 169, *170*, 195, 240
chemical fertiliser 200
chemicals 30, 44, 46, 51–2, 60, 62, 67, 90, 94, 137, 142, 152, 161, 174, 183; bleaches 162; fragrances 137; "happy brain" 88; harmless 43; hormone-disrupting 137; household 228; ingesting 150; non-sustainable 155; synthesised 51; toxic 62, 120, 127, 146, 177
chicken feathers 43
chickens 104, 106–8, 216, 221, 236
chief executive officers 9, 29, 129, 213
child labour 190, 244, 264
childcare 9, 19, 25, 36, 57; centres 51; competition 21; intergenerational 248; professionals 6, 163; providers 76–7, 227, 237; settings 101, 110, 142
Childcare Expos Conference 215
childminders 17, 212, 217, 237
children 1–4, 9–10, 34–41, 57–60, 74–7, 84–91, 98–101, 104–14, 132–42, 147–53, 167–70, 183–5, 215–19, 221–5, 232–7; birthday parties 50; books 273; developing 219, 227, 251, 253; fluoride toothpaste 147; gardening 87–102; gardening at Tops, Musgrove Park Hospital, Taunton *100*; neglected 266; nursery 91; over-feeding 165; paint containing toxins, chemicals and plastics 52; and parents 13, 252; part-time 64; primary-aged 226; school-aged 185; teaching 86, 93, 109, 147, 274; transporting 191; traumatising 41;

woodwork 173; young 21, 34, 100, 103, 106, 124, 167, 185, 216, 222, 236, 248, 274
Children's Environmental Health Network 219, 227
China 53, 55, 148, 162, 174, 178
choices 6–7, 27, 124, 127, 148, 155, 160–1, 163–5, 183, 187; healthy food 165, 221, 233; informed 175, 216; lifestyle 160; sustainable 35, 57, 144, 151, 155–6, 165, 177, 190, 203
Christmas 50–1, 54
Christmas cactus 96, *97*
clay 38, 43, 49, 52, 54, 81–2, 125; coloured 81; cosmetic 76; pink 150; quarry 126; slurry 82; tiles 126
cleaners 196, 230
cleaning 39, 53, 74, 79, 81, 110, 134, 136–53, 195; carbon dioxide 95; chemicals 94; hands 40; liquids 48; materials 39, 48; non-toxic materials 48; products 136, 142–4, 151, 196
Clegg, Brian 75
climate change 4, 14, 21, 45, 103, 109, 125, 187, 204, 207, 215, 226, 249; and the Conference of the Parties 4; crisis 103; and fossil burning 61; global 3–4, 239; reduction of 180; and sustainability 4
ClimateCare 129
cling film 43, 48–9, 240
cloth nappies 11, 14, 61–4, 66
clothes 15, 49, 55, 77, 144–6, *170*, 174, 178, 193; bad 114; children's 145; dryers 61, 145–6, 197, 233; lines 233; non-polyester/nylon 145; tight-fitting 62; wet/soiled 52, 65
Co-operative Community Fund 91
CO_2 emissions 120, 125–6, 129, 159, 174, 188–9, 202
coconut oil 140, 150, 152
COEL *see* characteristics of effective learning
coffee grounds 99, 139, 197
Coleus *98*
commercial brands 143
community 7, 32, 35, 39–41, 88, 91, 101, 209–10, 220–1, 224, 226, 241, 243, 246–7, 249–51; empowered 206; events 211, 248; global 220; involvement 87, 101; organisations 215; resources 222
companies 23, 26, 29–32, 51–2, 105–6, 119–21, 171–2, 174–8, 188, 190–2, 202, 213–15, 245–6, 248–53, 255–6; collection 195, 197; for-profit 213; insurance 101; limited 213; local 167; networking 214; printer 119–20; recycling 99; responsible 241; sustainable 171

compost 38, 67, 78, 89, 91–3, 147–8, 176–7, 197–200, 226, 235; activators 199; bark 92–3; certified plastics 45; ericaceous 92; food scraps 15; green 92; heaps 201; label instructions 92; liquid 201; loam-based 92; makers 199; multipurpose 93; organic 93; packaging 148, 175; peat-based 92; peat-free 92–3; potting 92
compostable alternatives 50
compostable plastics 44, 54
composters 10, 148, 200, 202
composting 15, 27, 85, 110, 197, 199–200, 203, 220–1; containers 200; descriptors 167; nursery *199*; organisms 198
computer waste company 119
computers 14, 43, 54, 73, 116–23, 173, 240; games 84–5; manufacturing companies 119; programs 159; search times 24; table-sized touch-screens 54
conferences 2, 4, 6, 27, 29, 215
construction activities 53, 73, **82**, 83
consumers 83, 119, 143, 162, 172, 175, 203, 246
containers 49, 52, 67–8, 87, 92–3, 107, 147, 152, 159, 178, 196, 200; large 48, 52, 168; old wipes 67–8; plastic 48, 52, 67, 143, 230; powder paint 76; water 75
Cora Ball filter 90
coral 3, 6, 24, 51, 73
corporate social environmental responsibility 28, 32, 133, 137, 144, 206, 215, 241, 243, 245, 254
corporate social responsibility *see* corporate social environmental responsibility
costs 54–5, 57, 60, 65–7, 70, 78, 81, 133, 174, 177, 191–2, 203, 205, 232, 252; charges 217; extra 60, 62; installing 132; running 118, 208; savings 192
cotton 54–5, 62–3, 65, 67, 81, 144, 174, 181, 197
cotton production 178
cows 5–6, 79, 161
craft activities 13, 53, 73, 80, 85, 114
creativity 36, 38–9, 226, 231
crockery 49, 79, 169
Croft, Anita 225
crops 92, 157, 181
CSER *see* corporate social environmental responsibility
CSR *see* corporate social environmental responsibility
cultural changes 17, 19, 22, 29, 32, 40, 70, 241
cultures 1, 19–20, 27, 40, 93, 113, 122, 178, 184, 220, 222–3, 249–50

curricula 219, 225, 238; and accreditation 219–38; national 34
customers 9, 16, 21, 123, 128, 178, 182, 187, 202, 204, 242, 245, 249
cutlery 49–50, 79, 169, 202
cycling 185

daffodil bulbs 94
dairies 161, 163, 197
dairy cows 161; methane-producing 3; and plastic milk bottles of milk 162
damage 4, 6, 34, 38, 61, 71–2, 84, 122, 125, 136, 140, 146, 157, 162, 173; environmental 152; human 103
Davies, Sarah 37
day nurseries 51–2, 57, 59, 104, 107, 151, 155, 159, 161, 165, 185, 209, 212, 224, 226
decomposition 44, 202
DEET 152
denatonium benzoate 75–6
dentists 147–8
deodorants 140
detergents 145
diesel 6, 29, 71, 157, 162, 188–92, 243, 251, 257; ban 189; cars 93, 188–9, 191, 241; emissions 188; old 29; vehicle exhausts 188; vehicles 162, 189–90
digital table 84, *116*
directors 19–20, 22, 25, 205, 209, 251; commercial 22, 132; finance 21, 132–3; human resources 21
diseases 11, 65, 91–2, 136, 152, 198
dishwashers 14, 49, 53, 134, 236
disposables 15, 62, 65
distance learning 2
distributors 46, 72, 122, 159, 174, 203, 241, 244
dogs 95, 112–13, 139, 197, 216
donations 18, 32, 213, 243, 248
Dow Chemicals 46
Dragon tree *96*
drains 39, 49, 62, 66, 70, 77, 81–2, 137, 141, 145, 173–4, 199
drinking water 180–1, 229, 247; *see also* water
dryer balls 145
dryers 61, 145–6, 197, 233
ducks 106
dust 75, 77, 134, 139–42
duty of care 1, 3, 7, 9, 16–17, 72–3, 75, 77–83, 86, 103–4, 109–10, 113, 164, 245–6, 264–5; about the environment 10, 19; of pets 240; of plants 101; to protect the planet for the children 17

EA *see* Environment Agency

early childhood 25, 40, 222, 275; curriculum 224; education 2, 21, 40, 222, 231, 262, 274; institutions 209; sector 3, 6
Early Childhood Education for Sustainability Development Framework 231
Early Years Alliance 212, 215
Early Years Award 164
Early Years Best Practice 212
Early Years Foundation Stage 18, 35, 87, 122, 219, 221, 231, 275
Early Years Learning Framework (early childhood curriculum) 224
Early Years Practitioners 114
early years sector 9, 17, 43, 57, 60, 103, 183, 231, 239, 248
earth microbes 197, 200
ECEfS see Early Childhood Education for Sustainability Development Framework
eco 11, 54, 81, 129, 143, 171, 177–8, 226; brands 143; community 226; games 26, 27; paints 76, 135; products 11; stories 240; suppliers 54–5, 148; sustainability 23, 27
eco eggs 14, 144–5
eco-games 27
Eco-Healthy Child Care Program 2010 227
Eco-Schools 24, 219, 225–6, 231, 250, 253
Eco Wheel **237**
economic exchanges 222
Eden Project 199, 201, 206
education 7, 19, 40–1, 136, 161–3, 170, 194, 219, 223, 225, 227, 231, 245–6, 248, 250; child's 36; industry 265; institutions 204; opportunities 35; organisations 136; progress 40; sustainable 21, 23, 30, 211
Edwards, Fred 237
eggs 30, 52, 106–7, 160, 198, 221
El Nino 103
electric bicycles 31, 186, 186–7, 255
electric cars 7, 22, 133, 190, 191, 192–3, 241, 254
electric motors 189–90
electric vehicles 61, 133, 157, 162, 188–91, 193, 257
electricity 5, 14, 29–30, 71, 118, 121–2, 132, 157, 189–93, 205; bills 15, 28–9, 132; changing suppliers 240; grid 180; premium-time 180; purchasing 132; rates 133; usage 22, 180; wasting 138
electricity grid 180
electronic equipment 108, 116–23
Elizabeth Jarman's Communication Friendly Spaces 37
embodied energy costs 126–7
emergencies 57, 66, 70, 117, 217

emissions 4, 78, 126–7, 165, 174, 188, 192, 202; carbon 159, 187–8, 206; CO2, 120, 125–6, 129, 159, 174, 188–9, 202; diesel 188; greenhouse gas 4, 165, 274; noxious 126; toxic 126; world's carbon dioxide 126; zero tailpipe 189
EMS see energy management system
energy 60–1, 118, 121, 125, 128, 131, 133, 155, 157, 162, 180, 191, 205–6, 226, 232; assessment 204–5; assessment and savings scheme 204–5; conservation 140; consumption 121, 205; efficiency 14, 187; high embodied 126–7; importing 126; management system 174; production 60; renewable 4, 118, 158, 162, 180, 240; renewable sources 142, 157, 243–4; saving modes 121; star ratings 233
energy savings opportunity scheme 204–5, 252–3
environment 1, 3–4, 17–19, 34–6, 55, 62, 66–8, 72, 83–4, 86–7, 113–15, 120–2, 126, 220–5, 249–50; family-styled 223; healthiest 217, 219, 227–8; marine 77, 125; natural 223, 225, 234, 249–50; safe 223; sustainable 136, 158, 217
Environment Agency 120, 204–5
Environment Bill 2019 207–8
environmental damage 152
environmental health officers 65, 227
environmental pollutants 43
Environmental Product Declaration 129
environmental stewardship 10
EPD see Environmental Product Declaration
equipment 4, 22, 79, 83, 87, 90–1, 117, 119–23, 169, 185, 199–200, 236; electronic 108, 116–23; medical 56; playground 230; radio-telemetry tracking 41; recycle 119; suppliers 171
ESOS see energy savings opportunity scheme
essential oils 68, 138–9, 150
ethane 44
Ethical Corporation 56, 214
EV see electric vehicle
EYA see Early Years Alliance
EYFS see Early Years Foundation Stage

fabrics 36, 44, 49, 52, 62, 67, 79–81, 143, 174, 177–8; conditioners 145; softening 145; sustainable 174; synthetic 145
Facebook groups 12, 29–30, 51, 117, 164, 212, 251
facility 119, 228–30; bottle recycling 45, 143; hazardous waste 229; industrial composting 176

families 2–3, 7, 23, 28, 34, 39, 54, 58, 209,
213, 218, 223, 230–6, 240, 275; and
attitudes towards animals 113; and
awards 28; encouraging eco-healthy
practices 231; Muslim 54; opinions on
introducing animals to the workplace
113; vegetarian 156
farm animals 109
farm sustainability 160
farmers 91, 156–9, 216
farms 39, 107, 109, 157, 159, 216, 234
feathers 43, 54, 80, 177
Featherstone, Sally 37
Federer, Roger 216
FEE *see* Foundation for Environmental
Education
ferns *95*
fertilised eggs 106
fertilisers 62, 92, 127, 200
fibres 67, 93, 146–7, 177
fish 24, 46, 51, 61, 106, 109, 114, 125, 160,
163, 170, 176, 198, 216, 220; certified
sustainable 160; eating human beings 46;
shell fish 46, 51, 160, 170
fishing 80, 160
food 3–4, 14–15, 48–9, 79, 104–6, 110–11,
137, 151–2, 155–6, 158–61, 163–5, 200,
225, 239–40, 263–6; businesses 159;
composted 199; organic 21, 158, 160;
plant-based 155, 163; plastic 79;
sustainable 4, 155–66, 263
food packaging 196, 235
food services 47, 50, 155
food standards 160
food waste 38, 165, 197, 203, 215, 221
footprint, electricity usage/carbon 22
Forest School 25, 34, 113–14, 275
Forest Stewardship Council 128, 172
forestry certification 172, 265
Foundation for Environmental Education
225, 264
freedom 1, 158, 224, 254, 263
French, Jess 84
FSC *see* Forest Stewardship Council

gardening 10, 39, 87–8, *89*, 90–1, 220;
activities 87, 89, 91, 101, 164; home 87;
supplies 138
gardening tools *90*
gardens 72, 75, 78, 87–91, 93, 104, 107–8,
110, 193, 197, 200, 221, 225, 232, 236
Gasbarrino, Melaina 84
Gates, Melinda 216
GECCO *see* Green Early Years Choices
Champion Organisation
general waste 45, 48, 60–1, 66, 73, 75, 77,
122, 147–8, 162, 195–6, 202

Generation X 21
Gerbera daisy *96*
German Passivhaus buildings 124
glass 15, 45, 49, 52, 54, 80, 85, 120, 158,
161–3, 169–70, 198, 200, 221, 230–1;
bottles 49, 91, 147, 161–3, 196, 241; low
emissivity 128; panels 128; products
162; sharp 196
glitter 27, 50–1, 76, 80–1, 145, 224, 240
global reporting initiative 206
gloves 43, 50, 90, 152, 226
glue 51, 73, **78**, 79, 117
glycerine 77, 79, 150–1
Godsey, Maria 84
Gold Standard 252
goldfish 104, 106
Goldschmied, Elinor 37
Good Energy Company (supplier) 180
governments 36, 41, 70, 132–3, 163, 181,
188, 193, 205, 209–10, 212, 239, 251, 255
grandparents 1, 9
Green Early Years Choices Champion
Organisation 7, 24, 32, 241, 248, 250–1,
253
Green Globe Company 171–2
greenhouse gases 4–5, 78, 146, 162, 165,
188–9, 220, 274
"greenwash" products and services 2, 7, 61,
81, 167, 174, 177, 182, 217
Greggs Foundation Environmental Grants 91
GRI *see* global reporting initiative
Guppyfriend wash bags 145–6

Hadland, Cheryl *211*, 253, 258
Hadland Care Group 257
hand washing 136, 140, 146, 149–50
Hazardous Waste Consignment Note 120
hazardous waste facilities 229
hazards 27, 149, 167, 185, 197, 229;
bacteria and bugs 75; environmental
health 60, 219, 227; human-made 5; and
risks 52–3, 99–100, 105, 108, 111, 113,
131, 133, 137, 141, 146–7, 153, 167–8,
183–4, 192; swallowing 123
health 4, 19, 25, 27, 74, 107, 129, 136, 141,
152–3, 155, 223, 247, 255–6; benefits 134,
254–5; environmental 227; human 79,
101, 153, 188; medical 247; risks 110, 141
heat exchangers 128, 240; *see also* heat
pumps
heat pumps 128, 131
heating 24–5, 44, 48, 61, 67, 124, 126, 129,
131, 133–4, 137–8, 170, 205, 233, 240;
bills 132; central 134; control 174;
efficient 131; engineers 131; infrared 31,
131, 134
helium 48

hemp 63, 126–8
herbicides 108, 141–2
herbs 76–7, 87, 100, 197, 240
home corner 73, **79**, 80, 85, 163
home energy assessments 31
hormone production 141
hospitals 57, 88, 248, 256
housekeepers 64–5
houseplants 94, 198
human resources 19, 21
human rights 206, 246–7, 266
humans 4, 78, 94, 103, 105, 122, 161, 216;
    and the biodiversity damage caused by
    103; and the capacity for thinking 'out of
    sight, out of mind' 6; killing almost all
    species of animal weighing over 50 kg
    108; poisons 125; and putting a value on
    nature 173
hybrid cars 189
hydro-electricity 131
hydrogen 140
hydrogen cars 192, 192–3

ICCC *see* International Conference on
    Climate Change
induction 20, 28, 196; and the five-year
    plan PowerPoint presentation 28; system
    for new employees 20, 28; for
    unqualified and qualified recruits 28
industrial composting facility 176
infrared heat 31, 134
ingredients 21, 38, 67–8, 92–3, 135, 137–8,
    143, 149, 151, 177; base 43, 92;
    biodegradable 143; natural 51; toxic 244
ingredients oxybenzone 152
insect houses 98
insect protection 136, 152
insects 24, 98, 104, 106–7, 112, 114, 134,
    153, 170, 198, 228, 232
International Conference on Climate
    Change 4
International Union for Conservation of
    Nature 193
investing *172*
investments 3, 22, 29, 49, 58, 64, 73, 75,
    77–83, 118, 132–3, 135, 174–5, 239, 242
ISO standards 129, 204, 206, 252
IUCN *see* International Union for
    Conservation of Nature

Jackson, Ellie 84
Jones, David 2, 7

Keep Britain Tidy (environmental charity)
    225

labels 2, 48, 129, 158, 160, 162, 168, 171–2

landfill 15, 45, 48, 57, 60, 67, 72, 81, 119,
    122, 162, 241
landscapes 48, 71, 73, 119, 125–7, 265
Lansbury, Janet 36
laundry 14, 47, 57, 61, 64–5, 70, 136, 144–5
Layton, Neal 84
learning 10, 13, 35, 41, 72–3, 86–9, 104,
    110, 113–14, 149, 220–1, 224, 250,
    263–4; active 26, 35, 87, 222; and
    development 221; distance 2; effective
    35, 87, 221; environment 3, 34, 101,
    235; outdoor 113, 128, 263;
    programmes 224
legislation 7–8, 208, 210
Lego 54, 73, 82
light table *131*
lighting 24, 124, 128–30, 205
liners 60, 62–3; *see also* bin liners
Lion Quality accreditation 160
liquid soaps 52, 149
liquids 67, 77, 142–3, 178
loam-based composts 92

magnifying glass *131*
manufacturers 46–8, 55, 60, 62, 70, 72, 119,
    125, 137, 140, 177–8, 188, 193, 203,
    241–2; plastic 208; resin 46; toy 168
Marquet, David 20
'Mass of Mismanaged Plastic Waste'
    (measurement for ranking of countries)
    45
meat 14, 156, 160, 163, 197–8, 220
MEM *see* modern educational movement
Members of Parliament 210–11, 214, 217,
    227, 266
metal gardening tools *90*
microfibres 55, 61–2, 65, 145–6
milk bottles 162–3, 196
millennial workers 21
millennials 21, 23
modelling clay **81**
modern educational movement 224
Monbiot, George 242
money 6, 14–15, 21, 47, 49–50, 65–6, 78,
    80, 122, 132, 197, 200, 203, 205–6, 213
Montessori ideology 34, 113
Montessori nurseries 76
MPs *see* Members of Parliament
multipurpose compost 93
mushrooms growing from coffee grounds)
    99
music 82, 248
musical instruments 54–5, 73, **82**, 83
Muslim families 54

NAHT *see* National Association of Head
    Teachers

nappies 29, 44, 47, 50, 52, 57–66, 138, 145, 240, 249, 251; absorbent 62; bio-degradable 60; cotton 63; disposable 57, 60, 70, 217, 241; distributors of 66, 70; easy-to-put-on 62; laundering of 145; microfibre 62; modern 59, 61; parent-provided 64; real 12, 32, 66, 70; reusable 15, 58, 61, 64–5, 70, 240; single 66; soiled 52; and wet wipes 57–70
nappy sacks 14, 25, 52, 60
NASA *see* National Aeronautics and Space Administration
National Aeronautics and Space Administration 94
National Association of Head Teachers 215, 262
National Day Nurseries Association 212, 215
national grid 131, 133, 190; *see also* electricity grid
NDNA *see* National Day Nurseries Association
New Zealand 11, 18, 34, 224–5; nature-based early years practice emerging within 114; and sustainability integrated into the curricula of 219; Te Whariki contained in the early year's curriculum 225; throw-away culture still prevalent in 178
newsletters 12, 30, 232–6
newspapers, recycled 127
NGOs *see* non-governmental organisations
NMT *see Nursery Management Today* magazine
non-governmental organisations 206, 213
non-recyclable plastics 196
non-toxic art supplies 230
Nursery Management Today magazine 215, 262
nutrients 15, 92–3, 200

OBC *see* Ofsted Big Conversation
OEP *see* Office for Environmental Protection
Office for Environmental Protection 207
Ofsted Big Conversation 212
oil 5, 43–6, 60, 62, 68, 71, 74, 78, 126, 131, 134–5, 143, 152, 158, 198; non-renewable 48, 127–8; plant-based 152; vegetable 43
old paint 170
Oldman, Liz 84
organic certification policy 158
organic composts 93
organic food 21, 158, 160
organic policy 157, 160
organic products 178

Orsted Company 180

packaging 52, 122, 136–7, 147, 151, 158, 167, 171, 175, 178, 197, 202–3, 234, 244, 246; compostable 148, 175; food 196, 235; plastic 60, 137, 147, 203, 217; sustainable 56, 122, 158; waste 171, 175, 234
paint 48–9, 52, 54, 72–3, 75–83, 85, 94, 118, 124, 128, 134–5, 149, 170, 226, 228–9; acrylic 226; children's 52; and glycerine 77; licking and swallowing of 75; lowest carbon footprint 135; non-toxit and eco-friendly 52; old 170; powder 75; ready-mixed 75; recipes 76; recycled 128; and shaving foam used by childcare providers 77
pallets 36, 168, 215
palm oil 161, 163
paper/card/cardboard **78**
parents 1, 9–16, 23, 25–6, 39–40, 50–1, 57–60, 63–6, 70, 86–9, 159–60, 164–5, 192, 209, 216–17; adoptive 9; and a child during a Tops Day Nurseries Bournemouth beach clean *13*; eco-minded 66; new or existing 10, 12; prospective 12; and staff 66, 70, 228; working 58
Paris Agreement on Climate Change 143
parks 103–4, 185, 187, 192, 209, 216, 256–7
Parliament 208, 210, 217
parrotfish 73
peat 92–3
peat-based compost 92
pedagogy 25, 33–41
Percival, Charlotte *27*
personal care 136–53
personal freedom 254
PET plastic 44
petrol 5–6, 29, 71, 157, 188–92, 243, 251, 257
petrol cars 162, 188–9
pets 39, 44, 94, 103–15, 196
phthalates 137, 141, 196
PLA plastic 44–5
plant biology *131*
plant foods 92–3
plants 10, 12, 14, 87–95, 98–102, 167–8, 170, 176, 178, 181, 198, 200, 221, 232, 235; acid-loving 92; air-cleaning 93; baby spider 95; fast-growing 62, 100; insect-ridden 198; living 95; renewable 174; *see also* houseplants
plastic *37*, 43–56, 60–2, 70–1, 80–5, 120–2, 134–5, 137, 143–4, 147, 151–2, 159–63, 173–7, 193, 198, 226–7; biodegradable 44; black 45; chemistry of *44*; compostable

44, 54; gloves 50, 152, 225; manufacturers 208; marine 51; melted 121; milk bottles 162; nappies 32, 57, 61; non-recyclable 196; oil-derived 44; packaging 60, 137, 147, 203, 217; particles 121; PET 44; PLA 44–5; plant-based 61; pollution 2, 4, 7, 24, 43, 46, 70, 146, 175, 193, 227, 249; products 46, 51, 208; recycled 47, 55–6, 244; single-use 23, 25–6, 32, 47, 56–7, 70, 150, 158, 175, 196, 205, 208, 219, 226–7, 249; straws 53, 162; toothbrushes 25, 148; toys 54, 83, 170, 195–6, 230; trash 126; waste 45, 143, 151, 239

plastic bags 11, 27, 38, 52, 84, 196, 203, 208, 227, 230, 234, 240; banning 208; crinkly 196; inflated 202; single-use 65

plastic bottles 43, 84, 91, 145, 181, 231, 273; for cleaning liquids 48; rigid 196; single-use 29; upcycling 85

plastic containers 48, 52, 67, 143, 230

plastic food 79

Plastic Free Schools 219, 226, 250

A Plastic Ocean (film) 2, 24, 32, 46, 240

plastic resources 54

plates 14, 49, 165, 197, 202–3; children's 165; of food 49; plastic-coated paper 50

poisoning 1, 220, 239

poisons 3, 107, 125; addictive 139; of humans 125; rat 139; risk assessment for 81

policies 12, 28, 136, 153, 179, 194, 208, 217, 245, 251, 254; anti-discrimination 252; internal 246; popular 217; protective 227; purchasing 136–7, 179, 246, 249; recruitment and retention 247, 252; sustainable transport 252

politicians 3–4, 6, 8, 58, 209–14, 217, 241; and the banning of wet wipes containing plastic 70; local 251; national 251; and the plastic pollution crisis 46, 56; protecting the planet with sustainable policies 6, 8

politics 209, 266

pollen 137, 139

pollution 24, 45, 95, 119–20, 183, 188, 192–3, 217, 249; noise 55; plastic 2, 4, 7, 24, 43, 46, 70, 146, 175, 193, 227, 249; shoreline 145

pot plants 89–90

potty training 58–9

poverty 3–4, 6, 207

powder paint 75

power 6, 8, 14, 61, 63, 120–1, 131, 137, 142, 169, 182, 189, 193; companies 180; electrical 223; group consumers 3; water-based 157

Prayer plant 96, *97*

preschools 40, 161–2, 180, 212, 224, 226

printers 116, 118, 120–2

problems 43, 45, 48–50, 52–4, 57, 60, 64, 66, 68, 159, 161, 180, 184, 187, 190; disposing of nuclear waste 132; micro-waste 145; odour 198; palm oil 161; perfumes and aftershaves 137; respiratory 141; of storage and overordering 163; of tooth decay in children 147

producers 156, 159, 176, 244

production systems 148

products 43–5, 83, 86–7, 129, 135–7, 140, 142–4, 161, 171–9, 181–2, 203, 227, 229–30, 244–6, 263–4; animal 81, 177; antiseptic 140; bio-plastic 176; biodegradable 176; compostable 176; dairy 163, 198; disinfecting 228; edible 150; grading of 244; new 54, 81, 153; non-biodegradable 175; plastic 46, 51, 208; PVC 196; single-use 61; sourcing of 22, 159; sustainable 78; unsustainable 217; wood 172

programmes 116, 136, 164, 206, 226, 248; environmental 264; preschool 113

projects 40–1, 108, 110, 116, 224; behaviour change 205; capital investment 205; conservation 104, 109; lemur 109

public transport 15, 183, 187, 251, 254–6

puffy paint 76

purchasing policies 136–7, 179, 246, 249

PVA 51, 78–9

PVC 128, 196, 230

rabbits at Tops Day Nurseries *111*

rainwater 126, 181

rat poison 139

re-use 15, 40, 48, 50, 62, 72, 74, 82, 85, 119, 195, 197, 221, 235; of chemicals 62; of silicon food bags 49; of smaller containers 48; of wet bags 14, 52

recyclers 99, 119, 167

recycling 13, 45, 77–8, 84–5, 118–20, 123, 143, 147, 196, 203, 220–1, 231, 240–1, 243–4, 273–4; batteries 123; bottles 143, 208; cardboard 56, 159; collections 196, 249; containers 85; equipment 119; games 240; materials 71, 135, 143, 162, 235, 244; newspapers 127; paint 128; paper 151; posters 13; rain water 181; systems 77, 162; tyres 126

Red emerald philodendron *97*

Reggio ideology 34

renewable energy 4, 118, 158, 162, 180, 240

research 17, 21, 23, 48, 50–1, 86, 88, 104–5, 110–11, 129, 136, 144, 147, 149–50, 227; alternatives to plastic 53; of Anita Croft 225; organisations 212; papers 145; scientific 72

resin manufacturers 46
resources 6–7, 13–14, 34, 37, 59–60, 78–83,
    114, 122, 167–9, *170*, 171–3, 221–2,
    224–5, 230–1, 262–5; community 222;
    digital 164; existing 71; improving 29;
    innovative 231; metal 37; natural 44;
    plastic 54; precious 74; renewable 125;
    repaired 72; shared 249; sustainable 170;
    unsustainable 83, 114; waste 157
Rock, David 20
RSPCA Assured accreditation 160

sand 12, 36, 40, 50, 54, 72–4, 81, 92, 125,
    162, 168, 195, 225, 240
sand cleaners 75
sanitising 136–53
Santos, Alexandra 137
SAS *see* Surfers Against Sewage
Save Water to Help the Earth (video) 226
Scandinavian Forest Schools 114
schools 20, 35, 50–1, 58–9, 91, 161–2, 164,
    185, 191, 221, 225–7, 248, 262–3, 275;
    cooking 155; government nursery 211
scientific research 72
SDGs *see* sustainable development goals
shellfish 46, 51, 160, 170
shopping trips *170*
SIDS *see* small island developing states
single-use nappies 47, 57, 60–1, 63–6, 70,
    251, 253
single-use plastic 23, 25–6, 32, 47, 56–7, 70,
    150, 158, 175, 196, 205, 208, 219, 226–7,
    249
Siraj-Blatchford, John 25, 33, 222
small island developing states 5
soap nuts 144–5; *see also* eco-eggs
soaps 38, 49, 52, 68, 144–5, 149–50, 153,
    196; antibacterial 149–50; blocks of 26,
    149; children's 150; liquid 52, 149;
    natural 49; scented 153
social media 209, 211, 250
soda ash processing plants 146
soil 15, 91–2, 95, 120, 157, 176, 197
solar panels 2, 7, 10, 15, 61, 124, 131–3,
    180, 240
special scientific interest 216
spheres of influence *33*
Spider plant *95*
SSIs *see* special scientific interest
staff training 253
standards 129, 143, 159, 213, 219–38, 252;
    applying environmental 204; food 160;
    international 129; self-certified 178
Steiner ideology 34
sticker for placing near light switch *13*
stickle bricks 54
stories 4, 12, 59, 84–6, 88, 210, 241, 273

suppliers 52, 55, 67, 72, 76, 129–30, 144,
    147, 151, 172–4, 179–80, 182, 202–3,
    244–6, 249; eco 54–5, 148; educational
    144; ethical 173; hardware 181;
    renewable energy 61, 121; sustainable
    energy 14, 31, 131
supply chains 174, 177–8, 246, 249, 265
sustainability 8–9, 11–14, 17–20, 25–7,
    29–30, 33–6, 38–41, 83–6, 133–6, 156–8,
    160–1, 205–6, 208–10, 212–16, 218–22;
    awards 28; certification 206; checklists
    208, 267; ecological 18, 206; education
    for 225; environmental 4, 231; ethos 19,
    39, 223; farming 160; financial 24, 113,
    212; initiatives 250, 252; integrated 20;
    journey 10, 12, 16, 171; teaching 224–5;
    vision 30, 32; work 5, 204, 208
Sustainability Action Plan 245
sustainable choices 35, 57, 144, 151, 155–6,
    165, 177, 190, 203
sustainable development goals 4, *5*, 40, *207*
sustainable farming 157–8
sustainable fishing 264
sustainable food 4, 155–66, 263
sustainable packaging 56, 122, 158
sustainable resourcing 167–82
systems 59, 119, 131–4, 175, 180–1, 219,
    226, 240; energy management 174; key
    worker 59; solar water 129

tablets 54, 117–19, 122
Tassoni, Penny 37
Tesla 190, 192
thermostatic mixing valves 181
Thunberg, Greta 103
TMVs *see* thermostatic mixing valves
toilet paper 151, 196
toilets 58, 63–5, 67, 134, 139, 142, 146, 149,
    178, 181, 237; rinsing poo into the 64–5;
    and shower sprays 65; training 58; and
    wet wipes 57
toothbrushes 53–4, 136, 147–8, *149*
toothpaste 39, 147
Tops, Parkstone *89*
Tops Day Nurseries 1, 13, *27*, *31*, 111, 114,
    118, *148*, *149*, 161, *186*, *201*, 204, 241
toxic air 93–4, 184
training 19–20, 25–6, 40, 53, 58, 196, 235,
    245, 249–51, 257, 265; materials 40;
    potty 57–9; staff 253; teams 28;
    vocational 223
treasure baskets 37, 73, 82, **83**, 275
Turner, Andrew 170
tyres 193–4

UK 50–3, 73–4, 119–20, 133–5, 149–51,
    161–2, 164–5, 181, 183–5, 187–9, 208,

212, 219, 221–3, 225–7; councils 196; diesel car sales 189; government 159, 161, 184; law 119; nurseries 89, 164; Parliament 204, 210; post-Brexit 208; recycling facilities 196; residents 119; Standards 219; subsidies 133
ULEVs *see* ultra-low emission vehicles
ultra-low emission vehicles 188
UNGC *see* United Nations Global Compact
UNICEF 93, 184, 213
United Kingdom *see* UK
United Nations Climate Change Conference 1995 (Conference of the Parties) 4
United Nations Convention on the Rights of Children 36
United Nations Global Compact 206, 251
United Nations Sustainability Goals 246–7
United Nations Sustainable Development Solutions Network 2019 World Happiness Report 178
USDA Organic and Soil Association Organic Standard 160

vegan food triangle *156*
vegans 26, 29, 54, 109, 148, 151–2, 156, 177, 197, 216, 220, 247
vegetables 10, 15, 81, 87, 92, 111, 114, 159, 161, 163–4, 197–8, 201, 221, 224, 228
vegetarian families 156
vegetarians 54, 106, 109, 216, 220, 259
Velcro 62–3
ventilation 75, 124, 128–9, 205, 228, 232
vocational training 223
VOCs *see* volatile organic compounds
volatile organic compounds 78, 137, 141, 146, 228–9

Waldorf Steiner ideology 76
walking trains or crocodiles 184–5
Walsh, Melanie 84
washing 47, 49–50, 53, 55, 61–5, 134, 136–7, 140, 145–6, 149–50, 162, 174, 224, 233, 236
washing machines 14, 30, 39, 49, 52, 55, 61–5, 90, 142, 145–6, 180, 193, 236–7
Waste Electronic and Electrical Equipment Regulations 2006 119–20
waste food 3, 220
waste management 176, 195–203, 210
waste packaging 171, 175, 234
waste plastic 45, 239

waste treatment plants 145
waste water 74, 124, 134
watch batteries 123
water 50–1, 53–5, 60–3, 66–8, 72, 74–9, 81–2, 90–2, 108–9, 125, 134–5, 176–8, 180–1, 192–3, 236; bills 181, 236; boiling 74, 141–2; butt 90, 134, 181, 237; clean 223; conserving 157, 181, 187; consumption 181, 187, 206; containers 75; drinking 180–1, 229, 247; grey 134; reclaimed 157; saving 226; supply 55, 147, 224; waste 74, 124, 134
water bottles 15, 25, 47, 114, 227; boycotting one-use 227; single-use 47, 114
watering 38, 74–5, 90, 93, 101, 181, 221, 235
watering cans 90
websites and Facebook pages 24, 219, 227, 250, 253
WEEE *see* Waste Electrical and Electronic Equipment
wet bags 64–5
wet wipe fabric 67
wet wipe liquid 67
wet wipes 57–68, *69*, 70, 114, 145
WHO *see* World Health Organization
wildlife 204, 207, 209, 263
wood 36–7, 52, 54–5, 78, 80, 90, 125, 128, 131, 142, 144, 147, 151, 167–70, 172–3; blocks 82; fibre 92; and metal resources *37*; natural 127; products 172; pulp 60, 67, 174; solid 127, 229; sustainable 56, 98, 173
wooden 82, 167, 195; bowls 170; cup holders 170; floor boards 127; gardening tools *90*; kitchen roll holders 170; pallets 168; resources *172*; spoons 83
Woodland Trust 108
workers 158, 244, 266; first shift 187; key 10–11, 169; millennial 21
workplaces 6, 113, 185, 254
World Commission on Environment and Development 4
World Economic Forum Annual Meeting 2018 21
World Food Day 260
World Habitat Day 260
World Health Organization 184
worm farms 235
wormeries 26, 30, 106, 169, *201*, 202, 220–1, 240

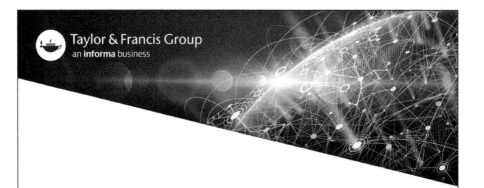